EXECUTIVE'S GUIDE TO MARKETING, SALES, AND ADVERTISING LAW

EXECUTIVE'S GUIDE TO MARKETING, SALES, AND ADVERTISING LAW

David C. Hjelmfelt

Prentice-Hall International (UK) Limited, *London*
Prentice-Hall of Australia Pty. Limited, *Sydney*
Prentice-Hall Canada Inc., *Toronto*
Prentice-Hall Hispanoamericana, S.A., *Mexico*
Prentice-Hall of India Private Limited, *New Delhi*
Prentice-Hall of Japan, Inc., *Tokyo*
Simon & Schuster Asia Pte. Ltd., *Singapore*
Editora Prentice-Hall do Brasil, Ltda., *Rio de Janeiro*

© 1990 *by*

PRENTICE-HALL, Inc.

Englewood Cliffs, N.J.

10 9 8 7 6 5 4 3 2 1

Library of Congress Cataloging-in-Publication Data

Hjelmfelt, David C.

   Executive's guide to marketing, sales & advertising law
David C. Hjelmfelt.
   p. cm.
   ISBN 0-13-296450-3
   1. Advertising laws–United States. 2. Marketing–Law and
legislation–United States. 3. Competition, Unfair–United States.
4. Executives–United States–Handbooks, manuals, etc. I. Title.
KF1614.H56 1990
343.73'084–dc20
[347.30384]
                                        90-34633
                                          CIP

ISBN 0-13-296450-3

PRINTED IN THE UNITED STATES OF AMERICA

For Mom and Dad

ABOUT THE AUTHOR

David C. Hjelmfelt is the author of numerous published articles on topics ranging from franchise contracts to taxation to the application of the antitrust laws to regulated industries including the highly regarded books *Antitrust and Regulated Industries*, and *Understanding Franchise Contracts*. This new book grew out of his experience in advising small business on the legal issues involved in marketing their products.

Mr. Hjelmfelt completed his undergraduate work at Kansas State University and received his law degree from Duke University. From 1971 to 1972 he was a visiting professor of law at the University of Oklahoma.

He now resides in Fort Collins, Colorado, where he was an assistant attorney general for that state in 1983.

At the present he is a partner in the firm of Hjelmfelt & Larson and of counsel to the Washington, DC firm of Goldberg, Fieldman and Letham, P.C. Mr. Hjelmfelt specializes in antitrust litigation and counseling to firms throughout the United States.

WHAT THIS BOOK WILL DO FOR YOU

In the quick-to-litigate atmosphere of the modern business world, marketing managers are pressed by competition to walk along the precipice of legal restraint. A misstep can result in a violation of the Sherman Act, Federal Trade Commission Act, or the Robinson-Patman Act, subjecting one to fines, imprisonment, and treble damages. On the other hand, a too cautious approach to marketing problems can result in lost sales and lost jobs. Now, more than ever, the marketing specialist needs a quick ready reference to use as a guide through the mine field of laws regulating the market function. To help meet that need this book shows how to reduce the risks of litigation when you terminate a distributor, determine pricing policies, establish discounts, award sales territories, refuse to deal and handle the other day-to-day problems involved in managing a marketing program.

This book is the result of many years of practicing antitrust law both in litigation and in advising businesses on how to avoid antitrust problems. This antitrust experience has been augmented by consulting with new business in the process of developing a marketing system and assisting others in the establishment of franchise programs.

The material covered is of particular interest to those engaged in marketing consumer items. While many of the chapters are also of interest to marketers of commercial and industrial items, the book principally covers marketing of consumer goods.

The aim is to provide a quick reference for a particular problem. Each chapter, other than the introductory chapter, is written to answer questions regarding a particular marketing problem. For example, for concerns with terminating a dealer, refer to the chapter discussing dealer terminations. It will not be necessary to read a great deal of material not directly related to your immediate problem.

Every effort has been made to provide today's legal requirements. Lengthy dissertations on legal history are avoided except when necessary to provide an understanding of the directions the law is taking.

Reading the appropriate chapters of this book before making marketing decisions will assist in designing an aggressive marketing program that will not violate the law. We hope to prevent anyone from blundering into a litigation quagmire. Nothing can halt a promising career in marketing faster than a treble damage antitrust case and the accompanying million-dollar legal fees.

This book then will tell you what you can and cannot do to meet competitive pricing. It will tell you what you can do about price discounters. When you can refuse to deal with a distributor? What steps can be taken to reduce the likelihood of litigation when it is necessary to terminate a dealer? This book will answer these questions and guide dealings with associations of distributors to prevent the appearance of participating in a conspiracy. The chapters dealing with market territories, exclusive dealing agreements, dual distribution systems, and franchising are invaluable for designing a new distribution system or implementing a new marketing strategy.

Advertising can expand sales but it can also spawn lawsuits. This book will advise on promoting a product without violating federal laws concerning the use of endorsements and testimonials. The legal use of comparative advertising is discussed.

Nearly every marketing program makes use of credit sales. Chapter 13 explains obligations in extending credit and pitfalls to avoid in debt collection.

What warranties are offered for your product? Some warranties are imposed by law. When and how can you limit them? What federal regulations are applied to warranties? These questions are answered in Chapter 14.

How do you label your product? What do you have to do to protect your trademark, trade name or copyright? These and other questions are covered by Chapter 19.

In recent years there has been a tremendous growth in sales by mail. Both the U. S. Post Office and the Federal Trade Commission have issued mail regulations. The 30-day rule and the negative option rule are explained in Chapter 16.

Chapters 17 and 18 cover unfair practices and misrepresentation. Among the topics discussed are lotteries, the shipment of unordered goods, product substitution, failure to fill orders promptly, "free" offers, contests, and the health or medical claims.

ACKNOWLEDGMENTS

Books like this are seldom the accomplishment of a single person—this one is no exception. My editor at Prentice-Hall, the late Bette Schwartzberg, provided valuable guidance regarding both scope and format. Research assistance has been provided by Tod Huckaby and Scott Sterkel. Typing and proofreading have been ably handled by Pat Alsum. I have had the invaluable prayer support of my good friend Dan Knab.

No acknowledgment would be complete without giving recognition to the burden this effort has placed on my family. Weekend after weekend they have foregone what I like to think of as the pleasure of my company. I thank them for their support.

CONTENTS

CHAPTER 11   Dealing with Advertising and Promotional Allowances 139

CHAPTER 12   How to Avoid Advertising Pitfalls 150

chapter one

ANTITRUST OVERVIEW

Of the many laws touching on various aspects of marketing, the antitrust laws, and in particular sections 1 and 2 of the Sherman Antitrust Act[1] and the Robinson-Patman Act,[2] have the most pervasive impact on the marketing function. These statutes cut a broad swath and will be mentioned frequently where particular aspects of marketing are treated. Chapters 2–8 deal primarily with the antitrust aspects of establishing, organizing, and maintaining a marketing system. At this point, these principal antitrust statutes will be discussed in a more general fashion to provide a basis for a better understanding of the later chapters.

PURPOSE OF THE SHERMAN ACT

In understanding and predicting the impact of sections 1 and 2 of the Sherman Act on various marketing activities it is helpful to keep in mind the fundamental purpose of the act. The basic premise of the Sherman Act is

> that the unrestrained interaction of competitive forces will yield the best allocation of our economic resources, the lowest prices, the highest quality and the greatest material progress, while at the same time providing an environment conducive to the preservation of our democratic political and social institutions.[3]

In short, the purpose of the Sherman Act is to protect the competitive process.

1

While it is sometimes said that the goal of antitrust laws is to achieve the best allocation of resources, this is at most an indirect goal which is believed to be achieved through the competitive process. The Supreme Court made this point in the landmark case of *Brown Shoe Co.* v. *United States*[4] in which it said:

> we cannot fail to recognize Congress' desire to promote competition through the protection of viable, small, locally owned businesses. Congress anticipated that occasional higher costs and prices might result from the maintenance of fragmented industries and markets. It resolved these competing considerations in favor of decentralization.

The Second Circuit in a famous decision written by Judge Learned Hand in *United States* v. *Aluminum Co. of America*[5] identified three policies underlying the Sherman Act:

1. Unchallenged economic power deadens initiative, discourages thrift, and depresses energy.
2. Competitors versed in the craft will be quick to detect opportunities for savings and new shifts in production.
3. A system of small producers, each dependent for success upon its own skill and character, is preferable for its indirect social and moral effects to one in which the great mass of those engaged in commerce must accept the direction of the few.

There is a tension between the promotion of competition and the efficient allocation of resources at times.

Key Point: Nevertheless, the courts have continually reaffirmed that the goal of the Sherman Act is the promotion of competition.

Efforts to defend anticompetitive conduct on the basis that it promotes efficiencies or ensures quality have been rebuffed. Such arguments must be addressed to Congress rather than to the courts. Throughout this book we will have occasion after occasion to refer to laws, rules, and regulations designed to preserve and enhance the competitive process. Some laws preserve competition directly by prohibiting anticompetitive restraints. Other laws such as the Federal Trade Commission Act do so indirectly by ensuring that consumers have access to full and truthful information.

PURPOSE OF THE ROBINSON-PATMAN ACT

The Robinson-Patman Act, which amended section 2 of the Clayton Act dealing with price discrimination, was enacted in 1936. As a piece of depression era legislation, it reflects goals and purposes which are at odds with the procompetitive purpose of the Sherman Act. The rise of the chain store with its mass purchasing power and resultant ability to reduce its costs threatened to drive the small locally owned retailer out of business. Section 2 of the Clayton Act was inadequate to combat local or regional level price cutting by chain stores. Following an investigation by the Federal Trade Commission (FTC), the Robinson-Patman Act was enacted. In very brief terms, the act:

1. Prohibits price discrimination but does permit price adjustments reflecting cost of service differences and to meet the competition

2. Requires that promotional allowances or facilities provided by a supplier be made available to all distributors on proportionately equal terms

3. Prohibits distributors, such as chain stores, from using their purchasing power to induce a discriminatory price from their supplier

Key Point: The purpose of Robinson-Patman then is not to protect competition but to protect the small independent distributor even at the cost of less vigorous competition.

The act has been severely criticized for its potential for thwarting the most efficient method of operation. Government agencies, the Federal Trade Commission, and the Department of Justice, have not enforced the Robinson-Patman Act vigorously in recent years. However, private parties may and do bring treble damage actions under the act. Robinson-Patman Act issues are discussed primarily in Chapters 10 and 11.

SHERMAN ACT SECTION I

Section 1 of the Sherman Act provides in part that "Every contract, combination in the form of trust or otherwise, or conspiracy in restraint of trade or commerce among the several states, or with foreign nations, is hereby declared to be illegal."

In popular terms section 1 deals with conspiracies although it applies to situations which would not fit a technical definition of conspiracy.

Key Point: Section 1 only comes into play when there are two or more parties involved.

The two parties required for section 1 application may be individuals, partnerships, corporations, or other legal entities. However, since the Supreme Court's decision in *Copperweld Corp.* v. *Independence Tube Corp.*,[6] it has been clear that a corporation cannot conspire with its wholly owned subsidiaries. The Court reasoned in *Copperweld* that a parent corporation so dominates its wholly owned subsidiaries that in reality there is only one actor. Since the decision in *Copperweld* lower courts have held that sister subsidiaries cannot conspire and a corporation cannot conspire with a subsidiary in which it owns 51 percent of the stock.

Similarly, a corporation cannot conspire with an officer or director acting within the scope of employment unless the officer or director has some independent economic interest in the conspiracy.

The law has always viewed conspiracy as a special danger to society because it brings the power and ability of a plurality of actors to bear on a transaction. Therefore actions lawful when done unilaterally may be unlawful if done jointly. Since it is concerted action that the law fears, a section 1 offense does not occur unless the parties contemplated concerted action. That is, there must be a unity of purpose. The conspiracy must be intended to restrain trade or commerce which is in or affects interstate commerce. Moreover the restraint must be unreasonable.

In summary, then, the elements of a section 1 violation are:

1. At least two persons must act
2. There must be a restraint of trade or commerce
3. The trade or commerce must be interstate
4. The restraint of trade or commerce must be unreasonable

PER SE VIOLATIONS OF SECTION I

Although we said that one of the elements of a section 1 violation is an unreasonable restraint of trade, proof of unreasonableness is often a massive undertaking. Therefore the courts have created so-called *per se violations* which dispense with proof of unreasonableness and effect on commerce. Some activities "because of their pernicious effect on competition and lack of any redeeming virtue are conclusively presumed to be unreasonable and therefore illegal without elaborate inquiry as to the precise harm they have caused or the business excuse for their use."[7]

Among the activities which have been held to be illegal per se are:

1. Price fixing (Chapter 9)
2. Market allocations (Chapter 3)
3. Boycotts and refusals to deal (Chapter 6)
4. Exclusive dealing (Chapter 5)
5. Tying arrangements (Chapter 8)

Since 1970 the trend of the law has been to find exceptions to the per se rules and to require more cases to be decided under a full rule of reason analysis.

Nevertheless the per se rules maintain their vitality and provide an attractive vehicle for plaintiffs to obtain a short-cut method of proof in seeking treble damages under the antitrust laws. Moreover, the activities which have been declared per se violations are most likely to trigger criminal prosecution brought by the Department of Justice. This is especially true of per se violations involving price restraints such as price fixing or bid rigging.

RULE OF REASON

In a very strict and technical sense, all business agreements or contracts restrain commerce. If company A sells a widget to company B, company C is restrained from supplying B's demand for that widget. To consider any contract to buy or sell as a restraint of commerce is a hypertechnical approach. Therefore the Supreme Court has held that only *unreasonable* restraints violate the Sherman Act. A more practical analysis would imply that a contract to buy and sell does not restrain commerce; rather it is commerce. Nonetheless, it is now a part of the law of Sherman Act section 1 that only *unreasonable* restraints of commerce are unlawful.

How does one know that a restraint of commerce is unreasonable? If the restraint falls into one of the per se categories, it is clearly unreasonable. For other restraints, it is necessary to engage in a lengthy and sometimes complex analysis of the activity to determine whether, under all of the circumstances of the case, the restraint is unreasonable. Among the matters considered are the facts peculiar to the business, the history of and the reason for the restrictive practice, and the market impact of the practice and any business justification for the challenged practice.

A rule of reason analysis focuses on the market effect of the restraint which is measured in economic terms for antitrust violations. Market definitions are discussed below in reference to section 2, monopolization offenses, but are equally relevant to section 1 analysis.

INTENT

For most Sherman Act offenses no specific intent is required. Rather, a general intent to do the act complained of is sufficient. Accordingly, acts done negligently would not provide the required general intent. The required general intent may be presumed from the fact that the conduct in question restrained trade. It has been said that no monopolist monopolizes unconscious of what he or she is doing. While a general intent is sufficient for most civil violations of the Sherman Act, the offense of attempt to monopolize does require a specific intent to monopolize.

MONOPOLIZATION

Unlike section 1 offenses which require at least two actors to join in a restraint of trade, the offense of monopolization under section 2 requires only a single actor. Section 2 of the Sherman Act provides in part that "Every person who shall monopolize, or attempt to monopolize, or combine or conspire with any other person or persons, to monopolize any part of trade or commerce . . . shall be deemed guilty of a felony." There are three distinct offenses under section 2:

1. Monopolization
2. Attempt to monopolize
3. Conspiracy to monopolize

In the Supreme Court's classic definition of monopolization in *United States v. Grinnell Corp.*,[8] the Court said monopolization has two elements:

1. The possession of monopoly power in the relevant market
2. The wilful acquisition or maintenance of that power as distinguished from the growth or development of a superior product, business acumen, or historic accident

It is also monopolization for a party with monopoly power, no matter how the power is acquired, to use that power to gain a competitive advantage or to destroy a competitor.

Key Point: Monopoly power by itself may be entirely lawful. For example, patents and copyrights create lawful monopoly power in the holder of the patent or copyright.

A lawful monopoly may become unlawful monopolization when it is used to restrain trade or destroy a competitor. For example, even a lawful monopolist violates the Sherman Act by requiring a customer to purchase an unpatented product which has competitive substitutes in order to purchase the patented product. This would be a use of lawful monopoly power to restrain trade or commerce in another product. The law will not permit such efforts to extend monopoly power.

Monopoly Power and How to Measure It

The first element of monopolization is the possession of monopoly power. Technically, *monopoly power* is defined as the power to control prices or to exclude or restrain competitors. Competitors need not actually be excluded nor prices actually controlled, so long as the power to do so exists. In other words, a firm will have monopoly power if it can impose a significant price increase above a competitive price level and not lose significant sales to its competitors. Or, a firm has monopoly power if it can protect or increase its share of a market by excluding potential rivals from the market. For example, a firm may own all of the available distribution outlets for a product within a certain market area. The existence of monopoly power is determined with reference to a particular market. For antitrust purposes a relevant market is made up of a geographic area and a product.

The geographic limits of a market may range from a single community, in the case of hospital services, to a worldwide market for diamonds. The extent of the geographic market is determined by examining the patterns of business of the parties involved, the market structure, and the industry. A market is an economic construct used to describe an arena in which competitive strength or market power is measured. It must reflect the area in which the seller operates and to which the purchaser can practicably turn for supplies. Among the factors to be considered in defining markets is the influence of competition and pricing of the firms on market behavior. The importance of defining the geographic market is that it identifies the buyers and sellers who participate in the market and whose strength and behavior will be analyzed.

For example, the geographic market for diamonds may be worldwide because the product is highly valuable and can be readily transported at low cost. On the other hand, the market for redimix concrete is a small local area because of the high cost of transportation. Geographic features such as mountain ranges, oceans, deserts, and lakes can create barriers to trade that will define the geographic limits of a market. Customer preferences may also determine a geographic market. Consumers may be willing to travel five miles to eat at a fast food restaurant but refuse to travel ten miles even if doing so would permit them to take advantage of a lower price or to obtain better quality. Additional evidence that two restaurants are in different geographic markets may be found in the fact that a substantial price reduction by one restaurant will not result in a loss of customers to the other. This is because customers will not drive the additional miles to the cheaper restaurant.

A relevant product market is comprised of all products that have reasonable functional interchangeability. For products to be interchangeable for purposes of market definition their physical properties must be such that they can be used for the same purpose and purchasers must be willing to substitute one product for the other. In economic terms products are placed in the same market if a relatively small increase in the cost of one product will cause buyers to substitute another product. Economists refer to this as the *cross-elasticity of demand* which is the measure of the degree to which the sales of one product vary with the change of price in another product. If a slight decrease in the price of product A causes a considerable number of customers of B, C, and D to switch to product A there is a high degree of cross-elasticity of demand and the products are in the same market.

Typically a single item or product will be placed in a market. However, in some circumstances a cluster of products or services may be grouped together as a single product. For example, the diverse banking services of loans, deposit accounts, estate and trust planning, safe deposit boxes, account reconciliation services, investment advice, and checking accounts have been clustered as the product of commercial banking.

Products may be placed in different markets by perceived differences in quality. Thus, it may be proper to distinguish between $10 wristwatches and $250 wristwatches. It may be necessary to separate products based on their qualities and functions. Stores selling men's business suits probably do not compete directly with stores selling blue jeans and bib overalls. For a more extreme example, an automobile dealership is not in the same market as a seller of motor boats although both products are used for transportation.

In summary, definition of a market in terms of product and geography means that if prices were increased significantly or if volume of the product was reduced significantly within a given area while demand for the product remained constant, then supply from other sources would not enter quickly enough or in sufficient volume to return the price or volume of sales to the prior level.

Once the product is identified and the geographic area described, the existence of monopoly power can be measured. Traditionally market power has been measured by the market share held by a party. The Supreme Court has refused to establish a bright line measure of the market share necessary for monopoly power. A 90 percent market share is almost certainly sufficient for a finding of monopoly power. A 65 percent market share creates monopoly power when the rest of the market is divided by 50 other firms.

Market share is not the only means of measuring monopoly power. Monopoly power may be shown by conduct which actually excludes competitors or raises prices. Other evidence of market power may be found in the structure of the market. For example, if there are high barriers to the entry of new firms into the market, the power of the firms already in the market is of more concern. Barriers to market entry include regulatory controls such as licensing, large economies of scale which preclude entry on a small scale, heavy capital requirements, or heavy advertising. Courts are more concerned with potential restraints on competition in a market having high entry barriers and few competitors. On the other hand, a restraint may have little effect on market prices when other firms can readily enter the market. Potential competition from firms which can readily enter the market will preclude monopolistic pricing by existing firms in the market.

Acquiring or Maintaining Monopoly Power

In addition to having monopoly power the offense of monopolization under section 2 of the Sherman Act requires that the firm has taken some action to acquire or maintain its monopoly power. The conduct required is conduct designed to exclude competitors using the types of unreasonable restraints which violate section 1 and other exclusionary practices designed to foreclose competition. In antitrust language such conduct is referred to as "predatory," "exclusionary," or "not honest industrial" conduct. Acts which would be entirely lawful if done by a firm lacking monopoly power may be unlawful if done by a firm possessing monopoly power. The courts have recognized that size carries with it an opportunity for abuse.

Key Point: The marketing professional must consider the structure of the market and whether the firm possesses monopoly power in designing a marketing program.

A firm with a large market share must be more circumspect in its conduct. Such firms will probably want to establish vigorous antitrust compliance programs to reduce the risk of antitrust violation. Moreover in dealing with large powerful firms courts are:

> to be wary of conduct which in the hands of a smaller participant might be considered harmless or honestly industrial, but when taken by a monopolist tends to destroy competition.[9]

A firm with monopoly power must refrain from conduct directed at smothering the competition or tightening its hold on the market. Additionally, acts done by a firm with monopoly power which are lawful when examined alone may be illegal when it is part of a course of conduct which maintains the firm's monopoly power.

What Is Exclusionary Conduct?

It is impossible to provide an exhaustive list of all conduct which might be held to be exclusionary because the analysis of conduct is very situation specific. However, some types of conduct that can be identified as having been held to be exclusionary are:

1. Monopoly leveraging or the cross market use of monopoly power is unlawful under section 2 of the Sherman Act. Monopoly leveraging occurs when a firm having monopoly power in one market uses that power to obtain an economic advantage in another market. Often

the monopoly power in the first market will be the lawful result of patent, copyright, license, or regulation. For example, a firm lawfully having a television broadcast monopoly pursuant to a Federal Communication Commission license was found guilty of leveraging its broadcast monopoly to obtain an advantage in the market for the production of television commercials. The broadcaster refused to air commercials which it had not produced.

A pharmaceutical company was held guilty of monopoly leveraging when it tied the discount offered on the purchase of two patented products to the purchase of a nonpatented product. The highly technical requirements of tie-in sales (see Chapter 8) were not met, but the conduct was an unlawful leveraging of the lawful patent monopoly into the market for the nonpatented product.

2. Selective refusals to deal may be unlawful if done with a view toward acquiring or maintaining monopoly power. Refusals to deal are discussed in detail in Chapter 6. As a general rule a firm has the right to select the parties with whom it will deal. However, refusals to deal become unlawful when done for monopolistic purposes. Moreover, if the refusal to deal is the result of a joint decision rather than a unilateral action it may even result in a group boycott which is a per se violation of section 1.

3. Bottleneck resources and essential facilities may create a duty to deal with a competitor. Occasionally a firm will control a resource or facility which is essential to participation in a market. If that resource cannot be duplicated economically, the owner of the resource may be required to permit its competitors to have access to the facility on a plane of equality. The classic example of an essential facility occurred in a case in which a group of railroads controlled the only suitable railroad bridge across the Mississippi River into the city of St. Louis. The railroads also controlled the railroad terminal in St. Louis. Competing railroads were greatly disadvantaged by a denial of access to the bridge and terminal. The Supreme Court required the owner-railroads to grant access to the bridge and terminal to the competing nonowner-railroads on a plane of equality with the access of the owner-railroads.

4. Predatory pricing or pricing below cost is unlawful but is exceedingly difficult to prove. Pricing issues are discussed in detail in Chapters 9 and 10. The purpose of the Sherman Act is to improve consumer welfare through competition. Price reductions are in the interest of consumers and are favored by the courts. Therefore courts are very

reluctant to find that a price reduction violates the Sherman Act. There are circumstances, however, when a price reduction is not in the long run interest of consumers. This can occur when a financially strong firm can cut its prices to drive existing competitors from the market and then, because entry barriers keep new firms from competing, the firm can raise its prices to collect monopoly profits. As a general proposition prices will not be held to be predatory unless they are below average variable costs. Average variable costs are the costs that vary with changes in output divided by the output.

Note. While predatory pricing is seldom established as a violation of federal antitrust laws, many states have specific statutes prohibiting sales below cost. These statutes may prove more troublesome than the Sherman Act.

5. So-called dirty tricks can constitute the necessary predatory or exclusionary acts to support a finding of monopolization. Dirty tricks include such activities as commercial bribery, product disparagement, intimidation, industrial espionage, and the hiring away of a competitor's key employees.

In a case involving an electric utility which sold at retail in competition with one of its wholesale customers, the court found that statements by the wholesaler that in the event of power shortages it would cut its wholesale customers before reducing service to its retail customers was a dirty trick. The court found anticompetitive the wholesalers "deliberate statements threatening plaintiffs power supply" which cast "doubt on the plaintiffs ability to offer adequate service to existing and potential customers."

In a case involving the business of the wholesale distribution of periodicals, the dirty tricks included below cost or predatory pricing, disparagement of the competitor's financial ability to continue operation, removal of the plaintiff's periodicals from display racks, intimidation of plaintiff's customers, and threats against persons who helped the plaintiffs obtain supplies.

It has been said that evidence of dirty tricks will go a long way toward establishing a violation of section 2 of the Sherman Act.

ROBINSON-PATMAN ACT

The Robinson-Patman Act was enacted in 1936 to cure perceived defects in section 2 of the Clayton Act to prevent discriminatory pricing. The statute is designed to provide small businesses protection from price discrimination by suppliers induced by the larger purchases of their chain-store competitors. However, the act affects a much broader array of transactions. In outline form, the Robinson-Patman Act prohibits the following discriminatory activities:

1. Price discrimination by the seller subject to cost justification and changed condition defenses. Price discrimination is the subject of Chapter 10.

2. Places restrictions on the payment of brokerage which can be used to conceal price discrimination.

3. Limits advertising and promotional allowances paid by the seller. The use of seller provided advertising is the subject of Chapter 11.

4. Limits promotional allowances paid by the seller. Promotional allowances are treated in Chapter 11.

5. Makes unlawful discriminatory prices knowingly accepted or induced by the purchaser.

The statute contains limited exemptions for cooperatives and nonprofit organizations.

Key Point: In very general terms the Robinson-Patman Act requires that:

1. Any price discounts be cost justified by savings from volume sales or delivery terms or be offered to meet a competitive offer.

2. That advertising and promotional assistance be made available to all customers on a proportionally equal basis. That is, a firm offering a promotional program designed for use by large purchasers must also design a proportionately equal promotional program for use by smaller purchasers.

Unlike the Sherman Act which reaches broadly to cover activities that affect interstate commerce as well as those activities that are actually in interstate commerce, the Robinson-Patman Act reaches only those transactions actually within interstate commerce. Moreover, the effect of discrimination must be "to lessen competition or tend to create a monopoly in any line of commerce" or "to injure, destroy or prevent competition with any person who either grants or knowingly receives the benefit of such discrimination, or with customers of either of them."

_____ **ANTITRUST COMPLIANCE PROGRAM** _____

An antitrust compliance program is simply a management tool for avoiding the expense incurred as a result of a violation of the antitrust laws. But why should a business or its employees concern themselves with avoiding a violation of the antitrust laws? There are a number of very important reasons.

First, a violation of the Sherman Act, the principal antitrust statute, is a felony for which a corporation may be fined up to $1 million and the individuals involved may be fined up to $100,000. Moreover, individuals may be sentenced to up to three years in prison.

How realistic is it that a criminal antitrust case will be brought? In March 1984 the Department of Justice had more than 110 Grand Juries empaneled investigating a variety of antitrust claims. As expected, these Grand Juries produced several hundred indictments of corporations and individuals. It is also important to note that the department's inquiries are expanding into new industries in addition to the construction bid rigging which has produced most criminal cases in recent years. For all of 1984 the department brought more antitrust criminal cases than in any other year of its existence.

Moreover, the Department of Justice believes strongly in prison sentences. Assistant Attorney General Paul McGrath in February of 1984 referred to price-fixers as thieves and felons who ought to be behind bars. Frequently, antitrust charges are joined with other criminal charges such as mail fraud.

Here are some sentences for individuals meted out in 1983.

- $20,000 fine, 2 years probation
- $10,000 fine, 120 days in prison, 6 months probation
- 120 days plus 3 years probation
- 1 year all suspended except 45 days
- $50,000 and 2 years probation
- $50,000 and 5 years probation
- 120 days in jail
- 2 days per week in community service for 3 years
- 60 days in federal prison
- 6 months in jail and 3 years of community service (2 days per month)
- $20,000 fine, 5 years probation with 500 hours of community service
- 5 months in jail

The sentencing trend is toward tougher criminal sentences for both firms and individuals.

Second, a firm convicted of price fixing or bid rigging on a government contract may be barred from bidding on future government contracts.

Third, treble damage civil actions have resulted. Enormous civil judgments have been obtained in recent years:

1. MCI obtained a $1.8 billion judgment from AT & T.
2. Litton obtained a judgment of more than $200 million from AT & T.

Fourth, litigation costs alone can be large. A major Sherman Act antitrust case can consume up to a million dollars a year in legal fees for several years. To this must be added the cost of hiring expert witnesses. Additionally, there is a large commitment of managerial time needed to defend an antitrust case. Managerial employees will be asked to search their files for documents, assist counsel in trial preparation, attend depositions which can last several days, answer interrogatories, and testify at trial. At least one senior managerial official will be asked to be present at all times during trial. All of this effort diverts time from the productive tasks normally assigned to these employees.

Surveys show that firms institute antitrust compliance programs for four reasons:

- Protect top management
- Avoid antitrust violations
- Previous involvement in antitrust litigation
- History of antitrust litigation within the firm's industry

To be effective an antitrust compliance program must be designed to attack the common causes of antitrust violations. The three most common causes are:

1. Pursuit of corporate gain
2. Ignorance of the law and failure to seek advice of counsel
3. Failure of subordinate employees to believe that management is serious about antitrust compliance

Clearly the first and third reasons are closely related. Subordinate employees—e.g., regional sales managers—agree to fix prices because they believe their firm will gain and they believe management is more interested in corporate gain than in antitrust compliance. These types of violations are sometimes called rational violations.

The best defense against rational antitrust violations is a general corporate atmosphere of abiding by law and being a good corporate citizen. These virtues should be taught in employee handbooks, in periodic memoranda from the chief executive officer, by lectures at company conventions, in employee newsletters, through formal antitrust compliance programs, and with the use of training films. Building an image of corporate law abidance will engender corporate pride as well as improve antitrust compliance.

The single most important element in an effective antitrust compliance program is a commitment by management to make it work. Top management may also consider adopting a number of compliance strategies including:

- Standardization of operating procedures which has the effect of limiting the decision making responsibility of lower level employees.

- Dismissal of employees involved in antitrust violations.

- Changing the company's reward system. For example, placing sales-persons on salary rather than commission.

- Moving decision making, particularly pricing decisions, to a higher corporate level.

- Encouraging employees to report suspicious conduct directly to cor-porate counsel without going through the chain of command. Here it should be pointed out that in the Ninth Circuit—which includes California, Washington, Oregon, Arizona, Idaho, Alaska, and Ha-waii—an employee who is fired because of refusing to participate in a price-fixing scheme can sue the former employer for price-fixing and obtain treble damages.

- Conducting antitrust compliance audits of likely trouble spots—e. g., sales managers, marketing and market research, corporate planning, and senior executives. The audit should also review the firms doc-ument retention policy.

AUDITS

It is not necessary to conduct an antitrust audit as a part of an antitrust compliance program. However, an antitrust audit can be an invaluable tool both for creating a new program and evaluating an existing program. An audit is particularly important in an industry that is chronically beset by antitrust problems or for a firm with a history of antitrust violations. Because of the possibility of treble damages in a civil antitrust action, an antitrust audit is cost effective.

Even when top management has carefully observed the letter and spirit of the antitrust laws, they may be unaware of antitrust problems created by middle management or sales personnel. Moreover, if the firm has acquired another company, it has also acquired the company's business practices and documents. At the least an antitrust audit of the acquired company should be conducted.

An antitrust audit will consist of a systematic review of preselected company documents and business practices. It is accomplished by reviewing files and interviewing employees. The expense of an audit can be reduced by identifying areas of the company of greatest antitrust concern as the focus of the audit. Areas of particular concern may include the following:

1. Employees who attend bid openings
2. Compliance with prior Department of Justice Business Review letters and prior antitrust consent decrees or judgments affecting the company's operations
3. Intracompany meetings of credit managers, sales managers, transportation managers, and so on
4. Relations with subcontractors who might be competitors
5. Relations with customers who are also competitors
6. Patent licensing
7. Trade associations
8. Low profit operations
9. Dealer terminations

What sorts of things should the audit look for? Complaints from other dealers? What sort of comments do the salespeople make in their daily call reports? Do they analyze the competition? Is there adequate support for price changes?

The antitrust audit should be designed to preserve corporate confidentiality to the fullest extent possible. It should be conducted or supervised by outside legal counsel. When employees are being audited:

- Employees should be given a written statement from highest management.

- Employees should be urged to cooperate with counsel or his agents.

- Matters only within the scope of employment should be discussed.

- Make known that the purpose of the audit is to permit the company to obtain legal advice.

- Communication should be classified as confidential.

The purpose of the following letter is to invoke the attorney–client privilege to preserve the confidentiality of statements made to counsel during the audit.

> Dear (employee)
>
> XYZ company is currently undergoing an antitrust audit conducted by outside counsel. It is a part of your duty to cooperate fully with counsel in making this audit successful. As you are aware, XYZ company is committed to full compliance with both the letter and spirit of our nation's antitrust laws.
>
> In order to make this audit successful, it is necessary for you to discuss matters within the scope of your employment freely with the legal counsel conducting the audit. These discussions will be held confidential and are for the purpose of enabling XYZ company to obtain legal advice.
>
> Very truly yours,
>
> President
> XYZ Corporation

DOCUMENT RETENTION PROGRAMS

Document retention programs have an important impact on antitrust compliance. A document retention program should be created if one does not presently exist. An extant one should be reviewed periodically and should be adhered to in practice.

Corporate document retention plans must be applied throughout the company on an even and comprehensive basis. Employees should be made aware that there are *no* private documents related to business. Thus items like desk calendars and work diaries are subject to discovery in antitrust proceedings. Documents ready for destruction under a document retention program should not be destroyed without consulting legal counsel if antitrust charges are pending or threatened.

Destruction of documents to avoid an antitrust conviction or civil action can itself be a criminal offense in some circumstances.

- It may constitute obstruction of justice in violation of 18 U. S. C. sections 1503 or 1505.
- It may violate the general injunction against conspiracy, 18 U. S. C. section 371.
- It may be contempt of court, 18 U. S. C. section 401.

- It may be misprision of felony, 18 U. S. C. section 4.

- It may be deemed a violation of section 10 of the Federal Trade Commission Act which makes it a crime to falsify certain documentary evidence.

Consider some situations a company might face regarding document destruction.

Example 1. Suppose a firm has an ongoing document destruction program and then receives a subpoena from a grand jury requesting documents. Should the firm continue to destroy documents?

Answer. No, unless the document is clearly unrelated to the grand jury inquiry. The assistance of legal counsel should be sought before any more documents are destroyed.

Example 2. As is often the case, the company receives a letter from the Department of Justice or Federal Trade Commission saying that a subpoena is on the way. Should the company continue to destroy documents under its document retention plan?

Answer. No, this should be treated as if the subpoena itself had been served on the company.

Example 3. The company learns that one of its employees has gone to the Department of Justice Antitrust Division for a chat. No court proceeding is pending. Should the company continue to destroy documents under its document retention plan?

Answer. It is probably safe to continue destroying documents but this is a close call. It may depend on how much the company knows. Definitely consult counsel.

Example 4. A company discovers an antitrust violation during the course of an antitrust compliance audit. There is no investigation of the company or a coconspirator pending. Should the company continue to destroy documents under its document retention plan?

Answer. It is probably safe to continue the firm's document destruction program.

DOCUMENT CREATION

All documents should be created with the expectation that the document will some day be seen by the company's enemies. Therefore, documents should be prepared in such a way as to avoid the appearance of evil. Legal counsel should be consulted in the drafting of certain documents. Counsel should review drafts of the following documents:

1. Documents relating to possible corporate acquisitions
2. Long-range plans
3. Marketing plans
4. Market research
5. Capital expenditure plans
6. Trade press advertisements
7. Training manuals
8. Sales manuals
9. In-house publications

POLICY STATEMENTS

In addition to the organizational strategies and the antitrust audit discussed above, the antitrust compliance program should also provide a formal written antitrust compliance policy statement to each managerial or sales and marketing employee. The method and detail of compliance policies differ widely with companies. For example, IBM simply includes a section on dealing with competitors in their Business Conduct Guidelines.

Control Data, on the other hand, utilizes a 12-page guideline for compliance with trade regulation laws covering price discrimination, licensing of technology, unfair methods of competition, monopolization, and mergers.

Other antitrust compliance policy statements contain lists of specifically prohibited activities. For example, one such policy states that no employee shall enter into any agreement or understanding with a competitor respecting prices, costs, profits, product or service offerings, terms or conditions of sale, deliveries, production facilities, production or sales volumes, market shares, decisions to quote or not to quote, sales territories, or distribution methods. With respect to certain other subjects, agreements with competitors can be reached only with approval of legal counsel.

The purpose of the compliance policy statement is not only to inform employees that the corporation does care about antitrust compliance but also to inform them in a general way of the content of the antitrust laws.

ANTITRUST SENSITIVE EMPLOYEES

Employees who are sensitive to antitrust problems are more likely to avoid inadvertent remarks that can create antitrust problems later. Alert employees will avoid the use of antitrust buzz words that create an appearance of impropriety even where none exists. Antitrust specialist Josh Greenberg tells the story of a client who was called before a grand jury and confronted with a letter that said:

> Dear Joe,
> Thank you for helping us to fix the price.
> Sincerely, Sam.

When a Department of Justice lawyer or a plaintiff's lawyer sees a document like that his heart races. The document has all the indicia of a smoking gun complete with identifiable fingerprints. In this particular case the document was innocent. Joe had testified for Sam in a case involving a dispute over mining royalties. The moral, however, is clear. With a little forethought, Sam could have chosen words less loaded with antitrust significance and Joe would have avoided a grand jury appearance.

Administrative Law Judge Steve Charno relates that while he was with the Antitrust Division of the Department of Justice a contract produced during discovery by a potential defendant carried this marginal notation by a corporate vice president:

> We will use this clause as a club if they ever try to compete with us.

The document was tantamount to a confession of an anticompetitive intent and an important element of proof of an antitrust violation.

Documents from the files of corporate executives have been found setting forth proposed corporate policies with a cryptic marginal notation "anticompetitive." By itself that notation is ambiguous but if the firm subsequently adopts the proposed policy, a jury may readily conclude that the corporation acted wilfully and knowingly to violate the antitrust laws.

The problem could have easily been avoided by expanding the notation to read "May be anticompetitive. Clear with counsel." Then if the policy is adopted by the firm, it can later be explained that prior to adopting the policy the firm secured a legal opinion that it could do so without violating the law.

When employees are alert to the requirements of the antitrust laws, they will be alert also to the importance of avoiding the use of language that raises an antitrust red flag. Obviously, there would be no references to "price fixing," or similar phrases like "price agreement" or "agreed upon price" unless the document also carefully explains the innocent meaning of those terms.

Documents should not be marked "Read and destroy"—all the copies will not be destroyed in this age of the photocopier. The language will only serve to emphasize any dangerous language contained in the document. Similarly, do not mark documents "For your eyes only" or "Confidential." "Confidential" should only be used for documents which might be subject to claims of privilege such as attorney work product or attorney–client. If the document is marked confidential it should be treated as confidential and filed separately.

What should be done if a dangerous document such as one containing antitrust buzz words is found during an antitrust audit? What should be done if a document is found with an incorrect or ambiguous statement of facts and it is not yet ready for destruction under the document retention program? First, it is dangerous to destroy the document on a selective basis. Other copies are likely to be found and selective destruction could result in a criminal charge for misprision of felony. Moreover, any ambiguity or incorrect fact statement will probably be construed against the company by a jury. Why? Because the jurors will infer a guilty intent from the selective destruction of the documents.

One way to handle such problem documents is to attach a subsequent clarifying memorandum to the document. If the clarifying memorandum predates any antitrust investigation or litigation it may successfully defuse the time bomb in the company files.

ASSOCIATION MEMBERSHIPS

An area which is particularly sensitive for antitrust concern is participation in trade associations. Trade association meetings are fertile grounds for conspiracy to divide markets or fix prices. Therefore, any antitrust compliance program should pay particular attention to trade association activities.

Personnel who attend trade association meetings must be trained to avoid any possible compromising discussions. Company personnel should be specifically and repeatedly instructed to avoid all discussions with competitors involving:

1. Future prices
2. Current production levels
3. Price stability

4. Terms of sales

5. Geographic areas

6. Specific customers

7. Products which are not for sale

If such topics are raised at either formal trade association meetings or at informal social gatherings in conjunction with trade association meetings, company employees should protest and refuse to participate. If the conversation persists, the employee should make a production out of leaving the room. The importance of creating a scene when withdrawing is to impress on the memory of all those present that the employee withdrew.

Certain trade association activities are more likely to spawn antitrust concern than are others. Among the areas which the Federal Trade Commission considers sensitive are:

1. Pricing activities

2. Certification and standard setting

3. Availability of membership, services and association information to nonmembers

4. Codes of ethics and industry self-regulation

5. Research and development programs

6. Lobbying activities

7. Labor negotiations

Pricing activities which may be subject to attack by the commission or the Department of Justice include matters which only indirectly affect the price such as:

1. Adoption of standard terms and conditions of sale

2. Higher retainages

3. Length of credit terms

4. Shorter warranty periods

5. Limited warranties

Any antitrust compliance program should include a review of all trade association memberships and activities. Unless there is a clear benefit to the company from membership in the association, the membership should be dropped.

Review of association activities should include the association's own antitrust compliance program. Attention also must be paid to the true objective of the association and the attitude of the association members toward compliance with the antitrust laws. Do the members conduct the real business of the association at informal meetings? Employees attending association gatherings should be warned that "minutes" of even the most informal gatherings are likely to exist. Some people are inveterate note takers and memo-to-the-files writers. Of course in reviewing association activities formal minutes of the proceedings should be reviewed. The antitrust risks vary somewhat depending on the personnel attending the association meetings. For example, one might expect a higher risk at a meeting attended by marketing and sales personnel than at one attended by engineering and technical people. However, engineers may run amok in standard setting or discouraging product innovation.

Membership restrictions can in themselves be anticompetitive. Therefore restraints on membership must be carefully scrutinized. Antitrust concerns can be avoided if any association membership restrictions have a legitimate procompetitive purpose and are tailored narrowly to achieve that purpose.

CHECKLIST FOR REVIEWING TRADE ASSOCIATION ACTIVITIES

_____ Does the trade association retain experienced antitrust counsel?

_____ Does association counsel regularly review the resolutions, minutes, by-laws, publications and policy statements of the association?

_____ Does association counsel attend the meetings of the association? General meetings? Board meetings? Committee meetings?

_____ Do the association leaders seek and follow the advice of the association's antitrust counsel?

_____ Does association counsel explain to the association antitrust risks to the members from time to time?

_____ Has the association had an antitrust audit? When?

_____ Has the association been subject to an antitrust investigation or complaint by a law enforcement agency?

_____ Does the association have an antitrust policy statement?

_____ Has the policy statement been distributed to the members?

_____ Does the association have antitrust guidelines? Are the guidelines readily available to the members?

_____ Are the guidelines referred to and followed?

_____ Are formal agendas prepared and/or reviewed by antitrust counsel?

Are the agendas followed?

_____ Are the true objectives of the association lawful?

_____ Do the association members have positive attitudes regarding antitrust compliance?

_____ Is the business of the association done only at formal meetings?

_____ Who attends meetings of the association?

_____ Are there any restraints on association membership?

STANDARD SETTING

Often trade associations will establish industry standards. There is no inherent conflict between standard setting and the antitrust laws. Ordinarily, standard setting will not raise antitrust concerns unless compliance with the standard is required to successfully bring a product to market.

> *Example.* An industry establishes a code which is then adopted by state and local legislative bodies. Since adherence to the standard is now mandatory, the standard-setting process has the potential for abuse in denying a new competitor access to the market either through changing the standard or refusing to certify compliance with the standard.

Key Point: Compliance with industry standard may be required as a practical matter even without formal legislative adoption. Wide-spread adoption and adherence to the standards on a voluntary basis may make it impossible to market a product that does not meet industry standards.

Antitrust concerns in the area of standard setting are greatly reduced if there are at least two competing standard-setting bodies. This ensures that companies who feel that their products have been unfairly or inappropriately excluded by one standard-setting body have an alternative. When there are competing standard-setting organizations, there is an incentive for each to establish the most credible and effective standard and a disincentive to exclude products or services for anticompetitive reason.

In the absence of competing standard-setting agencies, the Department of Justice considers two other factors crucial. First, does the standard-setting association provide due process to those challenging the standards or seeking certification? That is, does the association follow a procedure that:

1. Provides for input from most interested parties

2. Provide adequate record keeping of the basis for the decision
3. Require some justification based on the observed performance of the product or service

Second, the Department of Justice considers the nature of the criteria used in the standards. Standards based on performance rather than design criteria are more likely to enhance competition. Standards that establish minimum performance criteria are preferable from a competitive standpoint to those that establish maximum criteria or minimum and maximum criteria.

REQUIREMENTS FOR A SUCCESSFUL ANTITRUST COMPLIANCE PROGRAM

To be successful, an antitrust compliance program must be conducted by experienced antitrust counsel who approach client counseling with a "can do" attitude. That is, antitrust counsel must establish credibility with company personnel that they are not merely naysayers but are dedicated to helping company personnel achieve their goal through lawful means. Only then can the company be assured that company personnel from top to bottom will be sold on the absolute necessity of establishing and following an antitrust compliance program.

The antitrust compliance program must successfully educate company personnel to be sensitive to areas of antitrust risk. Antitrust counsel must be made available for confidential consultation with employees who have encountered an antitrust risk situation.

Once the program has been put in place it must be carefully and continuously monitored. Monitoring must include periodic spot checks of company files and update seminars.

Antitrust compliance programs like safety programs and quality assurance programs will not guarantee that no antitrust violations will occur. However, they have proven to be a cost-effective method of risk reduction when conducted by experienced antitrust counsel.

CONCLUSION

This chapter provides a framework of knowledge of antitrust law in which to understand the issues discussed in Chapters 2–12. Moreover, it will help in raising red flags indicating the need for legal counsel. The reader will find in subsequent chapters that certain acts may be lawful if done by a firm lacking monopoly power but which become unlawful when done by a firm having monopoly power.

Key Point: The marketing professional with some knowledge of how courts define markets and measure monopoly power is better equipped to gauge the legality of proposed marketing activity.

However, this book should not be used as a self-diagnostic antitrust handbook. Except for the bright line situations, antitrust law is a matter of shading and nuance requiring expert analysis.

Chapter 1 Footnotes

1. 15 U. S. C. §§ 1 and 2.
2. 15 U. S. C. §§ 13–13b, 21a.
3. *Northern Pacific Railway* v. *United States,* 356 U.S. 1, 4 (1958).
4. 370 U. S. 294, 344 (1962).
5. 148 F.2d 416 (2d Circuit 1945).
6. 104 S. Ct. 2731 (1984).
7. *Northern Pacific Railway* v. *United States,* 356 U. S. 1 (1958).
8. 384 U. S. 563, 570–71 (1966).
9. *G. A. F. Corporation* v. *Eastman Kodak Company,* 1981 Trade Cases (CCH) paragraph 64,025 (S. D. N. Y. 1981).

CREATING A DISTRIBUTION SYSTEM

The method chosen for distribution of a firm's product is determined by such factors as the existing and anticipated competition, firm's access to capital, firm size, industry custom and tradition, functional level at which the firm commences business, price of the product, need for product service and/or a trained sales staff, and rate of growth of the firm. Thus a manufacturer of curios may rely on independent wholesalers and jobbers while a firm which began as a local retailer may expand either by franchising additional outlets or by establishing new company-owned outlets or both. It is beyond the scope of this book to provide business advice regarding the best marketing program for a business at its various stages of development. Rather, it is the purpose of this chapter to discuss some of the legal pitfalls of various marketing programs. A particular emphasis of this chapter is franchising. Other chapters provide discussions related to selecting a marketing program—Chapters 3 (Territories), 4 (Dual Distribution), 5 (Exclusive Dealing), and 16 (Sales by Mail).

There are an infinite variety of methods by which a firm can market its product or services. A marketing program can be devised to meet the legitimate needs of any lawful marketing objective. Frequently legal problems arise when a marketing program is designed and implemented without careful attention to the laws of marketing. Legal pitfalls often can be avoided by changing minor aspects of the marketing plan.

One obstacle that often leads a firm to transgress the law is the lack of capital to adequately finance the expansion of the firms' marketing program. The firm sees potential distributors of the product as a source of the capital required to finance expanded distribution. This is one of the major attractions of franchising from the viewpoint of the franchisor. However, to attempt to utilize distributors as a source of capital raises a number of serious legal problems.

HOW TO AVOID SELLING A SECURITY

An important legal problem arising from a firm's efforts to use distributors as a capital source is the impact of state and federal securities laws. Most people only think of stocks and bonds as subject to securities laws. This is not the case. The legal definition of securities is extremely broad. The regulation of the sale of securities is a legal specialty which is itself the subject of multivolume treaties. However, the marketing professional should be alert to the potential for securities violations so that legal counsel can be sought. This section is designed to equip the marketing professional to identify potential problems. Even when the marketing plan presents securities law issues, a lawful marketing program in full compliance with the law may be desirable. In such cases the assistance of a securities law specialist should be obtained.

The broad definition given to the word "security" in federal and state securities laws can make these laws a trap for the unwary. The applicability of securities laws is often overlooked by lawyers, accountants, and businesspersons. Courts have acknowledged that "a security is not always an easily recognized creature." Nevertheless, failure to identify a transaction as one involving a security does not excuse compliance with registration and antifraud provisions of the securities laws. Even if the security is, fortuitously, exempt from regulation, the fraud provisions of the securities laws apply.

It has been said that "Whether the contemplated transaction constitutes a security should be a primary consideration in planning any significant business venture." The purpose of this section is to alert the nonsecurities specialist to some of the indicia of securities. It does not provide comprehensive coverage of the subject.

The Supreme Court has said in *SEC* v. *Howey* that the definition of a security

> embodies a flexible rather than a static principle, one that is capable of adaptation to meet the countless and variable schemes devised by those who seek the use of the money of others on the promise of profits.

Securities are defined broadly in §2 (1) of the Securities Act of 1933 to include "any note, stock, treasury stock, bond, debenture, evidence of indebtedness, certificate of interest or participation in any profit-sharing agreement, collateral-trust certificate, preorganization certificate of subscription, transferable share, investment contract, voting-trust certificate, certificate of deposit for a security, fractional undivided interest in oil, gas, or other mineral rights, or in general any interest or instrument commonly known as a 'security,' or any certificate of interest of participation in, temporary or interim certificate for, receipt for, guarantee of, or warrant or right to subscribe to or purchase, any of the foregoing." Similar definitions are found in §3(a)(10) of the Securities Exchange Act of 1934 and state securities laws. In construing the Securities Act, courts will be guided by the fact that the Act is remedial, that Congress directed that the Act be construed liberally and that form should be disregarded for substance and emphasis should be on economic reality. Among the more difficult securities law problems is the identification of investment contracts which are subject to the securities laws.

State statutes may define securities even more broadly than does federal law. For example, the California Corporations Code contains the following definition of securities:

> Security means any note; stock; treasury stock; membership in an incorporated or unincorporated association; bond; debenture; evidence of indebtedness; certificate of interest or participation in any profit-sharing agreement; collateral trust certificate, preorganization certificate or subscription; transferable share; investment contract; voting trust certificate; certificate of deposit for a security; certificate of interest or participation in an oil, gas or mining title or lease or in payments out of production under such a title or lease; put, call, straddle, option or privilege on any security, certificate of deposit, or group or index of securities (including any interest therein or based on the value thereof); or any put, call, straddle, option or privilege entered into on a national securities exchange relating to foreign currency; any beneficial interest or other security issued in connection with a funded employees' pension, profit sharing, stock bonus, or similar benefit plan; or, in general, any interest or instrument commonly known as a "security", or any certificate of interest or participation in, temporary or interim certificate for, receipt for, guarantee of, or warrant or right to subscribe to or purchase, any of the foregoing. All of the foregoing are securities whether or not evidenced by a written document. "Security" does not include: (1) any beneficial interest in any voluntary inter vivos trust which is not created for the purpose of carrying on any business or solely for the purpose of voting, or (2) any beneficial interest in any testamentary trust, or (3) any insurance or endowment policy or annuity contract under which an insurance company admitted in this state promises to pay a sum of money (whether or not based upon the investment performance of a segregated fund) either in a lump sum or periodically for life or some other specified period, or (4) any franchise subject to registration under the Franchise Investment Law, or exempted from such registration by Section 31100 or 31101 of that law.

_____ WHAT ARE INVESTMENT CONTRACTS? _____

For purposes of the Securities Act, the Supreme Court has said that an investment contract "means a contract, transaction or scheme whereby a person invests his [or her] money in a common enterprise and is led to expect profits solely from the efforts of the promoter or a third party." Thus there are three requirements for an investment contract (1) investment, (2) common enterprise, and (3) profits solely from the efforts of the promoter or a third party. However, it has been held that in addition to the foregoing factors, courts should also consider the economic reality. Under the definition of an investment contract, the SEC routinely treats limited partnership interests as securities.

The first requirement, that there be an investment, has been broadly construed. It often seems that courts will strain to find that an investment has been made. For example, it has been held that an employer's contribution on behalf of an employee to a pension plan is an investment by the employee.

The Supreme Court's formulation of the investment contract indicia as requiring an expectation of profits *solely* from the efforts of the promoters or third parties would seem on its face to create an easy escape through the assignment of some duties to the investor. In practice, District and Circuit courts have not followed the Supreme Court's rigid formulation. The SEC has taken the position that the assignment of nominal or limited responsibilities to the investor does not negate the existence of an investment contract. Where the duties assigned to the investor are so narrowly circumscribed as to leave little real choice of action or where the duties assigned would have little effect on the receipt of the promised benefits, a security may be found to exist. Even if the investor must exert substantial efforts, a security exists if the profit potential depends on the efforts of the promoter or a third party. Moreover, it has been said that "the issue is not what efforts in fact, were required of them. Rather, it is what efforts the (investors) were reasonably led to believe were required of them at the time they entered the contracts." However, where realization of the hoped for profits depends at least in part on the substantial efforts of the investor, no investment contract exists. The substantial efforts need not be the personal efforts of the investor if they are the efforts of someone controlled by the investor.

The third general requirement of a "common enterprise" has caused greater difficulty. That an investor's return is independent of that of other investors does not mean there is no common enterprise.

> Rather the requisite commonality is evidenced by the fact that the fortunes of all investors are inextricably tied to the efficacy of the (promoter's activities).

This formulation has been referred to as vertical commonality (between investor and promoter) as contrasted to horizontal commonality (among multiple investors), and has been adopted by the 9th circuit. The 6th and 7th circuits have rejected vertical commonality requiring horizontal commonality as has the State of Colorado. It has been observed that determining whether a "common enterprise" is present is a difficult matter under Colorado law.

Courts have stated the test for commonality in a variety of formulations. Thus it has been held that a common enterprise requires both a pooling of interest and multiple investors, a common enterprise does not require sale of undivided investments, a common enterprise can take the form of a trust fund investing in capital markets where the beneficiaries' common relationship with the enterprise is an undivided interest in the trust.

EXAMPLES OF INVESTMENT CONTRACTS

It is helpful to consider some fact situations that have led courts to find or reject finding an arrangement as an investment contract. The following examples will illustrate application of the law to particular marketing plans.

For example, the sale of portfolios of rare coins was held to be a sale of securities when the seller selected the coins for their investment value to the buyer and the seller provided such ancillary services as (1) resale assistance, (2) accounting, (3) insurance, (4) tax advice, (5) a depository for the coins, and (6) estate planning. The court noted that "coins do not appreciate in value at the same rate and accordingly their selection is the most crucial factor in determining how much profit an investor in coins will make."

In *Lowery* v. *Ford Hill Investment Company,* the sale of condominium units was determined to be an investment contract when the sale of the unit was tied to a mandatory exclusive management and rental agreement. The five-year rental agreement called for rentals to be made in a manner fair to all unit owners at rates fixed by the manager. The rental management fee was paid out of gross rentals and six-months' notice had to be given prior to the owner's using the unit. Court held that the purchaser's primary reason for buying a unit was the expectation of profit.

In another case, plaintiffs claimed that misrepresentations were made to induce them to purchase breeding chinchillas at inflated prices with the promise that defendants would buy back the progeny at an inflated price. The market was such that the defendant could pay the buy-back price only if it could resell them to new purchasers at inflated prices.

A real estate marketing program became entangled in securities law when, in selling the lots, defendant promised that the lots would increase in volume through the defendant's activities in developing and providing amenities. Defendant had led the purchasers to believe that a trust would be established to construct and operate facilities for the common benefit of all lot owners. The court said that central to the identification of a security "is the promotional emphasis of the developer."

However, in another real estate marketing venture the court held that the sale of a lot in a planned residential community was not a security when the developer was under no contractual obligation to do acts that would enhance the value of the lots. The developer's only obligation was to deliver title to the lots and any benefits resulting from the developers other acts to promote the development were incidental.

An investment contract existed when the promoter sold earthworms for breeding at ten times the market price. The promoter offered to purchase worms at a price too great to sell to any but new investors. Purchasers were told they would have to do no more work than in raising a garden.

In summary, any marketing plan in which capital is raised from the distributors should be designed to ensure that the profits anticipated from the investor–distributor arise from the investor–distributor's efforts and not from the manufacturer/supplier's efforts. This does not mean that the manufacturer/supplier cannot engage in advertising and promotional activities which will result in profits to the investor–distributor.

AVOIDING PYRAMID SALES

In 1966 the National Better Business Bureau identified pyramid sales and chain referral schemes as third on its list of the ten most serious consumer frauds. In 1971, the Securities and Exchange Commission called multilevel distributorships "inherently fraudulent." The SEC said such marketing programs typically involve the use of investment contracts which must be registered under the federal securities laws. Clearly, it is important that the marketing professional avoid designing a marketing plan that will be deemed to be an unlawful pyramid scheme.

There is no concise definition of pyramid sales. Perhaps this is because the courts want to be free from a rigid formula that would limit their ability to react to new variants of pyramid or chain referral schemes. Pyramid schemes come in at least two basic styles. In one style, the purchaser–investor must continually locate new recruits to qualify for shares in the venture profits. The only ceiling on participation is the total number of potential recruits.

An example of this style of pyramid scheme is found in the sale of Glenn W. Turner's Dare to Be Great motivational programs. Certain portions of the marketing program were held to involve the sale of unregistered investment contracts. Participants in the Dare to Be Great program were offered an opportunity to buy a sales position which entitled them to invite potential purchasers to revival-style opportunity meetings at which Dare to Be Great sales personnel made hard-sell presentations. If the potential purchaser bought into the program, the participant who invited the purchaser received a share of the purchase price. All of the sales efforts were made by Dare to Be Great personnel. The participants were instructed to tell the prospective clients very little about the opportunity meeting. They were instructed to use such phrases as "I have seen the money tree and I would like you to see it too."

When the Dare to Be Great program was tested in court, the court found that more was involved than the normal sale of a business motivation course. What the purchaser was really buying was the "possibility of deriving money from the sale of the plans by Dare to individuals whom the purchaser has brought to Dare." The court found that an investment contract was involved because the purchaser relied on the efforts of others to earn a return on investment and the efforts of others were "the undeniably significant ones, those essential managerial efforts which affect the failure or success of the enterprise."

A very similar pyramid arrangement was present in Koscot Interplanetary, Inc.'s cosmetic marketing program. This was ostensibly a plan for the retail marketing of cosmetics. However, on payment of a fee, a retailer could advance to a higher level of the marketing organization and earn money by recruiting new salespersons. As was the case in Dare to Be Great, the Koscot sales personnel assumed responsibility for selling the program to the new recruits. The court said its holding that an unregistered investment contact was present was limited to this and other schemes "in which promoters retain immediate control over the essential managerial conduct of an enterprise and where the investor's realization of profits is inextricably tied to the success of the promotional scheme."

The second style of pyramid scheme is that in which only a limited number of founder-memberships are sold. Prospects are urged to purchase early in order to profit from the relatively large returns based on the sale of memberships. Those who buy late in the pyramid are relegated to earning profits from the sale of the actual product.

Quite similar problems can be presented by chain referral marketing programs. In these marketing programs those purchasing the product for themselves are offered the opportunity to obtain fees for referring potential customers who will listen to a sales presentation. For example, in one marketing plan, the purchaser of a vacuum cleaner was offered $10 for each referral who would view a demonstration. When referral fees did not materialize as expected the purchaser sued claiming that in addition to purchasing a vacuum, he had also purchased an investment contract. The court held that on facts such as these the "essential efforts" were the efforts expended in getting the referral to watch the demonstration.

Thus, in determining whether an unregistered investment contract was present, it was necessary to determine whether the purchaser of the vacuum convinced the referral to watch the demonstration or merely provided names to the salesperson.

In addition to running afoul of the federal securities laws, pyramid or chain referral schemes may also violate the federal Mail Fraud Statute (see Chapter 16) or the federal Mail Lottery Statute (see Chapter 17). In addition, several states including California, Florida, Tennessee, and Texas have specific statutes applicable to pyramid and chain referral schemes.

The lesson for the marketing professional is that any multilevel marketing program must be carefully designed to avoid creating an "investment contract." A number of steps can be taken to permit both the use of multilevel marketing and to avoid the creation of an "investment contract." These include:

1. Emphasize the sale of the product rather than the sale of distributorships.

2. Do not charge a fee (investment) to move to a higher level in the organization.

3. Provide that profits come from the product sales, not the sale of distributorships.

4. Require participants to make significant efforts which are essential to their success.

Of course, it should go without saying that fair and honest dealing with one's distributors will go a long way toward avoiding trouble. If there is any question at all that an investment contract may be involved, legal counsel should be consulted. Remember that in addition to court orders requiring a firm to cease use of a pyramid scheme, the Securities Act and the Exchange Act provide civil remedies to defrauded purchasers. Further, treble damages may be awarded in a suit brought under the civil Racketeering Influenced Corrupt Organization Act (RICO) provisions.

CREATING A FRANCHISE SYSTEM

A popular form of product distribution is franchise sale. Franchising presents some unique legal issues which can be avoided by other marketing programs. At the same time, franchising provides opportunities not available with other marketing systems.

The essence of a franchise is a license from a franchisor of a trademark or trade name permitting the franchisee to sell a product or service under the trademark or trade name. The license must be accompanied by an agreement permitting the franchisor to ensure the quality of the product or service marketed under the trademark or trade name. The Federal Trade Commission has decreed that "some form of control over the franchisee is an essential ingredient of the franchise system." However several states have adopted other definitions of franchising to suit their own regulatory purposes. While most franchises are used for the sale of retail products there is no legal requirement restricting franchising to the retail sector or the economy.

One of the great advantages of franchising is that it permits the franchisor to make use of the franchisee's capital to finance business expansion. This permits the franchisor to expand the business more rapidly and into more markets than would be possible using only the franchisor's capital and credit. However, the use of the franchisee's capital raises legal questions regarding the potential sale of a security. The sale of the franchise must be structured to ensure that the franchisor is not actually selling a security which must be registered either with the federal government or the states or both.

Franchising can be looked on as an alternative to expansion through opening branch outlets. The advantage of a branch outlet is that it is subject to greater control. In branching, the owner retains almost complete control over pricing and purchasing and incompetent management can be removed and unprofitable operations can be closed or relocated at will. On the other hand, no matter how complex the franchise, the entrepreneur must surrender a great deal of control of day-to-day operations to the franchisee. The franchisee functions as an independent businessperson and is ordinarily free to set prices, locate sources of supply and to some extent decide how much capital should be spent in building up the business. Moreover, limits are placed by many state statutes on the ability to terminate or refuse to renew a franchise. Further, if expansion through franchising is desired, regulations issued by the Federal Trade Commission require a disclosure document be delivered to each prospective franchisee prior to the sale of any franchise. Because most businesses establish several company-owned branch outlets prior to undertaking franchising, most franchise systems consist of both company-owned and franchised outlets. Special problems can develop if company-owned branches operate in competition with franchised outlets.

WHAT IS A FRANCHISE?

A franchise is not a clearly defined business entity. The Federal Trade Commission applies its franchise rule to two types of commercial franchise relationships. These business relationships are (1) business opportunity ventures and (2) package and product franchises. Business opportunity franchises are business format franchises in which the franchisee is licensed to do business under a business format established by the franchisor and which is identified with the franchisor's trademark. Product franchises are businesses in which the franchisee is licensed to distribute goods produced directly by or under control of the franchisor. Either the business or goods themselves bear the franchisor's trademark. Automobile and gasoline station dealerships are common examples of product franchises.

Under the Federal Trade Commission rules there are three elements of a product or package franchise. One, there must be the distribution of goods or services associated with the franchisor's trademark. Two, there must be significant control or assistance provided with respect to the franchisee's method of operation. Three, the franchisee must pay a fee in excess of $500 to the franchisor prior to or during the first six months of the franchisee's operation. With respect to fee payments, such payments do not include reasonable amounts paid for inventory at true wholesale prices. However, payments for other items such as rent, advertising, equipment, supplies, training, escrow deposits, bookkeeping charges, promotional literature, equipment rental, and other noninventory items will count toward the $500.

State definitions of franchises show little uniformity in their precise language. Most definitions, however, can be identified as either a marketing plan definition or community of interest definition.

Marketing plan definitions typically revolve around the presence of uniform standards and centralized management for a prescribed marketing plan or system. Among the states employing a marketing plan definition are California, Illinois, Michigan, Indiana, Maryland, North Dakota, Rhode Island, and Wisconsin. For example, under the California statute a franchise is defined as a contract or agreement under which (1) a franchisee is granted the right to engage in the business of offering, selling, or distributing goods or services under a marketing plan or system prescribed in substantial part by the franchisor or its affiliate; (2) the operation of the franchisee's business pursuant to such a plan or system is associated with the franchisor's trademark, service mark, trade name, logo, or other commercial symbol designating the franchisor; and (3) the franchisee is required to pay directly or indirectly a franchise fee. It is clear that the greater the degree of control exercised by the franchisor, the more likely the franchise system will be a marketing plan franchise within the California definition. The franchise fee requirement does not include the purchase or agreement to purchase goods at a bona fide wholesale price. The Virginia law does not require the payment of a franchise fee but only contains the first two elements in the definition of a marketing plan or system franchise. Thus, many more sales programs would be treated as franchises under the Virginia statute than under the California statute.

The community of interest type definition of a franchise is employed in

Hawaii, Minnesota, South Dakota, and Washington. The Minnesota statutory definition of a franchise, which is typical of the community of interest type states, defines franchise as a contract (1) by which a franchisee is granted the right to engage in the business of offering or distributing goods or services using the franchisor's trade name, trademark, service mark, logo, advertising, or other commercial symbols; (2) in which the franchisor and the franchisee have a community of interest in the marketing of the goods and service; and (3) for which the franchisees pay directly or indirectly a franchise fee. The community of interest requirement of the definition is generally understood to be satisfied if the franchisor and franchisee have a common financial interest.

There are limited exemptions available from both state and federal statutes. For example, under the Federal Trade Commission Act a franchisor may petition for exemption from the coverage of the Federal Trade Commission's rules. Pursuant to such petitions, the commission has exempted certain automobile distributors based on a finding that sales of automobile franchises did not involve the same conditions ordinarily found in situations in which unfair and deceptive acts and practices had taken place. However, many states have enacted specific statutes dealing with automobile franchises. The commission has also exempted a group of major oil companies finding that the abuses taking place in the sale of petroleum franchises had already been specifically addressed by the Federal Petroleum Marketing Practices Act.

Red Flag: Although exempt from FTC rules, major oil companies may still be subject to various state franchise laws.

COMMON LEGAL ISSUES TO CONSIDER IN DESIGNING A FRANCHISE PROGRAM

As an initial step in franchising, the trademark or trade name should be registered. In several states, if the sale of the franchise is coupled with the license to use a registered trademark or trade name, the franchise offering itself need not be registered with the state. Much time can be saved if registration of franchises in each state is not required. However, registration of the franchise is required by some states even if the trademark or trade name itself is registered.

The design of the franchise system will itself determine whether certain legal issues will be presented. For example, among the decisions to be made by the franchisor is whether the franchise requires special architectural features for the outlets. For some franchises, a specially built building will be required which will be unsuited for other uses and have little resale value. If the franchisee is required to build or construct according to the franchisor's plans and specifications the franchisor should be prepared to grant a lengthy initial franchise term with liberal renewal options. Termination of such a franchise would leave a franchisee with a large capital investment which cannot be recovered readily and is likely to result in litigation.

Another franchisor decision is whether to grant the franchisee an exclusive territory and if an exclusive territory is granted, what size territory. Exclusive territories will generally be lawful, particularly for businesses which face competition from other outlets not a part of the franchise system.

The franchisor must also develop methods of maintaining quality. One method of maintaining quality frequently utilized in franchise systems is the requirement that the franchisee purchase supplies from the franchisor or from approved vendors. Purchase restrictions raise an antitrust "red flag" and have been a fertile source of litigation; however, such restrictions may be imposed if necessary to maintain quality. Restrictions to maintain quality generally will be lawful if sources of supply other than the franchisor are approved. This may require the franchisor to license other suppliers to manufacture items utilizing the franchisor's trademark and trade name.

The franchisor will also be required to determine whether cooperative advertising programs will be offered. Cooperative advertising programs are frequently a source of friction between the franchisee and the franchisor. On the other hand, cooperative advertising programs can assist the franchisee in developing business and at the same time provide the franchisor with substantial control of advertising content. Program details must be worked out in advance and the program should be firmly administered. To avoid Robinson-Patman Act problems the advertising program should be made available to all franchisees on a proportionately equal basis. Most cooperative advertising programs require the franchisees to make a contribution to the fund with the franchisor also making a contribution to the fund. The franchisor should hold the money in a restricted fund that it is obligated to expend for the benefit of the franchisees in accordance with the advertising program. The advertising program, spelling out the obligations of both the franchisee and the franchisor, should be set forth in writing. Funds should be kept in a separate account showing receipts and expenditures and the franchisor should report the advertising activities to the franchisees.

Franchises can be broken into two types. The first type is the business method type of franchise in which the franchisor is offering the franchisee a particular way of conducting a business. The other type of franchise is the product franchise in which the franchisee is licensed to sell a specific product manufactured by the franchisor or a licensee of the franchisor. Usually a franchisor of a business method franchise will seek to exercise greater control of the franchisee's operations. The degree of control exercised should be sufficient in either case to preserve quality and to protect the franchisor's trademark and trade name. It is possible that a franchisor can exercise so much control over the franchisee's activities that the franchisee will be an employee of the franchisor for some purposes.

A commonly used test for determining whether the person is an employee or an independent contractor is the so called ABC test. A person who meets all of the following requirements is considered an independent contractor:

a. He or she has been and in the future will be free from direction and control in the performance of services;

b. He or she performs services which are either outside of the usual course of business of the party contracted with or performs outside of all the places of business of the party contracted; and

c. He or she is customarily engaged in a trade occupation profession or business which is independently established.

Another problem area in determining how much control the franchisor should exercise over the franchisee is the risk of vicarious liability. If the franchisor exerts significant control over actions of a franchisee which injure a third party the franchisor may be found to be vicariously liable for the franchisee's actions.

SELLING FRANCHISES

The franchise cannot be offered for sale to prospective franchisees until a disclosure statement is completed in accordance with the Federal Trade Commission regulations. In many states, a franchise cannot be offered for sale until it has also been registered with the state. Typical registration statutes provide for the filing with the state of a copy of prescribed disclosure statement. In addition to preparing a disclosure statement, the franchise agreement itself should be prepared before the franchise is offered for sale. In considering information to include in sales material the franchisor should consult the consumer bulletin issued by the Federal Trade Commission entitled "Federal Trade Commission Advice for Persons Who Are Considering an Investment in a Franchise Business." This bulletin provides the franchisor with a checklist of the information that will be most important to a prospective franchisee. Much of this same information will be contained in the required disclosure statements. The Federal Trade Commission consumer bulletin suggests questions the prospective franchisee should ask and with which the franchisor should be prepared to deal. The questions are summarized and grouped as follows:

1. Who is the franchisor? What is the franchisor's reputation for fairness and honesty? Does he or she have all the franchises claimed? How do existing franchisees feel about the franchisor? Does the franchisor

deliver on promises? The prospective franchisee is advised to meet personally with the franchisor and to view a number of franchise outlets.

2. What about the franchise commodity? How long has the product or service been marketed? Is it a proven product, a fad, or a gimmick? Is it a luxury or a staple? How does it compare in price and quality with competing products? What is the consumer demand for the product? How reliable are the suppliers? Is the product safe? Is it patented? Will you be compelled to sell any new products developed by the franchisor?

3. What is the cost of the franchise? What is the initial fee? Is there a royalty fee? Is there an advertising fee? What equipment must be purchased? Is a special building required? What is covered by the franchise fee? Is the franchise fee justified by the business reputation of the franchisor? What supplies must be purchased? Must supplies be purchased from the franchisor? At what price?

4. What profits can reasonably be expected? The prospective franchisee is advised to ask to see the certified profit figures of franchisees operating on a level of activity reasonably expected?

5. What training and management assistance will be provided by the franchisor? How extensive is the training? How long does the training last? Where is the training given? Who pays the franchisee's expenses during the training period? Will the training include an opportunity to observe and work with a successful franchisee? Will the franchisee receive continuing management assistance? Will the franchisee receive advertising and promotional assistance? Will the franchisee be required to participate in franchisor sponsored promotions?

6. What about the franchise territory? What specific territory is being offered? Is it clearly defined? What is its potential? Does the franchisee have a choice of territories? What competition presently exists in the territory? Has the franchisor had a market survey done? Who prepared the market survey? How was the market survey prepared? Will the territory be exclusive? How will a specific site for the franchise be selected?

7. What provisions effecting termination, transfer, and renewal are contained in the franchise agreement? Under what circumstances can the franchisor terminate or refuse to renew the franchise? Can the franchise be terminated for failure to meet sales quotas? Does the agreement contain a covenant not to compete? Is the right to sell or

transfer the franchise restricted? Under what conditions can the franchisee renew the franchise? If the franchise is terminated or not renewed, will the franchisor purchase the franchise at a fair price?

8. Is the franchise attractive because it carries the name of a well-known personality? What is the extent of the personality's investment? Has the personality invested in the franchise? Will the personality devote substantial time and effort to the benefit of the franchisees? Would the franchise be a sound business venture if the personality were not involved?

9. Is the promoter primarily interested in selling distributorships? Is there a real market for the product or service? Will most profits be derived from subdistributorships?

10. Is it a route servicing promotion? If equipment such as vending machines must be purchased from the franchisor, how does the equipment compare in price and quality to equipment available from other sources?

11. Is the prospective franchisee qualified to operate the franchise business?

FEDERAL FRANCHISE DISCLOSURE REQUIREMENTS

Franchising experienced explosive growth during the 1960s and 1970s. Along with that explosive growth came a realization that many franchisors were engaging in abusive practices. The most common abusive practices fell into three categories—unfair termination or failure to renew the franchise, anticompetitive trade restraints, and failure to disclose relative facts to prospective franchisees. In 1979, the Federal Trade Commission, reacting to the abusive practices found to prevail in the industry, established rules relating to disclosure requirements and prohibitions concerning franchising and business opportunities. The Federal Trade Commission stated that the rules issued were in response to widespread evidence of deceptive and unfair practices in connection with the sale of franchises and business opportunities. The purpose of the rule was to reduce the opportunity for abuse by requiring disclosure of the facts needed by prospective franchisees to make an informed decision as to whether to enter into the franchise relationship. The commission rules require that a copy of the disclosure statement and a copy of the proposed franchise agreement must be given to the prospective franchisee ten working days prior to the signing of the franchise agreement and the receipt by the franchisor of any money from the franchisee. Failure to make the required disclosure is an unfair trade practice in violation of section 5 of the Federal Trade Commission Act.

Under the Federal Trade Commission rule, the disclosure statement must be provided to the prospective franchisee at the earlier of two time periods. The first period is the regulatory time period for making disclosures—ten business days prior to the execution by the prospective franchisee of the franchise agreement or any other agreement imposing a binding, legal obligation on the prospective franchisee, or ten days prior to the payment of any consideration by the prospective franchisee. The second one is the time of the first personal meeting between the prospective franchisee and the franchisor if it occurs sooner. Whether a meeting is considered to be the first personal meeting, thus requiring delivery of a disclosure statement, is determined by the following factors:

1. Whether the franchisor was prepared to discuss the sale of the franchise
2. Who initiated the meeting
3. Whether the meeting was limited to a brief and generalized discussion
4. Whether earnings claims were made

However, if the prospective franchisee already holds a franchise from that franchisor and merely seeks an additional franchise to establish a new outlet and the terms of the new franchise are not materially different from the existing franchise, a disclosure agreement need not be provided.

The Federal Trade Commission has taken the position that it is an unfair or deceptive trade practice under section 5 of the Federal Trade Commission Act for any franchisor or franchise broker to fail to furnish the prospective franchisee with the disclosure statement, to make any earnings claims except in accordance with the Federal Trade Commission rule, to make any claim or representation which is inconsistent with the information required to be disclosed, to fail to furnish the prospective franchisee with copies of the franchise or standard forms of franchise agreements and copies of the final agreements to be signed by the parties, or to fail to return to the prospective franchisee any funds identified as refundable in the prospectus. The commission has taken the position that violators will be subject to a civil penalty in actions brought by the commission with a fine of up to $10,000 per violation as well as actions for damages brought on behalf of the franchisee. Although the commission stated at the time the rule was established that there would be a private right of action available to franchisees under the Federal Trade Commission Act, the courts which have considered the matter to date have held that there is no private right of action under section 5 of the Federal Trade Commission Act for franchisees.

Key Point: Franchisees may bring suit for common law fraud.

The Federal Trade Commission disclosure requirements, which are set forth in the Federal Trade Commission Regulations, require the disclosure of some 20 items of information as follows:

1. Identification information. The disclosure requires that the official name and address of the franchisor and any parent company or holding company be disclosed along with the name under which the franchisor is doing business or intends to do business. Also the trade names, trademarks or service marks used in connection with the franchise must be disclosed.

2. The business experience of the franchise directors and the executive officers for the past five years must be individually stated along with the name of the employers for each director and executive officer.

3. The business experience of the franchisor and any parent company including the length of time that each has conducted a business of the nature of the business to be franchised and has offered or sold franchises and has conducted any business or offered or sold any franchises or business operated under any of the previously stated trade names, trademarks or service marks, or involving the sale or distribution of goods identified by any of those marks, or has offered for sale or sold franchises in other lines of business together with the description of other such lines of business must be disclosed.

4. The disclosure statement must also reveal who, if any, among the directors or executive officers of the franchisor has at any time in the past seven fiscal years been convicted or pleaded *nolo contendre* to a felony charge involving fraud, embezzlement, fraudulent conversion, misappropriation of property or restraint of trade. It must also be disclosed whether at any time in the past seven fiscal years any of the directors or executive officers has been held libel in a civil action resulting in a final judgment, or settled out of court, or is currently a party to any civil action pending which involves (a) charges of fraud, embezzlement, fraudulent conversion, misappropriation of property or restraint of trade or (b) which was brought by a present or former franchisee and which involved or involves the franchise relationship.

5. There must be a statement disclosing who, if any, among the directors and executive officers of the franchisor has at any time during the proceeding seven fiscal years (a) filed in bankruptcy, (b) been adjudicated of bankruptcy, (c) been reorganized due to insolvency, or (d) been a principle, director, executive officer, or partner of a firm that has so filed, been adjudged, or reorganized.

6. There must be a factual description of the franchise to be sold to the franchisee.

7. The disclosure statement must set forth all of the initial fees including franchise fees, down payments, prepaid rent, equipment, or inventory charges to be paid to the franchisor or to a person affiliated with the franchisor. The statement must also disclose the conditions, if any, under which fees are returnable.

8. Recurring funds required to be paid by the franchisee must be disclosed. Examples of such funds are royalties, leases, advertising, training, sign rental fees, and equipment or inventory purchases.

9. The disclosure statement must set forth the name of each affiliated person with whom the franchisee is directly or indirectly advised or required to do business with.

10. The franchisor must disclose any real estate, services, supplies, products, inventories, signs, fixtures, or equipment which the franchisee is required to purchase, lease, or rent from a specific source and the name and address of the source.

11. The franchisor must disclose revenues which it receives in consideration of the purchase by a franchisee from purchases made by an affiliate supplier or an approved supplier with whom the franchisee is required to do business.

12. The disclosure statement must include a statement of all the material terms and conditions of any financing arrangement offered to the prospective franchisee, either directly or indirectly, by the franchisor or an affiliate of the franchisor.

13. The disclosure statement must also describe the material terms of any restrictions placed on the franchisee (1) limiting the goods or services which may be offered for sale at the franchise outlet, (2) limiting the customers to whom the franchisee may sell, (3) limiting the geographic area in which the franchise may sell, and (4) granting territorial protection to the franchisee.

14. The extent to which the franchisor requires the franchisee to be personally involved in operating the franchise outlet must be described in the disclosure statement.

15. The disclosure statement must (1) set forth the terms of the franchise, (2) the conditions for renewal or extension of the franchise, (3) conditions under which renewal or extension may be denied, (4) conditions under which the franchisee may terminate, (5) conditions

under which the franchisor may terminate, (6) obligations of the franchisee which continue after termination or expiration of the franchise, (7) the franchisee's interest in the franchise upon expiration, termination, or refusal to renew, (8) the conditions under which the franchisor may repurchase the franchise from the franchisee whether by right of first refusal or otherwise, (9) the conditions or limitations under which the franchisee may sell or assign all or any part of his interest in the franchise, (10) conditions under which the franchisor may sell or assign, in whole or in part, its interest under the contract, (11) conditions under which the franchisee may modify the contract, (12) conditions under which the franchisor may modify the contract, (13) the rights of the heirs of the franchisee upon the death or incapacity of the franchisee, and (14) the provisions of any covenant not to compete.

16. The statement must also disclose certain statistical information concerning the number of franchises existing and the number of company-owned outlets. The statement must disclose (a) the total number of franchises operating at the end of the proceeding fiscal year, (b) the total number of company-owned outlets operating at the end of the proceeding fiscal year, (c) the names and addresses and telephone numbers of the ten franchise outlets nearest to the prospective franchisee or all franchises or all franchisees in the state of the prospective franchisee, (d) the number of franchisees who have voluntarily terminated or failed to renew their franchise during the preceding fiscal year, (e) the number of franchises required by the franchisor during the proceeding fiscal year, (f) the number of franchises for which renewal was refused during the preceding fiscal year, and (g) the number of franchises canceled or terminated during the preceding fiscal year. The disclosure statement must also list the general reasons for termination, cancellation and refusal to renew. For example, failure to comply with quality control standards, failure to make sufficient sales or other breeches of the contract agreement.

17. The disclosure statement must say whether the franchisor must approve any site selection and if site selection or approval is required, the statement must include a showing of the range of time elapsing between the signing of the franchise agreement and site selection or approval by the franchisor.

18. There must be a statement disclosing the type and nature of training and the minimal amount of training to be provided and the cost, if any, to the franchisee for the training.

19. When a public figure is used in connection with the franchise program, the franchisor must disclose in the disclosure statement the nature and the extent of the public figures involvement including promotional assistance, the total investment of the public figure in the franchise operation, and the amount of any fee or fees the franchisee will be obligated to pay for the public figure's involvement or assistance.

20. A balance sheet for the franchisor for the most recent fiscal year and an income statement and statement of changes in financial position for the franchisor for the most recent three fiscal years must be provided also.

A table of contents must be included with the disclosure statement. Additional requirements are applicable to any representation made with respect to the specific level of sales income, gross or net profits, actual or potential of existing or prospective outlets. Preparation of a franchise disclosure statement is an important step in preparing for the sale of franchises. The disclosure statement should not be utilized until it has been reviewed with legal counsel.

STATE LAW DISCLOSURE REQUIREMENTS

Many states have enacted statutes requiring the registration of disclosure documents with the state as well as delivery of the disclosure documents to the prospective franchisee prior to an offer of sale of the franchise. Michigan and Texas require only the filing of a notice of franchise "offering" or "an exemption statement." In other states there are statutes requiring registration and disclosure of "business opportunity" ventures that may also apply to certain franchises. Some registration or notification is required by the following states: Alabama, California, Connecticut, Florida, Georgia, Hawaii, Illinois, Indiana, Iowa, Kentucky, Louisiana, Maine, Maryland, Michigan, Minnesota, Nebraska, New Hampshire, New York, North Carolina, North Dakota, Ohio, Oklahoma, Oregon, Rhode Island, South Carolina, South Dakota, Texas, Utah, Virginia, Washington, and Wisconsin. There is substantial variety in the registration or disclosure requirements of the several states making it necessary for legal counsel to consult the statutes of each state in which the franchise is to be offered for sale or sold or in which a franchise outlet is to be located. The reference to state statutes should not be limited to the above list because additional states may from time to time enact statutes applicable to the franchise disclosure.

Registration requirements generally require the submission of all required information to a designated state office, frequently a portion of the state's securities commission. The registration period may take several months and is generally effective for one year. Renewal is ordinarily annual and if material changes occur which affect the registered offering circular an amendment of the registration is required. A material change that requires an amendment includes any facts, circumstance, or condition that would have a substantial likelihood of influencing a reasonable prospective franchisee in the making of the decision relating to the purchase of the franchise. The registration application typically consists of a copy of the offering circular to satisfy the disclosure requirements, a filing fee, appointment of a person located in the state to receive service of process, copies of all proposed contracts related to the sale of the franchise, copies of advertising proposed to be used in the state, an accountant's consent to use of audited financial statements, guarantee of performance where required, signature pages, tables of contents, identification of all persons who will sell franchises in the state, and other supplemental information as the state requires. Additionally, some states require a copy of the operating manual, articles of incorporation, certificate of incorporation, and certificate of assumed name and listing of all franchises sold during a specified time period be on file along with the other registration materials. The disclosures required to be made by states statutes are generally similar to the disclosures required by the Federal Trade Commission. A number of states have adopted the uniform franchise offering circular. Most states which accept the uniform franchise offering circular also permit use of the Federal Trade Commission disclosure statement.

States frequently provide that for failure to comply with state registration and disclosure acts injured franchisees may sue to obtain damages or recession of the franchise agreement. Also, the state authorities may enjoin the practices or enforce compliance. A registration statement may be suspended, revoked, or denied and the state may escrow or impound franchise fees or other funds paid by franchisees, until the franchisor meets its obligations. Some states provide also for civil penalties and permit the state to petition for a court-appointed receiver to operate the franchisor's business. Finally, some states provide for criminal penalties.

In addition to the remedies provided to franchisees by specific statutes, franchisees may also resort to the common law remedies for fraud and misrepresentation. In a suit for fraud, a franchisee may obtain not only actual damages but also punitive damages which may be greater than the actual penalties.

STATE REGULATION OF THE SUBSTANTIVE ASPECTS OF FRANCHISES

In addition to requiring the use of a disclosure statement and frequently registration of disclosure statements, offering circulars, advertising material, and form contracts, many states have enacted statutes regulating the terms and practices of the franchise relationship. Often these states prohibit certain franchise practices, such as in unreasonable conduct or unfair dealing with franchisees. Other more specific ones include prohibiting interference with the free association among franchisees or prohibiting a refusal to deal with franchisees or discrimination among franchisees, violating a franchisee's exclusive territory, or coercing a franchisee with threats of termination are all prohibited by some states. Other states prohibit a franchisor from failing to repurchase items on termination or nonrenewal of the franchise, or unreasonably prohibiting the transfer of the franchise, particularly unreasonably restricting transfer of the franchise to the heirs of the franchisee. Other states prohibit the unreasonable requirement of purchases from designated suppliers or others in relationship to the purchaser. In some states collecting but not using an advertising fee is unlawful. Indiana makes unlawful the imposition of a binding arbitration agreement in the franchise contract.

One franchise relationship that has received substantial state attention relates to termination and nonrenewal of a franchise. Frequently, states require that prior written notice be delivered to the franchisee setting forth reasons for termination or nonrenewal. Typically, notice requirements are 60 days or 90 days prior to termination although one state requires 180 days notice for nonrenewal of the franchise. Frequently, the statutes also require that the franchisee be given an opportunity to cure any defect, giving cause for the nonrenewal. However, these notice statutes also ordinarily provide exemptions permitting the franchisor to take quick action to terminate the franchise in an emergency situation such as adjudication of the franchisee as a bankrupt or abandonment of the franchise business.

Most state franchise statutes impose a good cause standard for termination or nonrenewal of the franchise by the franchisor. The definition of good cause varies, but frequently the definitions refer to failure by the franchisee to comply substantially with the franchise agreement, failure to act in good faith in a commercially reasonable manner, voluntary abandonment, conviction of the franchisee of an offense, franchisee impairment of the franchisor's trademarks or commercial insignia, loss of the right to occupy the franchised premises, or failure to pay the franchisor within ten days after receipt of notice of sums past due. Courts have also found that good cause was present when there was failure to achieve stated sales quotas or the dealership was unprofitable or there was failure to agree upon terms of a renewal where both parties acted in good faith.

Additionally, many states require the franchisor to compensate the franchisee for some franchise assets on termination or nonrenewal. There is no uniformity among such statutes. However, such statutes frequently require the franchisor to pay for the franchisee's inventories, supplies, and equipment obtained from the franchisor or approved sources.

Clearly the termination or nonrenewal of a franchisee is a matter subject to considerable regulation by the states. As might be expected, it is also subject to a great deal of litigation by disappointed franchisees. Legal counsel should be considered prior to terminating or refusing to renew a franchise.

SELLER-ASSISTED MARKETING PLANS

Another marketing program subject to great abuse and to some state regulation is seller-assisted marketing. A typical seller assisted marketing program involves the sale or lease of products, equipment or supplies to a purchaser who will use the products, equipment or supplies in beginning, maintaining or operating a business when the seller does any of the following:

1. Represented that the purchaser will earn an amount in excess of the initial investment
2. Represented that there is a market for the product
3. Represented that the seller will purchase the product

Seller-assisted marketing plans are sometimes regulated by states under the title of business opportunity statutes.

Seller-assisted marketing is often associated with the sale of vending machines, racks, or work-at-home paraphernailia. The California legislature found that the initial payment required was usually in the form of overpriced equipment or products. The purchasers/distributors often had little or no business experience and were frequently retirees who risked their life savings to supplement their pensions. To protect such persons, the California legislature enacted laws requiring disclosure of relevant information, prohibiting misleading practices, and prohibiting certain unfair contract provisions.

California statute requires filing a disclosure statement prior to making any sales offers. The disclosure statement must be updated annually. A list of the persons selling the program must also be filed with the state. In most respects, the disclosures which must be made are the same or very similar to the disclosures required under the franchise laws.

In marketing a seller-assisted marketing plan in California, a seller is prohibited from using the phrases "buy-back" or "secured investment" if the "security" is represented by the product sold to the purchaser/distributor. That is, if the only security the purchaser receives for an investment is the product purchased, the purchaser cannot be told the investment is secured. Further, the phrases cannot be used if there is any restriction whatsoever on the purchaser's right to invoke the buy back provision during the first year of the contract.

California law also prohibits the seller from making any representations regarding earnings unless the seller has data to substantiate the claims.

California further provides that the purchaser shall have three days from the date of contracting in which to cancel the seller-assisted marketing contract for any reason whatsoever.

The California statute is typical of state statutes regulating seller-assisted marketing or business opportunities. Of course it is necessary to consult each state's statutes to learn the state's unique statutory requirements. Among the states having statutes regulating the marketing of business opportunities are California, Connecticut, Florida, Georgia, Indiana, Iowa, Kentucky, Maine, Maryland, Michigan, Nebraska, New Hampshire, North Carolina, Ohio, Oklahoma, South Carolina, South Dakota, Texas, Utah, Virginia, and Washington.

PETROLEUM MARKETING

Congress has passed special legislation dealing with franchises for the marketing of motor fuel. The Petroleum Marketing Practices Act is designed to protect franchises of large oil companies from unjust terminations of their franchises or from refusals to renew their franchises. The Act accomplishes this purpose by making it unlawful for the franchisor to terminate or refuse to renew the franchise except in certain specified situations. The statute also provides specific time periods in which notice of termination or nonrenewal must be provided to the franchisee.

Several states have enacted legislation dealing with the marketing of motor fuels. For example, Delaware makes it unlawful for manufacturers and refiners to open company-owned retail outlets. The Delaware statute also requires that retail dealers receive uniform treatment with respect to the (a) extension of voluntary allowances, (b) equipment rental, and (c) allocation of gasoline and other fuels during periods of shortage. The manufacturer or refiner is specifically prohibited from setting the retail product price.

The Hawaii Gasoline Dealers Act forbids the franchisor from dictating retail prices, or requiring the franchisee to purchase tires, batteries, and accessories from the franchisor. Hawaii also requires the franchisor to buy back inventory of a terminated franchisee at 90 percent of cost.

Several states forbid the franchisor from requiring the franchisee to maintain any set hours of operation.

MOTOR VEHICLE FRANCHISORS

The relationship between motor vehicle manufacturers and motor vehicle distributors has been the subject of special legislation at both the state and federal levels. At the federal level, Congress has enacted the Automobile Dealers Day in

Court Act which creates a right in Automobile Dealers to sue in federal court for a manufacturer's failure to act in good faith in performing or complying with the terms of the franchise or in terminating or refusing to renew the franchise. Coercion, threats, or intimidation are evidence of bad faith.

The California Automobile Dealer's Act regulates the business dealings between automobile franchisors and franchisees and the termination of automobile franchises. Prior to termination, an automobile franchisee is entitled to a hearing before the Motor Vehicle Board. Similarly, existing franchisees are entitled to a hearing before the Motor Vehicle Board before a new franchise for the sale of the same line of vehicles is issued for their area.

The California Motor Vehicle Board has the power to hear disputes between franchisors and franchisees regarding payment for dealer preparation and warranty work.

Typically state statutes place limitations on the franchisor's right to terminate the franchise and require the franchisor to recognize and accept a family member as successor to a deceased or incapacitated franchisee. Franchisors are prohibited from discriminating among franchisees and must make reasonable deliveries of vehicles, parts or accessories that have been publically advertised.

Table 1 compares franchises and company-owned outlets.

TABLE 1
Franchises and Company-Owned Outlets Compared

COMPANY-OWNED	FRANCHISE
1. Can set prices.	1. Less control over prices.
2. Can hire and fire managers.	2. Can only remove management by terminating franchise.
3. Can close outlet at will.	3. Termination of franchise is controlled by contract and statute.
4. No state registration required.	4. In many states the franchise must be registered prior to sale.
5. Liable for state and local taxes.	5. Ordinarily the franchisee is liable for state and local taxes.
6. Company must provide the required capital.	6. Capital is provided by the franchisee.

TABLE 1 *(Continued)*
Franchises and Company-Owned Outlets Compared

COMPANY-OWNED	FRANCHISE
7. Company has complete quality control.	7. Must police franchisee to maintain control.
8. Liable for injuries caused by negligence.	8. Not liable for acts of franchisee unless franchisor exercised significant control over activity causing the injury.

chapter three

MARKETING ISSUES REGARDING SALES TERRITORIES

Among the many factors a manufacturer must consider in determining the best method of distributing its product is how to encourage distributors to offer the most point-of-sale service, and how to ensure that distributors will aggressively promote the product. One method of ensuring that distributors aggressively sell the manufacturer's product is to grant the distributor a particular sales territory. A written distribution agreement should delineate any territorial or customer restraints to be placed on a distributor. Such restraints would include restraints on transshipping and assignments of primary responsibility. Territorial restraints are particularly helpful when the distributor must make a large investment in capital items or in sales staff training to market the product. When the product requires a highly trained sales staff or a strong product service and maintenance capability, the manufacturer must anticipate the "free rider" problem.

FREE RIDERS

Free riders are distributors who are able to capture more sales by holding their costs down by not offering a trained sales staff or service department. The free rider assumes that customers visit the full service dealer for a complete explanation and demonstration of the product and then purchases from the lower priced free rider. If a manufacturer fails to prevent free riding, fewer distributors will provide trained sales staffs and service departments.

On the other hand, restraints placed on distributors by the manufacturer to prevent free riding tend to reduce *intra*brand competition although the same restraint may increase *inter*brand competition. *Inter*brand competition is increased because the product is supported by trained sales personnel and service departments. *Intra*brand competition is decreased because discounting free riders no longer offer an alternative to full service dealers.

A number of market restraints may be imposed to deal with free rider problems. One very common method is to assign specific markets to distributors. In this fashion a distributor may be assured that there will be no competition with a free rider and the economic value of the investment in marketing and servicing a product will not be siphoned off by a discounter. This chapter will discuss the use of sales territory strategies in dealing with free rider marketing problems. Legal principles involved are applicable to territorial restraints generally however whether imposed for free rider purpose or for other purposes. Moreover, territorial restraints are not the only method of dealing with free riders. Free rider problems may be avoided by using manufacturer-owned retail outlets or through refusals to deal with certain retailers or exclusive dealing agreements which are covered by Chapters 5 and 6.

VERTICAL RESTRAINTS

Largely in recognition of the free rider problem, courts now test nonprice vertical restraints under the rule of reason analysis rather than as per se violations. Other justifications for resorting to the rule of reason are that the restraints imposed on the distributor are simply restraints that could be freely imposed on the product distribution by the manufacturer if the manufacturer elected to distribute the product itself. Finally, many economists have argued that a manufacturer cannot gain from imposing restraints that do not promote efficiencies. Accordingly, vertical restraints that do not promote efficiency are unlikely to be imposed by manufacturers. On the other hand, restraints that do promote efficiency are unlikely to violate the purposes of the antitrust laws and should be permitted.

APPLYING THE RULE OF REASON

In reviewing nonprice vertical restraints courts have shown a willingness to apply a somewhat simplified rule of reason. The analysis focuses on the competitive effect of the restraint. Moreover, the courts are willing to suffer diminished *intra*brand competition to obtain increased *inter*brand competition. Accordingly, a balancing process is applied in which the anticompetitive impact is evaluated, the procompetitive impact is analyzed, and finally the anticompetitive impact and the procompetitive impact are balanced. If the procompetitive impact outweighs the anticompetitive impact, the restraint is lawful. In many cases the balancing analysis is not required because the plaintiff is unable to demonstrate any anticompetitive effects from the territorial division. To establish an anticompetitive effect the plaintiff must prove that the supplier's action in creating a market division had an impact on competition in a relevant market. This in turn requires showing that the supplier has market power in the relevant market.

HORIZONTAL RESTRAINTS

While nonprice vertical restraints on markets are tested under the rule of reason, horizontal restraints remain per se unlawful. Horizontal restraints are restraints agreed to and imposed by entities operating at the same level of the market.

For example, an agreement among the distributors of a product to divide the market geographically would be a horizontal restraint of trade and a per se violation of section 1 of the Sherman Act. However, if the manufacturer assigns exclusive sales territories to each distributor, a nonprice vertical restraint exists which is subject to the rule of reason analysis. Why are they treated differently? One reason is that the manufacturer is not likely to impose the restraint unless it promotes efficiencies, but the distributors acting horizontally would impose such a restraint to simply increase prices.

An obvious problem can arise in determining whether a restraint is horizontal or vertical when the manufacturer utilizes a dual distributor system, i. e., there are both manufacturer-owned distributors and independent distributors. When is the restraint imposed vertically by the manufacturer and when is it imposed horizontally by the distributor? At this point, it is sufficient to note that there is a dispute among the federal judicial circuits as to how to treat dual distributors. Dual distribution is discussed in Chapter 4.

A problem also arises in determining whether the restraint is vertical or horizontal when the impetus for the restraint arises from the distributors but is imposed by the manufacturer. In some instances distributors agree among themselves regarding a marketing restraint and then prevail on the manufacturer to impose the restraint vertically. Restraints originating with the distributors in such a fashion stand a high risk of per se condemnation as horizontal restraints. The economic theory is that if the restraint were likely to increase *inter*brand competition, it would probably have originated with the manufacturer rather than with the distributors. However, it is not unlawful for distributors to make suggestions regarding marketing nor is it unlawful for a manufacturer to adopt and act on such suggestions. Nevertheless, whenever the restraint is proposed by a distributor the manufacturer should proceed with caution.

Red Flag: Caution is especially required if the restraint, although suggested by only a single distributor, has been the subject of discussion among distributors. The manufacturer should carefully document its own independent efficiency-enhancing reasons for imposing the restraint vertically.

If a horizontal agreement among distributors is established and participation in that agreement by the manufacturer is established, the manufacturer as well as the distributors may be found guilty of a per se violation of section 1 of the Sherman Act. Participation by the manufacturer may be found if the manufacturer acts to enforce the distributor's horizontal agreement.

One circumstance in which a manufacturer may be drawn into a horizontal market restraint is when one distributor enlists the aid of the manufacturer to restrain another distributor. In form, the restraint may appear to be vertical but some courts have described it as horizontal, reasoning that merely enlisting the manufacturer to impose the restraint does not transform the restraint from horizontal to vertical. The manufacturer may be placed in a very awkward position. The action the manufacturer is being requested to take may be in the manufacturer's own best interest and may even be in furtherance of its own marketing program, but since it was first suggested by the distributor there is a danger that a court will find a horizontal element.

Key Point: In these cases, it is essential that the manufacturer establish, through documentation, that it has its own reasons for taking actions and that its actions are unilateral and not taken in concert with any distributor. Remember that a section 1 offense requires two or more parties acting in concert.

The importance of unilateral decision making and documenting the unilateral nature of the decision is discussed in Chapter 7 under dealer terminations.

HOW TO TELL WHAT MARKET DIVISIONS ARE ILLEGAL

Thus far we have seen that the use of territorial market divisions may provide an effective means of dealing with a free rider problem. It may also provide an incentive for a distributor to agree to handle the supplier's product. We have also seen that vertically imposed territorial market restraints will be judged under a rule of reason analysis in which the increase in *inter*brand competition will be weighed against the decrease in *intra*brand competition. Finally, we have seen that horizontal territorial agreements are per se violations of section 1 of the Sherman Act. Let us now look with greater specificity at illegal territorial market restraints.

First, it is clear that horizontal agreements between competitors at any level of production or distribution to divide markets on a product, customer, or geographic basis are per se unlawful. Such agreements are identified as naked restraints of trade. For example, the Supreme Court held unlawful an arrangement under which independent regional supermarket chains formed a cooperative to act as a purchasing agent and develop a private-label merchandising program. The court struck down the part of the arrangement which restricted each member of the cooperative to selling the private brand only in an exclusive territory and precluded resale of the private label brand to other retailers.

In yet another case, the Supreme Court found unlawful a horizontal restraint in which a group of bedding manufacturers established a jointly controlled subsidiary which adopted a trade name, a trademark, and product specifications and then licensed each manufacturer to manufacture and sell under the Sealy trade name and trademark only in a designated territory.

Similarly, a territorial restraint among lessors of over-the-road, long-haul trucks was held to be unlawful when the restraint, a location clause, was imposed by the lessor's national association. The association was formed to provide a vehicle through which small local truck leasing firms could guarantee nationwide servicing of trucks leased for long-haul use. Association members agreed to provide servicing for trucks leased from other members of the association. This permitted small lessor's to compete in long-haul truck leasing with national leasing firms. However, the association spaced member franchises at locations which precluded the franchisees from competing with each other.

In each of the foregoing examples, horizontal competitors formed and controlled the entity which imposed what might appear to be in a vertical relationship. In each instance, the court held that the restraint was horizontal and therefore illegal per se.

A horizontal restraint was also found when competitors agreed not to solicit each others' accounts and to balance among themselves accounts that voluntarily switched. Further, a franchisor was found to have engaged in a horizontal territorial allocation scheme when it permitted its franchisees to veto the granting of a new franchise in its territory.

Second, while horizontal restraints are routinely condemned, it is difficult to find cases since 1978 in which vertical territorial restraints have been condemned.

Key Point: It must be remembered that in a vertical restraint case, the plaintiff must establish as a threshold matter that the supplier has market power.

It is highly probable that a market share of less than 30 percent will not create the requisite market power. One court, however, did find a violation when the market share was as low as 12 percent.

Nonetheless, vertical territorial restraints will be found unlawful if they are an integral part of a resale price maintenance agreement. Resale price maintenance remains a per se violation (See Chapter 9). Further, a vertical territorial restraint disguised as a warranty-fee passover was held unlawful when it reduced *intra*brand competition and did not promote *inter*brand competition.

LAWFUL MARKET DIVISIONS

A short oversimplified list of lawful market divisions includes:

1. Horizontal market divisions are never lawful.

2. Market divisions imposed vertically by a firm having less than a 30 percent market share are nearly always lawful.

3. Vertical market divisions imposed by a firm with more than a 30 percent market share are lawful if the procompetitive effect on *inter*brand competition outweighs any restraint on *intra*brand competition.

Under the Patent Act, the owner of a patent may convey an exclusive right under the patent "to the whole or any specified part of the United States." Thus, a patentee may grant a license limiting the licensee's right to make, use or sell the patented product to a particular territory within the United States. However, a licensee agreement limiting the territories of both the patentee and the licensee might be treated as a horizontal market division in violation of the Sherman Act. Courts have also permitted a patentee to limit a manufacturing licensee to sell to only certain customers.

Red Flag: The field of patent licensing is quite complex and legal counsel should be sought regarding any specific marketing or licensing plan.

HOW TO USE AREAS OF PRIMARY RESPONSIBILITY

A supplier may wish to ensure that a distributor fully exploit a particular geographic market but at the same time may not wish to limit the distributor to sales only in a particular area. In such cases, the dealer may be assigned a primary sales territory. When it has satisfactorily exploited its primary area, the distributor may then make sales outside of the assigned territory.

Primary responsibility clauses may also impose specific sales quotas which must be met before outside sales begin. Or, they may simply require the distributor to exhaust all best efforts to sell the supplier's products in the area of primary responsibility. Primary responsibility clauses have generally been approved by courts and a distributor who fails to adequately exploit a territory may be terminated. The fact that the distributor is making a substantial number of sales outside of its area may be evidence of a failure to meet its primary responsibility obligations.

LOCATION CLAUSES

Another variation of assigning set territories for distributors is the use of location clauses. In these clauses the supplier limits the distributor to sales from a particular location and refuses to make shipments at any other location. When not a part of a resale price maintenance program or joined with other restraints, location clauses have been held lawful.

DROP SHIPMENTS

Drop shipments involve shipments by the manufacturer directly to the customer on behalf of the distributor. A ban on drop shipments is more problematical than is a location clause or an area of prime responsibility clause. A strict ban on drop shipments coupled with an area responsibility clause or a location clause may result in a de facto territorial division. The tenth circuit upheld a manufacturer's refusal to make drop shipments on behalf of a distributor into areas served by other distributors. In that case each distributor had been assigned an area of primary responsibility. While the distributor was permitted to make sales outside of its primary area of responsibility, the manufacturer refused to facilitate such sales by making drop shipments.

PROFIT PASSOVERS

Profit passover requires a dealer selling outside a territory to pass a portion of the profit over to the seller assigned to develop the territory in which the purchaser is located. The profit passover compensates the dealer's efforts in promoting the sale through advertising and providing postsale service in the territory. Under a profit passover program, there is no prohibition on making sales outside of the assigned territory. Profit passovers will usually be upheld. However, a profit passover was declared unlawful when it restrained *intra*brand competition without increasing *inter*brand competition.

HOW TO USE A BAN ON TRANSSHIPPING

Territorial market divisions may not provide a complete solution to the free rider problem. Even if a distributor sells only to customers within an assigned service territory, those customers may transship the goods into another territory for resale. This has led some manufacturers to reinforce territorial divisions by requiring their distributors to sell only to ultimate consumers or only to purchasers who agree not to transship. When transshipping prohibitions are not used to enforce a resale price maintenance scheme and are imposed unilaterally, they have been upheld as a legitimate effort to deal with the free rider problem. It is believed that the prohibition promotes *inter*brand competition sufficiently to counterbalance any diminished *intra*brand competition.

For example, when Viking Sewing Machine Company, Inc. refused to sell to a discounter located in an area already granted as an exclusive area to another dealer, the discounter purchased some Viking sewing machines from dealers in other areas which were transshipped to the discounter. The court found no per se violation when Viking enforced its policy that "Viking sewing machines shall not be shipped into another Viking dealer's territory. Viking sewing machines shall not be shipped to non-Viking dealers or distributors in any part of the world."

A manufacturer may even establish a ban on transshipping after receiving complaints from its distributors as long as the ban is imposed unilaterally. The ban on transshipping can be enforced with visits to wholesalers to discuss the policy and threats to consider whether the company's no transshipping policy has been observed when wholesale distributorships are up for renewal. Moreover, a ban on transshipping can be coupled with a ban on subdistribution.

In establishing a policy against transshipping the manufacturer should take the following steps:

1. Review its files to ensure that there are no materials which would evidence joint, as opposed to unilateral, decision making.
2. Document the legitimate business reasons for the policy such as to prevent free riding and to promote *inter*brand competition.
3. Enforce the policy without discrimination.

SOFT DRINK INTERBRAND COMPETITION

A specific statute, the Soft Drink Interbrand Competition Act (15 U. S. C. section 3501), exempts from antitrust inquiry the use of restraints on transshipment and the use of exclusive territorial areas in the soft drink industry. Exemption occurs so long as the soft drink product "is in substantial and effective competition with other products of the same general class in the relevant market or markets."

The statute provides that any trademark licensing agreement may grant the licensee the "exclusive right to manufacture, distribute and sell products in a defined geographic area. The licensee may also be limited, directly or indirectly, to the manufacture, distribution and sale of such products only for ultimate resale to consumers within a defined geographic area."

Courts have interpreted the statute as making boycotts used to enforce a ban on transshipping lawful.

For example, Pepsi Co. enforced its territorial restraints on retailers by use of the following practices held lawful under the Soft Drink Interbrand Competition Act:

1. Retailers were required to buy and sell Pepsi Co. products only within the geographic boundaries granted to the licensed bottlers in which the retailer was located.

2. Retailers could not sell to other retailers.

3. Retailers who did buy or sell Pepsi Co. products from or to other retailers were to be boycotted.

It has been held that a ban on transshipping can be applied to retailers as well as to bottlers.

However, the Soft Drink Act does not prevent antitrust charges of price fixing, horizontal restraints of trade or group boycotts which would otherwise be unlawful.

SALES TERRITORY CHECKLIST

_____ Is there a free rider problem?

_____ Who made the decision to allocate territories?

_____ Is there a dual distribution situation?

_____ Was the restraint suggested by a distributor?

_____ Have the distributors jointly proposed territorial restraints?

_____ Is the party imposing a "vertical restraint" a mere agent of horizontal competitors?

_____ Does the restraint increase interbrand competition?

USING DUAL DISTRIBUTION SYSTEMS

Firms sometimes distribute their products through both company-owned outlets and independent distributors. This is known as a dual distribution system. A dual distributor program may be the result of conscious choice or historical accident as when a distributor initially distributes through company-owned outlets and then begins to use independent distributors to rapidly expand its market penetration at less capital cost to itself. A dual distributorship may also result during a time of transition from the use of only company-owned outlets to only independent distributors, or vice versa. How the dual distributor program came into existence is unlikely to affect the outcome of marketing law issues.

The existence of a dual distribution system is not always readily apparent. However, in determining whether dual distribution type problems may arise can be determined by asking whether the firm operates on the same level as and in competition with any of its suppliers or customers. Thus it is relevant to consider two facts:

1. The firm must operate on at least two market levels.
2. The firm must compete with its supplier or customer.

There are many valid business reasons for utilizing a dual distribution system. The presence of valid business and economic rationale for dual distribution will provide an important element of proof in defending against an antitrust allegation of anticompetitive or predatory intent in marketing. Accordingly, the business or economic reasons for utilizing a dual distribution system should be documented in the company's files. The Antitrust Division of the Department of Justice in its 1985 Vertical Restraints Guidelines expressed the opinion that partial vertical integration resulting in dual distribution may permit a firm to realize both the efficiencies of vertical integration and the advantages of independent distributors. Among the benefits the Antitrust Division believes may result from dual distribution are better planning, lower transaction costs, better quality control, quicker response to market innovations, and greater access to market information.

Business reasons for utilizing a dual distribution system are present when participation in the second market level would provide useful information to the firm, encourage the provision of additional services to consumers by others, improve quality, or provide savings in the cost of distribution. Moreover, so long as resale price maintenance is a per se violation of the antitrust laws, vertical integration does provide a lawful means for a manufacturer to achieve a measure of control over the retail price.

Although there are many legitimate reasons why a firm would choose a dual distribution system, it is also well recognized that dual distribution provides opportunities for predation and collusion that cannot be ignored.

Key Point: The greater the market share of the dual distributor, the greater the likelihood that its activities will be harmful to competition.

In measuring market share, the firm's transfers from one level of the market to the other—i.e., internal sales—as well as its sales to independent distributors are counted.

HORIZONTAL OR VERTICAL RESTRAINTS

The presence of a dual distribution program frequently creates an ambiguity as to whether a market restraint imposed by a manufacturer on its distributors was imposed by the manufacturer in its role as a manufacturer and therefore is a vertical restraint or whether the restraint was imposed by the manufacturer in its role as distributor and therefore is a horizontal restraint. Whether the restraint is vertical or horizontal is of concern in the case of nonprice restraints because horizontal nonprice restraints are per se unlawful while vertical nonprice restraints are tested under the rule of reason. Since vertical as well as horizontal price restraints are per se unlawful the distinction is of less importance when a price restraint is at issue.

TERRITORIAL RESTRAINTS BY DUAL DISTRIBUTORS

Courts have not reached a clear consensus as to whether territorial restraints imposed by a dual distributor will be classified as horizontal or vertical. In the past it was generally held that all restraints imposed by a dual distributor were horizontal. However, since the Supreme Court's decision in the 1977 case, *Continental T. V. Inc.* vs. *GTE Sylvania, Inc.*, a number of courts, notably the second and fifth circuits, have decided that the dual distribution program is not relevant and that all manufacturer-imposed restraints are vertical. This approach may assume away the problem which is whether the entity imposing the restraint was acting as dealer or as manufacturer in imposing the restraint. Other courts, notably the ninth circuit and District of Columbia circuit, have taken the position that whether the restraint is horizontal or vertical is a fact issue to be decided on a case-by-case basis. A few courts may still find that restraints imposed by dual distributors are always horizontal.

More recent cases in circuits which still consider the presence of dual distribution a relevant consideration, all make a threshold determination as to whether the restraint is vertical or horizontal before deciding whether a per se or rule of reason test will be applied. Some courts consider the effect of the restraint before determining whether it is horizontal or vertical. If the restraint is one which lessens *inter*brand competition or will decrease output, it will be classified as horizontal.

TERMINATIONS OF INDEPENDENT DISTRIBUTORS

Dealer termination issues are discussed in depth in Chapter 7. Here the unique problems arising from the termination of an independent distributor in a dual distribution setting are discussed.

As a general proposition, courts recognize the right of a manufacturer to choose with whom it will deal. If the manufacturer can point to legitimate business reasons for the dealer termination, the termination is almost certain to be lawful. However, if a manufacturer attempts to drive the independent out of business or terminates them by unlawful means, a predatory intent may be found. Thus, it is lawful for a firm to change from a dual distribution system to a system using only wholly owned distributors, but the change cannot be done by unlawful means. It can also be unlawful to terminate an independent distributor if the manufacturer is aware that the independent cannot survive without access to a variety of competing products including those of the manufacturer. In such a case, termination of the relationship with the independent would cause the independent to go out of business, thus eliminating an outlet for competing goods. The termination would affect interbrand competition.

In analyzing dealer termination cases, courts are primarily concerned with the effects on interbrand competition rather than on intrabrand competition. On the other hand, when the manufacturer had monopoly power over the product so that there was very little interbrand competition, a dealer termination which limited intrabrand competition was held to be unlawful.

DUAL DISTRIBUTOR REFUSALS TO DEAL

Refusals to deal are treated in depth in Chapter 6. Here we consider matters of peculiar relevance to the dual distributor. Dual distributors who refuse to deal with an independent distributor may be charged with monopolization in violation of Section 2 of the Sherman Act under the following theories:

1. Leveraging monopoly power from one level into another level
2. Increasing barriers to entry by new firms by requiring new firms to enter at two market levels
3. Evading regulation of monopoly profits

Leveraging

Leveraging would occur when a dual distributor with monopoly power at the manufacturing level attempts to expand the impact of that monopoly into the distribution level by refusing to deal with an independent distributor who carries competing goods or who could not survive by carrying only competing goods.

Increasing Entry Barriers

A manufacturer may increase entry barriers to a potential competing manufacturer by refusing to deal with a distributor who carried other manufacturer's goods. If this destroyed or severely restricted the retail outlet available to a potential competitor at the manufacturing level, it would force a potential new manufacturing competitor to also enter the business at the retail outlet. The potential competitor's cost of entering the market would increase.

Evading Regulation

A firm that is subject to economic regulation at one market level and as a result of regulation has monopoly power may try to evade economic regulation of its profits by integrating vertically into an unregulated market. It may thereby avoid regulation aimed at precluding monopoly profits by using its regulated business to recover costs properly associated with the unregulated business. Other forms of cross-subsidization may also be available.

In each instance, it is important to consider whether legitimate business reasons exist for the refusal to deal and the effect, if any, on interbrand competition. Careful documentation should be maintained showing legitimate business reasons and any resultant operating efficiencies.

PRICE SQUEEZE

Dual distributors have a unique power to disadvantage independent distributors who must rely on them for supplies, by imposing a price squeeze. In a price squeeze, the supplier sells to the independent distributor at a price higher than the imputed transfer price from the supplier to its owned-distributor. This places the independent at a cost disadvantage in reselling in competition with the owned-distributor.

In the famous *Alcoa* case which gave rise to the price squeeze analysis in antitrust law, Alcoa controlled aluminum ingot which was the raw material for aluminum sheet. Alcoa both manufactured and sold aluminum sheet and sold ingot to competing manufacturers of aluminum sheet. Alcoa raised the price at which it sold ingot and at the same time lowered the price it charged for aluminum sheet. This placed its competitors in a price squeeze which violated Section 2 of the Sherman Act.

POTENTIAL ROBINSON-PATMAN PROBLEMS

It is with reference to the Robinson-Patman Act that dual distribution is most likely to create unique problems. In very brief terms, the Robinson-Patman Act prohibits a seller from discriminating in price among competing customers with respect to the sale of commodities of like grade and quality where the effect may be to substantially lessen competition. Robinson-Patman Act issues are also treated in Chapters 10, 11, and 12.

> *Note:* Although the Robinson-Patman Act applies only to the sale of commodities, some state unfair competition statutes apply to services as well as commodities. Calif. Bus. & Prof. Code Sections 17024, 17040 (Deering 1976); Colo. Rev. Stat. Section 6-2-103(1) (1973).

Before there can be Robinson-Patman price discrimination there must be two reasonably contemporaneous sales at different prices. For a dual distributor the issue often involves a claimed difference between the price paid by the independent distributor and the imputed internal transfer price to the owned-distributor. Unfortunately, the law is unsettled as to whether the transfer to the owned-distributor is a "sale" within the meaning of the Robinson-Patman Act. Generally such transfers have been deemed not to be "sales"; however, when the distribution subsidiary has substantial autonomy over purchasing some courts will find that the internal transfer is a sale. In determining whether the distributor has autonomy, courts look to the control exercised by the manufacturer. The elements of control courts have considered are:

1. Daily supervision of operations
2. Maintenance of distributor's business records
3. Maintenance of the distributor's payroll
4. Making of managerial decisions including retail pricing

Since the absence of a sale in an internal transfer will immediately obliviate many Robinson-Patman issues, those firms desiring to use a dual distribution system should carefully consider insuring sufficient control over the owned distributor to preclude internal transfers being deemed to be "sales."

WHEN PRICE DISCOUNTS ARE PERMITTED

The presence of dual distributors or distributors who are vertically integrated creates special Robinson-Patman Act problems when price discounts are offered. Price discounts may be permissible when cost justified. However, functional discounts have been held to be unlawful and cannot be cost justified. Price discounts become functional discounts when offered to a dual function purchaser who both retails and sells at wholesale to other retailers. If the discount is made available for services to be performed by the purchaser, and if the discount applies to the goods resold to others, it is lawful only if it is available to all buyers at the same level of distribution.

For example, assume manufacturer X sells widgets at $0.10 each to retailers, and retail distributor A integrates vertically to the wholesale level. Thus A now purchases widgets from X some of which it resells at retail and some of which it wholesales to retailers B and C. If X sells at wholesale to A at a price of $0.08 each there is an unlawful functional discount with respect to those widgets which A sells at retail. In this example, manufacturer X is guilty of unlawful price discrimination and the dual distributor A may be liable for knowingly receiving an unlawful price discount.

__ WHEN TO OFFER PROMOTIONAL ALLOWANCES AND SERVICES __

Under the Robinson-Patman Act a manufacturer making advertising and promotional allowances or services available must do so on proportionately equal terms for all competing customers. A difficult problem arises for the manufacturer who sells both to wholesalers and directly to retailers, i.e., a manufacturer who sells to owned-wholesalers and to independent wholesalers, who must ensure that the advertising or promotional allowance is available to the customers of the independent wholesaler as well as to its own distribution customers.

The Federal Trade Commission has issued guidelines for advertising allowances and other merchandising payments and services. Under the FTC guidelines, which are described in more detail in Chapter 11, the seller must ensure that the availability of the advertising allowance is made known to its indirect customers as well as its direct customers. To accomplish notification of its indirect customers, the seller may

1. Contract with the intervening wholesaler to provide the notification
2. Place notices in the shipping containers
3. Publish notices in trade publications

The seller may also directly notify indirect customers of the available promotional allowances. If the seller contracts with an intermediary to make a promotional plan available to an indirect purchaser, the seller should include provisions in the contract requiring the intermediary to:

1. Give notice to the seller's indirect customers in conformance with the FTC standards
2. Check customer performance in accordance with FTC standards
3. Implement the plan in a manner which will ensure its functional availability to the seller's customer in conformity with FTC standards
4. Provide certification in writing and at reasonable intervals that the seller's customers have been and are being treated in conformity with the agreement

In addition to including the above terms in its contract with the intermediary, the seller independently should make spot checks of its customers at least every 90 days to ensure that the FTC guidelines are being met.

The provisions of the Robinson-Patman Act dealing with advertising and promotional allowances can only be enforced against sellers. However, a customer who knowingly receives a promotional allowance that is not available on proportionately equal terms to its competitors may be subject to an action brought by the FTC under Section 5 of the Federal Trade Commission Act which prohibits unfair methods of competition.

STATE ENFORCEMENT

While the federal courts are treating dual distributors more permissively, the states have refused to follow the lead of federal law enforcement. The Vertical Restraints Guidelines adopted by the National Association of Attorneys General (NAAG) on December 4, 1985, takes a more restrictive view of dual distribution than do the federal guidelines.

First, under the NAAG guidelines, restraints by dual distributors are more likely to be treated as horizontal restraints. Thus, if the intent or predominant effect of the restraint is to prevent competition with the firm in its dealer capacity, the restraint will be treated as horizontal. In deciding whether the restraint is vertical or horizontal, the Attorneys General will evaluate three factors:

1. Whether a high percentage of brand sales at the dealer level are made by company-owned outlets

2. Whether the nonprice restriction diminishes interbrand competition because it restrains competing dealers who sell both the supplier's brand and competing brands

3. Whether the competing independent dealers are also intrabrand competitors of the firm at the supplier level

Many states prohibit sales made at a price below the cost to the seller. Such statutes may create special problems for dual distributors in determining costs at the functional level of wholesale sales or retail sales. Some state statutes provide specifically for dual distributors. For example, the Maryland Commercial Law Title 11, Section 11-401(H)(2) provides that the definition of wholesaler includes only the wholesale sales made by a dual distributor.

The California Unfair Practices Act under Section 17071.5 of the Business and Professions Code, which creates a presumption of an intent to injure competition for certain retail sales made below cost, applies only to retail sales made by a seller who does not manufacture the goods sold. The presumption does not apply to retail sales made by persons principally engaged in the sale to consumers of commodities of their own production or manufacture. In some dual distribution situations, it will be difficult to determine whether the presumption of an anti-competitive intent for a below-cost sale should apply.

As with so many situations in the law of marketing, we can provide general guidance and alert the reader to potential problem areas. However, there is no substitute for specific legal advice.

chapter five

HANDLING EXCLUSIVE DEALING ARRANGEMENTS

An exclusive dealership is an arrangement in which a supplier agrees to distribute products through a single distributor in a given sales territory. The supplier may also agree that it will not create additional distributorships in the area during the life of the distributorship agreement. An exclusive distributor marketing structure may result from the unilateral practice of a supplier to deal with only one distributor in each local market, or it may result from contractual agreements between the supplier and the distributor.

A number of procompetitive benefits may result from exclusive dealerships. The manufacturer/supplier may achieve greater control of distribution costs, encourage the provision of presale and postsale services, and encourage promotional efforts by distributors. Moreover, exclusive dealerships may be required if dealers are to make large capital investments. From the dealer's viewpoint, an exclusive distributorship protects and encourages capital investment and encourages the distributor to spend more on promoting and servicing the product. Obviously exclusive distributorships retard intrabrand competition while presumptively promoting interbrand competition.

Exclusive distributorships are almost always lawful. However, they are subject to challenge under sections 1 and 2 of the Sherman Act. In analyzing potential problems in exclusive marketing arrangements, it may be helpful to distinguish between exclusive distributorships and exclusive dealing. The latter refers to situations in which the supplier agrees to sell to a dealer only on condition that the dealer not carry a competing line of goods. The effects on competition of exclusive distributorships and exclusive dealing are somewhat different.

WHAT THE COURT SAYS ABOUT EXCLUSIVE DISTRIBUTORSHIPS

The Supreme Court has upheld the use of exclusive distributorships when nothing more is involved than a vertical restraint on the suppliers' right to sell to other distributors and there are other competing products available in the market. In determining whether an exclusive distributorship is lawful the courts have considered such factors as:

1. Strength of interbrand competition

2. Duration of the exclusive distributorship

3. Geographic extent of the distributorship

Absent evidence of monopolization, a manufacturer may lawfully grant an exclusive distributorship. Moreover, a manufacturer may terminate existing distributors to establish a new exclusive distributorship or to expand the territory of another distributor.

Red Flag: A court has found unlawful monopolization by a distributor when the distributor obtained exclusive dealerships from most of the competing manufacturer's of a product.

When a system of exclusive distributorships is being used, the termination of an existing distributor and replacement by another distributor is not unlawful.

Red Flag: If there is any evidence that exclusive distributorships and/or dealer terminations are being used to maintain retail prices, courts will examine the transaction very closely to determine whether the real purpose and effect is to fix prices.

If a nonexclusive agreement is desired, the parties may wish to include language similar to the following in their agreement:

> Supplier and distributor acknowledge that this is a nonexclusive agreement and nothing in this agreement will be construed as precluding or prohibiting distributor from carrying any other _____products.

EXCLUSIVE DEALING

Exclusive dealing is more troublesome than are exclusive dealerships. Exclusive dealing arrangements are subject to challenge under section 1 of the Sherman Act, section 3 of the Clayton Act (commodities only), and section 5 of the Federal

Trade Commission Act. Exclusive dealing arrangements usually take the form of agreements between a supplier and a distributor in which the distributor agrees to obtain all of its supplies of a product from the supplier and not to deal in the goods of a competing supplier. Such agreements may be harmful to competition because they tend to foreclose competing suppliers from access to the market.

A party complaining about an exclusive dealing contract must show that the opportunities for other traders to enter or remain in that market must be significantly limited by the exclusive dealing contract. What most concerns the courts about exclusive dealing is that a single manufacturer will gain control of all or a substantial number of the retail outlets for a product in a given geographic area. This will raise a high entry barrier to other manufacturers who may desire to break into the market by forcing a competing supplier to expand resources at both the manufacturing and distributing levels if it is to enter the market.

There is no fixed percentage of the market that must be foreclosed before an exclusive dealing arrangement becomes unlawful. Foreclosure of as much as 15 percent of the market have been upheld. On the other hand, one court held that foreclosure of 24 percent of the market was unlawful. The legality of an exclusive dealing contract will not turn on market shares alone. Rather the courts will also consider such factors as business justification and ease of market entry by creation of new dealerships or through other existing distributors.

Exclusive dealing arrangements are not per se unlawful because they may have procompetitive effects. Courts have recognized a number of legitimate business reasons for utilizing exclusive dealing such as requirements contracts. From the buyer's standpoint exclusive dealing:

1. May assure supply
2. Afford protection against price increases
3. Enable long-term planning on the basis of known costs
4. Eliminate or reduce the expense and risk of carrying a large inventory

From the seller's viewpoint exclusive dealing:

1. May reduce selling costs
2. Protect against price fluctuations
3. Offer a predictable market
4. Provide a means of obtaining a market foothold in the face of entrenched competitors

Key Point: When exclusive dealing agreements are used be sure to document in the files the legitimate business reasons for their use.

Judicial analysis of an exclusive dealing agreement requires (a) definition of the line of commerce affected, (b) definition of the market area involved and (c) a determination of whether the amount of competition foreclosed constitutes a qualitatively substantial share of the relevant market. The court will consider whether the opportunities for others to enter into or remain in the market are significantly limited by the exclusive dealing. Another factor courts will consider is the duration of the exclusive dealing arrangement. Ordinarily the shorter the duration of the arrangement the more likely it is to be upheld. However, in the context of the electric utility industry a 20-year requirements contract for coal supply for a particular generating plant was held lawful. One court said that exclusive dealing contracts which could be terminated in less than a year were presumptively lawful.

Section 3 of the Clayton Act expressly prohibits agreements not to deal in competitive products if the effect of the agreement is to probably lessen competition. The prohibition extends beyond explicit restraints on handling the goods of a competitor to encompass as well the setting of prices or the granting of rebates or discounts as incentives not to handle competing goods.

Whereas under the Sherman Act an exclusive dealing arrangement is lawful unless it actually restrains commerce, an exclusive dealing arrangement will violate section 3 of the Clayton Act if it will "probably lessen competition." Accordingly, a greater showing of anticompetitive effect is required to establish a violation of the Sherman Act than is required to establish a violation of the Clayton Act.

EXAMPLES OF EXCLUSIVE DEALING AGREEMENTS HELD UNLAWFUL

While the following examples show situations in which illegality may be found, remember that the other requirements of the statute such as a probable lessening of competition must also be satisfied.

1. A contract prohibiting the use of a competitor's goods unless they could be obtained at a price lower than that charged by the contracting supplier.

2. A discount of 50 percent for not handling the goods of a competitor; otherwise the discount was only 25 percent.

3. Leasing a machine on terms which required payment of royalties for the use of competing machines as well.

4. Forfeit of the right to use the seller's trade name if competitive goods were handled.

There must also be an agreement or understanding that the dealer will not handle the goods of a competitor. Courts have found no violation when:

1. The distributor voluntarily decides not to carry the goods of a competitor
2. A manufacturer unilaterally cancels a dealership which handle competitive goods
3. A manufacturer uses aggressive tactics to encourage distributors to give priority to the sale of its goods

On the other hand, the required agreement need not be contained in a specific written contractual provision. Rather, the agreement may be inferred from circumstantial evidence or from a general pattern of exclusion.

In determining whether an exclusive dealing contract is an unreasonable restraint of trade, the focus is on the amount of the relevant market that is foreclosed to competitors by the agreement. The exclusion of competitors from the market is of antitrust concern only if it harms competition. Thus an exclusive dealing agreement will not be unlawful unless:

1. It is likely to keep at least one significant competitor from doing business in the market
2. The probable effect of the exclusion will be to raise prices above the competitive level or otherwise harm competition

The factors considered in determining whether an exclusive dealing contract will probably result in substantial market foreclosure include:

1. Relative strength of the market participants
2. Amount of commerce involved in relation to the total volume of commerce in the geographic market
3. Probable immediate and future effects which the foreclosure might have on the market
4. Dominance of the seller in the market
5. Extent of actual market foreclosure resulting from the agreements
6. Ease of market entry by new distributors
7. Sales structure existing in the industry

8. Duration of the exclusive dealing agreement
9. Extent to which competition exists in the face of the exclusive dealing agreements

EXCLUSIVE DEALING UNDER STATE LAW

At least 17 states have "little FTC" laws modeled after the Federal Trade Commission Act. As a general rule, these states will consider Federal Trade Commission precedent in interpreting the state law. Accordingly, exclusive dealing contracts are likely to be treated under state law in very much the same way as they are treated under federal law.

Red Flag: Some states may require a lesser degree of proof to establish a violation of the state act.

ALL REQUIREMENTS CONTRACT

All requirements contracts are forms of exclusive dealing agreements in which a purchaser agrees to purchase all the needs for a certain product from one supplier. Requirements contracts have been upheld in the same circumstances in which other exclusive dealing contracts have been upheld.

To document the reasonableness of an all requirements contract a party should document its need for an assured source of supply, the desirability of price stability, the need for quality control or any other rationale for a single source of supply. Requirements contracts of a short-time duration are more likely to be upheld than are contracts of long duration although a 20-year requirements contract for coal for an electric generating station was upheld when less than one percent of the market for coal was foreclosed by the contract.

BLANKET CONTRACTS

Blanket contracts are price guarantee agreements in which a supplier agrees to sell to a distributor a certain product at a set price for a set period of time. The distributor usually must agree to purchase a certain minimum quantity which may approach its estimated requirements for the period of the contract. The distributor usually must promise to sell only to ultimate consumers. Such agreements benefit the distributor by providing an assured price that can be used to formulate bids for ultimate sales.

Although blanket contracts may have some similarity to exclusive dealing agreements, they do differ in that they do not preclude the distributor from dealing with others. Accordingly, blanket contracts are not unlawful exclusive dealing contracts.

RECIPROCAL DEALING

Reciprocal dealing is treated much like tying arrangements although it also has a resemblance to exclusive dealing. Reciprocity is subject to attack under sections 1 and 2 of the Sherman Act and section 5 of the Federal Trade Commission Act. The focus of antitrust attack has been on reciprocal purchasing agreements. A reciprocal purchasing agreement is one in which supplier A agrees to buy widgets from B in return for B's agreement to buy trinkets from A. There is harm to competition from such an agreement only if a party has sufficient market power to force the reciprocal purchase on the other party. The market ideal is that goods will be bought and sold on their own competitive merits and not on the basis of market power or bargaining strength. If firm A has sufficient market power as a purchaser of widgets to force the seller of widgets, B, to purchase trinkets from A then competition for the sale of trinkets is no longer on the merits. For reciprocity, as with tie-in sales (see Chapter 8), there must be two separate products involved.

Reciprocity restrains competition in the following respects:

1. Competitors of participants in the arrangement are foreclosed from the market
2. Price, quality, and service cease to be the determinants of purchases
3. An industry may become more concentrated

Courts have identified two types of reciprocity that raise antitrust concerns:

1. Coercive reciprocity in which one party leverages its power as a purchaser to compel another party to make reciprocal purchases
2. Material reciprocity in which parties of equal bargaining power agree to purchase from each other

To be unlawful, reciprocity must affect a not insubstantial amount of commerce. Such an agreement will be per se unlawful under the same circumstances as a tying arrangement.

Findings of actual violation of the antitrust laws through reciprocity have been rare.

chapter six

REFUSALS TO DEAL: WHEN IT'S LEGAL TO REFUSE

One of the most important tasks in establishing a marketing program is the selection of distributors. Manufacturers want to have the maximum amount of freedom to identify and select their distributors to create the most aggressive and most efficient marketing program possible. Manufacturers are also concerned with selecting distributors who will maintain an appropriate product image and will provide adequate presale product servicing. For the most part, the law does provide the manufacturer with the degree of freedom it desires.

It is a basic tenant of the law that "in the absence of any purpose to create or maintain a monopoly, the [Sherman] act does not restrict the long-recognized right of a trader or manufacturer engaged in an entirely private business, freely to exercise his own independent discretion as to the parties with whom he will deal."

As a general rule then, a company has the right under the antitrust laws to choose with whom it will deal. Moreover, in instances in which other brands are readily available to a would-be distributor, a manufacturer may not only refuse to deal with some would-be distributors but it can select certain dealers with whom it will deal exclusively.

Unless the seller has monopoly power or is likely to achieve monopoly power, a unilateral refusal to deal with a potential distributor is unlikely to contain a high degree of antitrust risk. So long as it acts unilaterally, the seller may refuse to sell to discounters or to those who will not adequately and properly present its product. Nonetheless, a seller should take care in communicating a refusal to deal to the would-be distributor. While no reason need be given, if a reason is given it should be a truthful one. Giving a false reason for a refusal to deal can create embarrassment in any subsequent litigation and could be construed by a jury as an attempt to conceal an unlawful reason—such as a conspiracy.

REFUSALS TO DEAL BY A DOMINANT SELLER

Refusals to deal become more problematical when the refusal is by a manufacturer with monopoly or a dominant market position. A refusal to deal by a monopoly seller violates the antitrust laws if the refusal is intended to maintain the seller's monopoly. A refusal to deal by a dominant seller (one with a large market share but not yet a monopolist) is unlawful if it is intended to create a monopoly in the seller. An example of such a refusal to deal was a refusal by Kodak to continue to offer a wholesale discount to a distributor when Kodak was trying to achieve control of the market for its own retail outlets.

Generally, an unlawful refusal to deal involves an effort by the monopolist to leverage its power in one market to obtain an economic advantage in a second market. For example, it was held that a refusal by Sunkist Growers, Inc., which had monopoly power over the supply of oranges, to sell oranges to a firm which would compete with Sunkist in exporting oranges to Hong Kong violated section 2 of the Sherman Act. Sunkist was faulted for using its control over the supply to extend its monopoly illegally into the distribution market.

One defense to a charge of unlawful refusal to deal which courts will consider is whether a monopolist engaging in vertical integration thereby achieves greater efficiencies. When efficiencies exist, courts are likely to approve the refusal to deal. On the other hand, the refusal would be condemned in the absence of any efficiencies of vertical integration.

A refusal to deal by a monopolist with a would-be customer who deals with a competitor of the monopolist is unlawful. Such a refusal to deal is inherently anticompetitive. Accordingly, it was unlawful for a newspaper, which was an indispensable means of advertising in a particular market and which enjoyed a substantial monopoly in the market, to refuse to sell advertising to local businesses which also advertised on a local radio station.

A unilateral refusal to deal can also be unlawful when the seller controls access to a facility which is essential to competition in the market place. A company having exclusive control over an essential or "bottleneck" facility which is necessary to effective competition cannot deny potential competitors access to that facility on reasonable terms and conditions if such a refusal would place the would-be competitor at a disadvantage. The facility must be one which is necessary to competition and which cannot practicably be duplicated.

A monopolist cannot insist on dealing only on discriminatory terms. That is, a monopolist cannot deal on one basis with those who do not compete with it and on other less favorable terms or not at all with those who do compete with it.

MONOPOLISTS' LAWFUL REFUSALS TO DEAL

There are a number of situations in which refusals to deal by monopolists have been found to be lawful. A monopolist may refuse to deal in the following situations:

1. A monopolist may refuse to deal with those it does not compete with.

2. A monopolist may refuse to deal so long as its unilateral refusal does not extend or maintain its monopoly power.

3. A monopolist may refuse to deal with a party which insists on preferential treatment.

4. A monopolist may refuse to deal for certain legitimate business reasons such as to avoid injury to innocent third parties.

5. A monopolist which is not a public utility may refuse to deal because it is shutting down its operations.

6. A monopolist may refuse to license its technology.

JOINT REFUSALS TO DEAL

Joint refusals to deal are more problematical than are unilateral refusals to deal. Joint horizontal refusals to deal may include refusals to enter into new business relationships, refusals by associations to approve or certify a product (for example, a refusal to certify a product as meeting an industry code), or a trade association's refusal to admit a new member or the expulsion of an existing member. Joint refusals to deal are often referred to as "group boycotts" or "concerted refusals to deal."

Courts have found that concerted refusals to deal are violations of the Sherman Act in a variety of situations. For example, the Supreme Court held an agreement among retail lumber dealers not to deal with wholesalers, who also sold to ultimate consumers in competition with the retailers, to be unlawful. The arrangement unlawfully used the combined strength of the retailers to coerce the wholesalers to stop competing.

In another instance the Supreme Court condemned an agreement among garment manufacturers to refuse to sell to stores which sold "style-pirated" garments. The court said the agreement violated the law by narrowing the outlets to which the manufacturers could sell, removed freedom of action from the manufacturers, subjected targeted retailers to a group boycott, and suppressed competition from the sale of unregistered textiles and copied designs.

A concerted refusal to deal was also held unlawful when a group of manufacturers and appliance distributors agreed that the manufacturer would not provide appliances to a particular discount dealer. In holding the group boycott unlawful, the court said that it could not be "saved by allegations that [it] . . . fixed or regulated prices, parceled out or limited production, or brought about a deterioration in quality."

Key Point: The crucial element in concerted refusals to deal which are per se unlawful is an effort to exclude or disadvantage a competitor by cutting it off from a trade relationship which is necessary for any firm trying to compete. The classic group boycott usually entails an effort by two or more suppliers or customers not to deal with the target.

So called classic group boycotts have been identified as falling within three groups:

1. Horizontal combinations at one market level, whose purpose is to exclude direct competitors from the market

2. Combinations among traders at different market levels, designed to exclude from the market direct competitors of some members of the combination

3. Combinations designed to coercively influence the target's trade practices rather than to eliminate the target as a competitor

Key Point: Often the presence of an anticompetitive or exclusionary purpose is critical to the court's analysis of concerted refusals to deal. Accordingly, any group refusing to deal should carefully establish a record of a nonexclusionary purpose.

In order to understand what a group can and cannot do in the way of concerted refusals to deal, it is important to understand what factors courts have considered in deciding whether to apply a per se rule to a concerted refusal to deal. Among the factors are:

1. Whether the refusal to deal arose in a commercial setting

2. The economic rationale for the joint conduct

3. Whether the conduct has a purpose other than the suppression of competition

4. What the relationship between the group and the target is

5. Whether the restraint is ancillary to joint, efficiency-creating conduct

Joint action within the context of a self-regulating trade association also may be examined for anticompetitive or exclusionary effect. Trouble spots for trade association activities include:

1. Membership requirements

2. Standard setting

3. Certification of products

4. Joint purchasing

The trade association's actions should be the least restrictive which can accomplish the goal of the justifying self-regulation.

AVOIDING THE JOINT REFUSAL TRAP

Since the likelihood of an antitrust violation is greatly reduced if action is taken unilaterally, any decision to refuse to deal should be unilateral if at all possible. Consider the following marketing problems.

Problem 1

A firm has granted an exclusive dealership to dealer A. B requests a dealership which would infringe upon A's exclusive dealership. Upon A's insistence, B is denied a dealership. Although this smacks of joint action, the prior existence of a lawful exclusive-dealership agreement makes the joint refusal lawful.

Problem 2

Dealer A has a nonexclusive dealership. Again when B requests a dealership, A protests. B is denied a dealership. This situation is more difficult. There are cases which indicate that this may be an unlawful joint refusal to deal.

Key Point: If you want to utilize exclusive distributorships make that a part of your written distributorship agreement. Enforce the agreement yourself and do not first consult your existing distributors.

Problem 3

Prior to deciding whether to accept the new dealer, the manufacturer consults with several of his existing distributors. In this situation antitrust risks increase dramatically. Any refusal to deal after consultation with others will look to the world like joint action—unless of course the manufacturer refuses to deal contrary to the advice of the distributors.

Red Flag: If the distributors have already engaged in a horizontal conspiracy to fix prices, allocate customers, or divide territories, the manufacturer may be deemed to have joined the unlawful conspiracy, if its refusal to deal advances the objectives of the distributor's conspiracy.

RESPONDING TO THE COMPLAINING DEALER

A chronic evidentiary problem when a disappointed would-be distributor sues a manufacturer claiming an unlawful refusal to deal is the presence in the manufacturer's files of letters from existing distributors protesting the appointment of a new distributor. Plaintiffs in such cases try to fashion a conspiracy from evidence of complaint followed by the manufacturer taking the action requested by the complaining distributor. Therefore, it is important that the manufacturer disassociate itself from the complaint. One way to do so is to respond to the complaint with a letter similar to that which follows.

> Dear Joe Smith,
>
> Your letter of January 25, 1988, regarding the potential appointment of additional distributors has been received in this office. As you are well aware, the appointment of distributors is a matter for the company alone to determine. This decision, like all previous decisions regarding the appointment of distributors, will be made unilaterally by the company.
>
> Sincerely,

Red Flag: A letter replying to a distributor's complaint about another existing or potential distributor should never state that the company has agreed to take the action requested.

Other actions a manufacturer can take to ensure that its refusals to deal will be unilateral and lawful include:

1. Establishing written business criteria for the selection and appointment of distributors

2. Establishing a management level committee which is insulated from direct contact with existing distributors to appoint new distributors

When written criteria for the selection and appointment of distributors exist, it is important that the firm follow those criteria. The reasons for any deviation from written criteria should be carefully documented.

RATIONING SCARCE SUPPLIES

On occasions a manufacturer or wholesaler may not be able to satisfy the product demand. This may be the result of a scarcity of raw materials or insufficient manufacturing capability. In such situations the supplier may establish a plan to allocate short supplies among existing distributors. Generally, the courts have upheld allocation programs against refusal to deal claims. Voluntary allocation programs are more likely to pass judicial muster than are terminations of selected dealers. Moreover, some courts will give great weight to equitable considerations particularly if the allocation of scarce supply is accomplished through dealer termination cases. If an effective allocation program could have been utilized a court is more likely to enjoin a termination.

Red Flag: An allocation scheme is unlawful if it is used, by a supplier having monopoly power, as a device to influence price or to maintain or extend its monopoly.

Courts have upheld the following supplier programs for dealing with a supply shortage:

1. There is withdrawal from a geographic area or market.
2. The allocation program was applied without discrimination among classes of dealers and there was no proof of a combination or conspiracy to raise prices or restrain competition.
3. The allocation scheme did nothing to enlarge the manufacturer's share of the market and the manufacturer had dedicated the increase in production capacity to its competitors.
4. An allocation of a popular sports car to dealers who sold more of a less popular model where there was no tying arrangement.
5. Rationing of steel was upheld since the rationing appeared to have been "no more than a move to meet the sudden change in the current business climate." The effect was to divide production among all customers, including defendants own fabricating division, equitably

and in a manner which maintained relative equality among all fabricators; neither the policies nor the manner in which they were carried out permit any implication that a defendant resorted to retaining in a calculated effort to exclude from competition independent fabricators.

REFUSAL TO DEAL CHECKLIST

_____ Does the supplier have a large market share?

_____ Are there other sources of supply?

_____ Are there valid business reasons for the refusal to deal?

_____ Will the refusal to deal harm competition?

_____ Has the decision to refuse to deal been made unilaterally?

_____ Have the business reasons for a refusal to deal been documented in the files?

_____ Does the file contain complaints from competing distributors?

_____ Does the refusal conform to the supplier's criteria for dealer selection?

chapter seven

HOW TO TERMINATE DISTRIBUTORS

Business relationships don't last forever. Sooner or later circumstances are likely to develop between a supplier and its distributor which make it desirable or necessary for the supplier to terminate the relationship. While there are many valid and lawful reasons for a supplier to terminate a particular distributor, there are also a number of unlawful reasons. Distributor terminations have provided a fertile spawning ground for litigation as disappointed distributors try to recoup from the loss of an important supplier. Typically such cases involve a number of claims against the supplier running the gamut from simple breach of contract, to fraud, to violation of state franchise or fair dealership laws, to violations of sections 1 and 2 of the Sherman Act. The frequent assertion of Sherman Act claims with the attendant risk of treble damages makes these cases expensive to defend. The trick, then, is to terminate the distributor and not get sued. Careful planning prior to termination can greatly reduce the danger of suit. This chapter examines problem areas in dealer terminations and then discusses ways to avoid problems and lawsuits.

SHERMAN ACT PROBLEMS AND HOW TO HANDLE THEM

Both sections 1 and 2 of the Sherman Act are implicated in dealer termination and refusal to deal cases (see Chapter 1, Antitrust Overview). Section 2, which applies in most instances to unilateral conduct, is less of a problem because courts have recognized the right of a trader or manufacturer engaged in a private business to freely exercise independent discretion as to the parties with whom he will deal.

Key Point: Most unilateral refusals to deal do not violate the antitrust laws. Dealer terminations are very similar to refusals to deal.

On the other hand, the law has long recognized that the danger of mischief is increased when two or more embark on a common course of conduct. Accordingly section 1 cases, which involve joint action, present more difficulties in dealer termination.

Key Point: Conduct which is lawful when done by a supplier unilaterally may become unlawful when the conduct is the product of an agreement or conspiracy with a third party.

Thus, as a threshold matter, it is necessary to determine whether the dealer termination is unilateral or joint.

Because section 1 of the Sherman Act requires proof of a contract, combination, or conspiracy, it requires that at least two parties have a unity of purpose. Once unity of purpose is shown, the distributor may have little difficulty in proving a violation because some section 1 offenses are per se violations, that is, the plaintiff does not have to prove that the acts done were harmful to competition. In such cases the law presumes that the act was harmful to competition. Some activities that have been declared per se violations of section 1 include price fixing, horizontal market or customer allocations, group boycotts, and some tying arrangements. The reduced level of proof necessary to meet the requirements of a per se section 1 offense coupled with the potential for recovering treble damages plus attorney's fees make section 1 an attractive claim for terminated distributors. The main line of defense for the supplier is to make sure the decision to terminate is unilateral.

It is an axiomatic principle of antitrust law that a firm lacking monopoly power has a right to either deal or refuse to deal with whomever it likes so long as it does so unilaterally. However, even unilateral refusal to deal can violate the Sherman Act if the refusal is accompanied by some unlawful conduct or conceived in some monopolistic purpose or to control a market. This is particularly true of a business with a large share of the market.

When section 1 claims are made, the terminated dealer frequently attempts to show the necessary unity of purpose by proving a conspiracy between the supplier and one or more competing distributors. For this reason, the supplier must exercise particular care in handling complaints made by distributors about other distributors. The supplier should respond to such complaints in a fashion that will clearly and unmistakably be understood by some future jury as showing that the supplier will not act against the target distributor on the basis of the complaints. Those making the complaint should be told:

- That the supplier will continue to make its own decisions independently
- That the supplier is quite capable of monitoring the market itself
- That those making the complaint ought to tend to their own distribution business

By no means should the supplier inform those making the complaint of its plan of action. Such action could be taken as an expression of a conspiratorial agreement. See Chapter 6 for a sample letter responding to a dealer complaint.

Prior to the Supreme Court's decision in *Monsanto Co.* v. *Spray-Rite Service Corp.*[1] in 1984, some courts held that the presence of complaint letters plus dealer termination alone was enough evidence to find a conspiracy. After *Monsanto*, a terminated dealer must present additional evidence which tends to exclude the possibility that the manufacturer was acting independently.

Key Point: Manufacturers should give their field personnel written instructions to never discuss with one distributor the marketing practices of another distributor.

HOW TO TERMINATE PRICE CUTTERS

Price fixing, including resale price maintenance, is a per se violation of section 1 of the Sherman Act. Terminated distributors frequently strain to characterize their terminations as having been done to enforce a price-fixing scheme. If the terminated distributor was a price cutter, the problem is particularly sensitive. Price cutting by distributor A is likely to bring complaints from distributors B, C, and D. If the supplier reacts to the complaints by terminating or disciplining the price cutter, the inference of a price-fixing conspiracy is apparent. When a dealer is terminated following complaints by other dealers, courts will apply a two-part test:

1. The terminated distributor must convince the court that the alleged conspiracy between the manufacturer and the complaining distributor is an economically reasonable allegation. That is, is the alleged conspiracy economically rational behavior?

2. The terminated distributor must produce evidence which tends to exclude the possibility that the manufacturer was acting independently. For example, it was held that a jury question was presented when a manufacturer replied to a distributor complaint: "Please be advised that corrective action has been taken regarding (name of company omitted) offering discounted parts on the international

market. Hopefully, the problem is resolved but should it recur please advise us." The complaining dealer responded: "Thank you for your prompt action in respect of the pirate spares supplier." The court held that the exchange could be held by the jury to constitute an agreement between the manufacturer and the complaining dealer. Accordingly, any action taken against a price cutting distributor must be clearly established as a unilateral action by contemporaneous documentation and should be supported by a commercially defensible rationale.

There is a particular trap for the unwary supplier in dealing with a price-cutting distributor. If the supplier threatens to terminate the distributor unless the price cutting ceases and the price cutter does stop cutting prices, the supplier has created very persuasive evidence of an agreement between the supplier and distributor to fix prices. With this sort of record the supplier may be very reluctant to terminate the price cutter if the discounting resumes.

Key Point: The single most important point to remember is that a supplier may take a number of actions unilaterally to establish the retail price of a product. (Such actions are discussed in Chapter 9, Pricing Decisions.) As soon as these actions cease to be unilateral and become the result of agreement, the supplier has become party to an unlawful resale price maintenance scheme.

TERMINATION TO ENFORCE UNLAWFUL AGREEMENTS

Just as termination of a dealer to enforce a price fixing agreement is unlawful, so to, is a termination to enforce other anticompetitive agreements. For example, a supplier was found to have violated the Sherman Act by refusing to deal any longer with a distributor except on the basis of an unlawful tying arrangement. The supplier insisted that the dealer purchase a certain number of flush doors for every six panel doors the dealer wanted to purchase.

Similarly it would be unlawful for a distributor to terminate a dealer to enforce a horizontal territorial agreement. If a market division is enforced by a manufacturer using a dual distribution system, i. e., both independent and supplier owned distributors, the legality depends on whether the enforcement is unilateral. If the action is not unilateral, the dual distributor will be deemed to have joined in a horizontal agreement with the independent distributors. Even a nondistributing supplier may be engaged in enforcing a horizontal market division if it polices the territorial agreement on the request of a distributor.

Courts have held that a distributor who contends that the supplier has refused to deal as a means of enforcing an anticompetitive practice, such as a tying arrangement or price fixing, may establish the requisite combination or conspiracy by showing that either:

1. The distributor had unwillingly complied with the practice.

2. Although the terminated dealer refused to comply, other dealers agreed to comply under threat of termination.

HOW TO HANDLE UNILATERAL REFUSALS TO DEAL

It is well settled in the law that as a general proposition a supplier may pick and choose with whom it will deal. As discussed above any refusal to deal should be a unilateral decision made by the supplier. However, there are a few situations in which even unilateral refusal to deal may be unlawful under the antitrust laws. Under section 2 of the Sherman Act determining whether the unilateral refusal to deal or termination of a dealer is unlawful depends first on whether the supplier has monopoly power in the relevant market.

Unilateral refusals to deal by a supplier with monopoly power have been found to be unlawful in certain limited circumstances. These circumstances are discussed below.

- An attempt by a supplier having monopoly power at one market level, such as manufacturing, to extend that lawful monopoly into another marketing level, such as retailing, is a section 2 violation.

  For example, a violation occurred when the sole manufacturer of linen rug material in the United States that operated a dual distribution system refused to provide material to a distributor who had bid against the manufacturer for the finishing and resale of rugs to the U. S. government.

  In another case, in which a regional wholesale distributor of periodicals refused to continue selling to a small jobber because the wholesaler wished to take over the jobber's business, the Sixth Circuit Court of Appeals stated the following test for determining lawfulness of a unilateral refusal to deal:

  > There are situations . . . where a refusal to deal as part of a vertical integration scheme is anticompetitive. This is, (1) where integration facilitates price discrimination so that a monopolist can reap the maximum monopoly profit from different customers; (2) where integration increases first-

level entry barriers so that potential competitors are stymied; and (3) where integration facilitates evasion of regulation of monopoly profits. In such cases, a court should not hesitate to find a section 2 violation.[2]

- Violations of section 2 have also been found when a monopolist refuses to deal with customers who deal with its rivals. In a leading case decided by the Supreme Court, *Lorain Journal* v. *United States*,[3] the Court found a violation when the *Lorain Journal* newspaper refused to sell advertising to local businesses which also advertised on the local radio station. The newspaper was an indispensable medium for advertising in the market and its refusal to deal was intended solely to destroy competition from the radio station.

- Dual distributors who take pricing actions which have the effect of limiting the ability of independent distributors to compete have been held to have violated the antitrust laws. A violation was found when Eastman Kodak Co. terminated a distributor's dealer discount when the distributor refused to sell its business to Kodak.[4]

A refusal to deal may take the form of termination of an existing business relationship. These refusal to deal problems therefore are equally relevant to dealer terminations.

HOW TO HANDLE FRANCHISE TERMINATIONS

Terminating a franchised distributor (see Chapter 2) imposes an additional legal hurdle over and above compliance with the Sherman Act. Over the years, a history of abusive treatment of franchises by franchisors have led most states to enact legislation providing special protection for franchises. Frequently state statutes regulating franchises have specific provisions dealing with termination of the franchise relationship. For example, an Illinois statute makes it unlawful to terminate a franchisee prior to the end of the term of the franchise agreement except for "good cause." The statute then defines "good cause" to mean failure of the franchisee to cure a default in performance under the franchise agreement within 30 days of notice of such default. Good cause under the Illinois statute also exists if:

1. The franchisee is adjudicated as bankrupt or insolvent.
2. The franchisee makes an assignment for the benefit of creditors.
3. The franchisee voluntarily abandons the franchise business.
4. The franchisee is convicted of a felony.

5. The franchisee repeatedly fails to comply with the lawful provisions of the franchise agreement.

California law also requires good cause for termination of a franchisee. The California statute defines good cause to mean, among other things, the failure to cure a default after 30 days notice but also lists circumstances in which the prior notice is not required.

Key Point: Prior to terminating a franchisee, it is essential that the franchisor carefully review the termination provisions of both the franchise agreement and the applicable state statute.

Prior to termination all notice provisions must be complied with. Moreover, the review of state statutes must include a check for special industry specific statutes. Examples of industry specific laws are the California Automobile Dealers Act, the California Business and Professions Code (Petroleum Dealers and Distributors), and the California Fair Dealership Law which makes it unlawful to terminate a distributor because of the race, color, religion, national origin, ancestry, or sex of the dealer.

Failure to renew a franchise is similar in effect to a termination. Thus it should come as no surprise that franchise renewals are often subject to special statutory protection. The Illinois Franchise Disclosure Act, for example, makes it unlawful to refuse to renew a franchise without compensating the franchisee where (a) the franchise agreement precludes the franchisee from conducting a substantially similar business under another trademark or commercial symbol in the same area or (b) where the franchisor did not receive at least six-months notice of the franchisor's intent not to renew the franchise.

Franchise renewals are also typically the subject of detailed contractual provisions. The contract provisions as well as the state statutory provisions must be satisfied.

Federal statutes must also be consulted if the franchisee is an automobile dealer (Automobile Dealer's Franchise Act) or a retailer of petroleum products (Federal Petroleum Marketing Practices Act).

Red Flag: The added technicalities affecting the termination or nonrenewal of a franchisee makes advice of counsel an integral part of the termination decision-making process.

Key Point: Special care must be taken to ensure compliance with all notice requirements before terminating a franchisee. The franchisee must be given adequate notice of noncompliance with the franchise agreement.

HANDLING STATE ANTITRUST LAWS

State antitrust laws, patterned after the federal statutes, are applicable to terminations of distributors. Generally the state courts have had little experience with antitrust law and follow federal court decisions. However, due to some differences in language and occasionally in interpretation it is necessary to consider the impact of state antitrust law as well as federal law.

LAWFUL TERMINATIONS

The bulk of this chapter has been devoted to a discussion of situations in which it is unlawful to terminate a distributor. The purpose of the discussion presented is to post red-flag warnings at danger points. However, it may be helpful and reassuring to pause for a brief look at lawful dealer terminations. The following list is not exhaustive but rather is provided by way of illustration.

1. Changes in the structure of a distribution system are lawful. Thus, a manufacturer which in the past has relied upon independent distributors may terminate the independent distributors and assume the distribution function itself.

2. A supplier may unilaterally terminate a price discounter.

3. A supplier may substitute one distributor for another.

4. A distributor may be terminated as a poor credit risk.

5. A distributor may be terminated for poor sales performance.

6. Failure to properly stock and advertise the supplier's product is a lawful reason for termination of a distributor.

7. A supplier may terminate a distributor who fails to promote the product in its area of primary responsibility.

8. A supplier may terminate an ineffective distributor.

9. A manufacturer may refuse to sell to a distributor who handles a private-brand version of competing goods. The manufacturer's brand is almost certain to be promoted less energetically than the competing private brand.

10. A distributor may be terminated for violation of a lawful exclusive dealing arrangement.

11. A desire to avoid losing the business of other disgruntled distributors has been held to be a valid independent business reason to terminate a discounter by at least one court.

12. A mail-order distributor was lawfully terminated to promote the manufacturer's policy of face-to-face sales.

PRACTICAL TIPS

Strictly aside from reviewing the applicable law to ensure that the termination is lawful there are a number of practical steps a supplier can take to avoid a lawsuit.

Key Point: An important precaution a supplier should take: Collect accounts receivable from the distributor prior to giving notice of termination.

After termination, a distributor will be reluctant to make further payments to the supplier. If the supplier is forced to sue the distributor to collect receivables, it is likely that the distributor will counterclaim alleging an unlawful termination. On the other hand, the terminated distributor may not initiate litigation on its own.

Another practical precaution a supplier should consider: The offer of generous terms for repurchase of inventory held by the terminated dealer.

A distributor left with a large inventory which it may have to sell at a loss is more likely to sue than is a distributor which has been treated generously.

If the distributor has made a large investment in display cases or special fixtures or materials to promote and service the product, the supplier should consider an offer to purchase the investment from the terminated distributor.

It is helpful to formulate a checklist for review prior to terminating a dealer. The use of a checklist is helpful in ensuring that a lawful basis for terminating the dealer exists.

CONTRACT PROVISIONS

Careful consideration should be given to a written distribution agreement. Distribution agreements are discussed in detail in Appendix A. If state laws regulate termination of the relationship any written distribution agreement should conform to state law. Where there is no statutory provision, state common law may require reasonable notice of termination or may permit termination of an order-to-order relationship at will.

Key Point: The Uniform Commercial Code provides that a relationship of indefinite duration can be terminated on good faith and on reasonable notice at any time.

Among the termination provisions to be covered in a written distribution agreement are the following:

1. A party's right, if any, to terminate without cause but upon reasonable notice
2. The supplier's right to terminate if the distributor fails to meet certain performance standards
3. Termination for contract breaches
4. Termination for changes in ownership of the distributor
5. Termination when the distributor encounters financial difficulties

CLAIMS FOR UNLAWFUL TERMINATION

A terminated dealer whose very livelihood is at stake is likely to fight to either maintain the dealership or recover damages. In any suit for damages a terminated dealer not only may claim damages for breach of contract but also treble damages for alleged violations of the Sherman Act and the Racketeer Influenced Corrupt Organizations Act (RICO). If such litigation occurs it will be expensive in management time and legal fees even if the dealer loses. Therefore great care must be taken in terminating a dealer.

CHECKLIST FOR TERMINATING A DEALER

The checklist should include the following items:

_____ Review all contracts between the supplier and the distributor to determine both the contractual grounds for termination and any notice requirements. This review should include not only the initial contract but any modifications or amendments as well.

_____ Review the requirements of any applicable state or federal statutes.

_____ Consider whether the asserted commercial justifications for the termination are the real reasons for termination. A file search and interviews should be conducted to determine whether other motivations are documented. The existence of unlawful motives or disguised motives will surface at trial. Early identification of these motives may permit structuring of a lawful termination.

_____ Do the company's files contain complaints against the distributor by other distributors? If so, special precaution should be taken to avoid antitrust problems.

_____ Has the company been consistent in its treatment of dealers. If other dealers were similarly situated, were they terminated?

_____ Have other distributors been involved in the decisions to terminate? The involvement of other dealers raises the possibility of a conspiracy in violation of section 1 of the Sherman Act.

_____ Are documents in the company's files that are relied on to support the termination credible? An example of documents which lack credibility are those which seem to have sprung up overnight to justify termination. Such documents suggest the existence of some hidden motive for the termination.

_____ Do the company files contain letters of commendation or positive reviews of the target distributor's performance?

_____ What is the impact of termination on the distributor? Will termination jeopardize a large investment made by the distributor? Are there alternative sources of supply? What percentage of the distributor's business will be jeopardized by the termination? How large are the potential damages to the distributor? These matters are a matter of practical rather than legal concern in assessing the likelihood of litigation.

_____ Is the distributor being treated reasonably? Is the dealer being given fair notice? Have there been prior warnings? Is the company willing to buy back the distributor's inventory?

_____ Does "good cause" exist for termination of a franchise? Have all notice requirements been satisfied?

Although no reason is required to terminate a distributor, unless required by contract or state statute, the absence of a valid commercial reason for the termination may lead a court to infer an unlawful reason. At the same time, the statement of a false reason or no reason at all does not compel a finding that the termination was unlawful.

Chapter 7 Footnotes

1. 104 S. Ct. 1464 (1984).
2. *Byars* v. *Bluff City News Co.*, 609 F. 2d 843, 861 (6th Cir. 1979).
3. 342 U. S. 143 (1951).
4. *Eastman Kodak Co.* v. *Southern Photo Materials Co.*, 273 U. S. 359 (1927).

chapter eight

HOW TO COMPLY WHEN HANDLING TIE-IN SALES

Arrangements in which a seller agrees to sell product A only on condition that the purchaser also purchase product B are known as tying arrangements. In this example, product A is the tying product and product B is the tied product. Tying arrangements may violate section 1 of the Sherman Act, section 3 of the Clayton Act (commodities only), and section 5 of the Federal Trade Commission Act. Tie-in claims may also be predatory acts which will support a finding of monopolization under section 2 of the Sherman Act.

However, the courts have recognized that tie-in sales also can be legitimate marketing tools which have no anticompetitive consequences. Therefore, tie-in sales are sometimes judged by a rule of reason standard rather than a per se standard. The Supreme Court has said that the "essential characteristic of an invalid tying arrangement lies in the seller's exploitation of its control over the tying product to force the buyer into the purchase of a tied product that the buyer either did not want at all, or might have preferred to purchase elsewhere on different terms."[1]

The Harm to Competition from Tying Arrangements

Tying agreements deny competitors free access to the market for the tied product because of the tying seller's market power, rather than because the tied product had a lower price or better quality. Further, the purchaser is forced to forego its free choice between competing products.

A tie-in will be per se unlawful if it meets the following criteria:

1. Two separate services or products are involved.

2. There is an agreement to sell one product or service conditioned on the purchase of another.

3. The seller has enough economic power over the tying product to enable it to restrain trade in the market for the tied product.

4. A substantial amount of interstate commerce in the tied product is affected.

Two-Products

The first requirement of a per se tying violation is that two separate products are involved. For example, it is not an unlawful tie-in sale to require that a customer purchasing a right shoe also purchase a left shoe—only one product is involved, a pair of shoes. Similarly, it is not unlawful to sell a stereo unit assembled with turn table, amplifier and speakers, although some customers desire to purchase components and assemble their own sound system. The Supreme Court has held that the question of whether one or two products are involved turns not upon the functional relations between the items, but rather on the character of the demand for the items.

Key Point: There must a sufficient demand for the tied product to identify it as a separate market.

In the past the Supreme Court has found two separate products involved despite a functional link as follows:

1. A heating system and stoker switch

2. Salt machine and salt

3. Process patent and material used in the patent process

4. Computer and computer punch cards

5. Gasoline and underground storage tanks

6. Shoe machinery and supplies, maintenance, and peripheral equipment

Lower courts have found the following items to be separate products:

1. Trailer homes and the lease of trailer sites

2. A condominium and a maintenance contract

3. Cemetery lots, gravemarkers, and installation services

4. An automobile dealership and replacement parts for automobiles

5. Photocopiers and supplies

On the other hand, courts have held that only a single product was involved in the sale of tickets to exhibition football games and the sale of regular season tickets; legal services rendered to a credit institution as part of loan processing; sale of a condominium and the leasing of an adjoining recreational facility.

It is apparent from the above list of product decisions that courts make an ad hoc decision regarding the existence of separate products. There are a number of factors that the courts consider in making this determination. Courts consider:

1. Whether other participants in the industry sell the products separately or together

2. Whether versions of the product differ in significant respects; whether efficiencies are gained by selling the items together

3. Whether the two items are regularly sold as a unit or in fixed proportions

None of these factors by itself is necessarily determinative in every situation.

One of the more difficult issues faced by the courts in the context of tie-in cases has arisen in franchise cases where the courts have been required to determine whether a trade mark license is a separate product. This is an area of the law in which the courts have been unable to agree on a common rule.

The ninth circuit has held that a trademark license could be a separate product in the business format type franchise situation. This is because in the case of a business format franchise the consumer has no reason to associate the component goods used in the franchised operation with the trademark. The Chicken Delight franchise agreement was characterized as a business format franchise in *Siegel* v. *Chicken Delight.*

The fourth circuit, on the other hand, has said that the determining factor in trademark license cases is whether the challenged aggregation of goods is an essential ingredient of the franchised system's formula for success.

Key Point: When the trademark serves merely to identify the claimed tied product, the quality of the trademark and the quality of the tied product are so inextricably intertwined in the mind of the consumer as to preclude a finding that the trademark is a separate product!

An example of such franchise is the Baskin-Robbins Ice Cream franchise considered by the ninth circuit in *Krehl* v. *Baskin-Robbins Ice Cream Company.* The court described the franchise as a distribution type of system in which the franchised stores serve merely as conduits through which trademarked goods manufactured by the franchisor or its licensee according to detailed specifications, are ultimately sold to the consumer.

Tied-Sale

The second requirement of a per se unlawful tying arrangement is that the availability of one product is conditioned on the purchase of the other. If both products are available separately, either from the challenged seller or from other sellers in the market, there is no unlawful tie-in. In a classic example, if the corner grocery refuses to sell flour unless the purchaser also buys sugar, but sugar and flour can be purchased separately from a number of other grocery stores in the market, there is no unlawful tie. Thus, one court held that there was no unlawful tie when reduced rate airfare was available only when a Budget Rent-a-Car was also taken because both air fare, although not discounted, and Budget cars could be obtained separately.

Courts have expressed differing opinions as to whether there is a tie when one of the products is available at a discount price only when purchased in conjunction with another product. The fourth circuit in holding that tying discounted goods to the purchase of another good was unlawful stated the rule to be that a tie-in is "noncoercive, and therefore legal, only if the components are separately available to the customer on a basis as favorable as the tie-in arrangement." On the other hand, the third circuit found no unlawful tie when a pharmaceutical company offered discounts on two patented drugs when a third nonpatented drug was also purchased.

Another issue which has been raised from time to time is whether there can be an unlawful tie-in when the seller of the tying product has no economic interest in the sale of the tied product. This can become an important issue when a franchisor requires that a franchisee purchase the tied product from approved vendors to ensure quality or uniformity. Or, in another context, a seller may want to restrict warranties on a product by insisting that only certain other products be used with this product. A number of courts have held that where the seller of the tying product has no economic interest in the tied product there is no unlawful tying arrangement. The lack of an economic interest in the tied product makes it very unlikely that such a tie would be imposed for exclusionary or predatory purposes.

Sufficient Power to Coerce the Tie

Another requirement for a per se unlawful tie is that the seller of the tying product must have sufficient economic power to coerce purchase of the tied product. Courts have generally looked to the following as indicia of sufficient power to coerce purchase of the tied product:

1. A dominant market position with respect to the tying product

2. A tying product so unique in terms of legal, physical, or economic characteristics as to give the seller a special advantage

3. A substantial number of buyers who have purchased both products when there is no explanation for their doing so other than the seller's market power

Note: Most courts have refused to find that a trademark by itself creates sufficient economic power to coerce a tie.

The courts are also split as to whether a copyright provides sufficient economic power; however, it is probably true that a copyright is more likely to provide the requisite power than is a trademark. But even copyrighted products may have close substitutes which defeat a finding of economic power in the copyright holder. Patents are more likely to create economic power than are either trademarks or copyrights.

Red Flag: Tying arrangements in which the tying product is a patented product should be carefully reviewed by antitrust counsel.

A dominant market position sufficient to create economic power for forcing may be found with a market share as low as 30 percent if the market share is held by the dominant firm. Market shares of less than 30 percent are unlikely to create sufficient economic power and therefore ties by firms with less than 30 percent are unlikely to be challenged by the Department of Justice or found to be unlawful by the courts.

Another indicia of sufficient economic power to coerce a tie is the acceptance of the tie by a large number of buyers. Widespread acceptance of a tie by itself is very equivocal evidence. It may simply mean that purchasers prefer to purchase the package.

Key Point: Before market power can be found based on buyer acceptance of the package, there must be evidence that negated reasons other than the sellers market power to explain the acceptance of the tie.

Effect on Commerce

The final element required to make a tie-in sale unlawful under the Sherman Act is that the tie-in must affect a "not insubstantial" amount of interstate commerce in the tied product. The Supreme Court has held that it is sufficient if more than a *de minimis* amount of commerce in the tied product is affected. Amounts as small as $10,000 have been held sufficient. Moreover, the value of all tied sales aggregated over time is used to determine whether more than a *de minimis* amount of commerce is affected.

However, if the purchaser is required to purchase a product he or she would not have otherwise purchased, even from another seller in the market, there is no effect on commerce in the tied product. Similarly, if the seller of the tying product has a monopoly on the tied product some courts have found that there can be no effect on interstate commerce because no other seller could have sold the product. For example, if the only manufacturer of portable radios is also the only manufacturer of batteries for those radios, it is not unlawful to tie the sale of batteries and radios.

FULL-LINE FORCING

Full-line forcing is a close cousin to tie-in sales in which a supplier requires the distributor to carry the full line of products offered by the supplier. For example, a supplier of hardware products may require its distributors to offer for sale the supplier's full line of hardware products. Full-line forcing arrangements generally do not prohibit the distributor from carrying competing products. This distinguishes full-line forcing from exclusive dealing (discussed in Chapter 5). Full-line forcing has not been held to be unlawful per se and has usually been upheld under a rule of reason analysis. Because the distributor is not precluded from carrying competing products, it is difficult to prove that any commerce was foreclosed by the practice. Full-line forcing had been upheld even when the supplier had a policy of pressuring the distributor to push its products and frowned on the distributor carrying competing products.

Key Point: Full-line forcing may become unlawful when it is coupled with minimum purchase requirements.

Requiring the dealer to purchase certain quantities of the supplier's full line may have the effect of preventing the dealer from carrying competing products. A requirement that a Ford dealer maintain a stock of Ford Motor Company's parts and accessories at a level "reasonably comparable to the current demand" was upheld but only because the court interpreted "current demand" to mean the current demand for genuine Ford Motor Company parts. Any broader interpretation would have interfered with the dealer's ability to carry parts manufactured by Ford's competitors.

WHEN TIE-IN SALES ARE LAWFUL

There are a large number of situations in which it is entirely lawful to require that two products be purchased together rather than separately. Many lawful tie-in arrangements are apparent from the foregoing discussion of the elements of an unlawful tie-in. For example, if the seller lacks sufficient market power to coerce the purchase of the tied product, a tie-in sale is not unlawful. Other examples follow.

- A seller may require the purchaser to purchase a tied product when the purchaser has no economic interest in the tied product. Thus, a franchisor may require that the franchisee purchase supplies from sources approved by the franchisor when the franchisee has no economic interest in the approved source.

- A seller may require a purchaser to purchase a tied product when use of the tied product is required for proper functioning of the tying product or to maintain quality control. For example, a manufacturer of a machine may require that supplies used in the machine be purchased only from the manufacturer to maintain the warranty or to protect quality.

- A seller may offer both products in a package and may even apply sales pressure to convince the buyer to purchase both products so long as the sales pressure is not coercive.

    When both products are readily available separately, it is generally lawful to sell them in a package. However, the courts are split regarding the lawfulness of offering a discounted price on a tied sale. If the discount does not reflect efficiencies inherent in the joint sale, there is greater likelihood that a court will find the requisite coercion.

- In a newly developing industry, a tie-in may be permitted for a limited period of time where the seller has a legitimate business interest in assuring the effective functioning of complex equipment by selling only an integrated system. For example, a dealer was permitted to sell components of a community television antenna system only as a unitary system including servicing.

- A seller was permitted to tie two products that had to be used together in order for either to function properly. Prior separate sales of the items had resulted in widespread consumer complaints.

- The licensing and the use of a product brand name by a distributor can be tied to a requirement that the distributor purchase and sell the brand name product. Accordingly, it has been held lawful to require that a gasoline dealer sell only Crown gasoline from pumps bearing the Crown trademark.

- Tying may be justified to protect good will when there are valid reasons for not providing product specifications for the tied product to permit its purchase from third parties. The use of product specifications instead of a tie-in will not be required when it would require disclosure of trade secrets, or because of the complexity of the product it would be impracticable or because customer dissatisfaction would result. However, whenever a tying arrangement is used for protecting good will or preserving a trademark the restraints imposed should not go beyond those minimally required to achieve protection.

The tenth circuit has upheld against tie-in claims a distribution arrangement which allocated popular and scarce sports car models to dealers based on the dealers prior sales of a less popular but more plentiful model car. The court noted that the allocation was based on the dealers sales rather than its purchases of the less popular model. Therefore, dealers could not acquire the popular sports car simply by purchasing the less popular model. Rather the dealer had to engage in the procompetitive activity for selling the tied product. However, it must be noted that certain aspects of the allocation scheme did violate the fair dealing requirements of the Automobile Dealers' Day in Court Act.

MONOPOLY LEVERAGING

Conduct which does not satisfy all of the requirements for a tie-in violation under section 1 of the Sherman Act may, nonetheless, constitute monopoly leveraging in violation of section 2 of the Sherman Act. Monopoly leveraging is the use of monopoly power in one market to obtain a competitive advantage in another market. This situation can best be understood by reviewing the facts of an actual case.

A pharmaceutical manufacturer had two patented products for which it faced no competition. Its sales of a third product, which was not patented, faced stiff competition. To increase its sales of the third product, the manufacturer offered a discount on its drug prices based in part on the quantity of purchases of the nonpatented drug. Thus, to obtain the discount, the purchaser had to purchase the nonpatented competitive drug. However, each drug was sold separately. The court held that there was no unlawful tying arrangement because each drug could be purchased separately. There was, however, a section 2 violation, because the manufacturer was leveraging its lawful monopoly over the patented drugs to obtain an economic advantage in the market, for the nonpatented drug.

It is unusual for a court to find that a marketing plan is a lawful tying arrangement under section 1 but is an unlawful monopoly leveraging under section 2. Nonetheless, the possibility does exist that a court might do so and that possibility should not be ignored.

Chapter 8 Footnotes

1. *Jefferson Parish Hospital District* v. *Hyde,* 104 S. Ct. 1551 (1984).

chapter nine

MAKING THE RIGHT PRICING DECISIONS

Price is the most sensitive part of the market mechanism. The Supreme Court has described restrictions on free and open price competition as a threat "to the central nervous system of the economy." Most price-fixing arrangements are illegal per se regardless of whether the price fixed is an upper or lower price or is an entirely reasonable price. As the Supreme Court explained in the famous *Trenton Potteries* case:

> The aim and result of every price-fixing agreement, if effective, is the elimination of one form of competition. The power to fix prices, whether reasonably exercised or not, involves the power to control the market and to fix arbitrary and unreasonable prices. The reasonable price fixed today may through economic and business changes become the unreasonable price of tomorrow. Once established, it may be maintained unchanged because of the absence of competition secured by the agreement for a price reasonable when fixed. Agreements which create such potential power may well be held to be in themselves unreasonable or unlawful restraints, without the necessity of minute inquiry whether a particular price is reasonable or unreasonable as fixed and without placing on the government in enforcing the Sherman Law the burden of ascertaining from day to day whether it has become unreasonable through the mere variation of economic conditions.

Red Flag: Nothing is more likely to trigger an action for a criminal violation of the Sherman Act than is a price-fixing agreement. A criminal conviction is a felony conviction and can result in both fines and imprisonment. Courts are increasingly willing to impose prison terms for such "white-collar" crimes.

The Supreme Court has defined price fixing as including any "combination formed for the purpose and with the effect of raising, depressing, fixing, or stabilizing" the price of a product. Price-fixing agreements are generally considered to be either horizontal, between competitors at the same market level, or vertical, between a manufacturer and retailer. Horizontal price fixing is the most readily condemned of all anticompetitive practices. It is the practice most likely to trigger an action by the Department of Justice. Frequently, a price-fixing case brought by the Department of Justice will be followed by numerous treble damage antitrust actions brought by private plaintiffs or even by state and municipal governments.

Vertical price fixing is less likely to trigger a Department of Justice action than is horizontal price fixing. However, claims of vertical price fixing are frequently brought by terminated distributors (see Chapter 7). In such cases, the distributor claims that its termination was unlawful because it was done to enforce a vertical price-fixing arrangement. Such claims are particularly troublesome when the terminated dealer was a price cutter or discounter.

HORIZONTAL PRICE FIXING

Horizontal price-fixing agreements between parties at the same market level are per se unlawful whether they are direct or indirect. Direct price fixing occurs when the price to be charged to a third party is fixed by express or tacit agreement. Indirect price fixing is an agreement that does not specifically fix prices but can be construed as being designed to fix prices. An example of an indirect price-fixing agreement is an agreement between oil companies to buy up all of the surplus gasoline on the spot market in order to raise gasoline prices.

PRICE FIXING BY SELLERS

Because the human mind is restlessly inventive, it is impossible to catalog all the possible agreements among sellers of goods which may constitute price fixing. However, the following examples may be helpful in flagging potential problems:

1. Agreements to use uniform price lists as a starting point in bargaining with customers
2. Agreements to require uniform cash down payment
3. Agreements to follow uniform rules in extending credit

4. Implicit agreements regarding price differentials between different grades of a product

5. Agreements to charge uniform costs or mark-ups

6. Agreements to charge a uniform price regardless of where goods are sold

7. Maximum price agreements

8. Agreements prohibiting discounts

9. Agreements establishing uniform discounts.

10. Agreements placing limits on the supply or production of a product

11. Agreements to reduce or to raise prices

12. Agreements between competitors to maintain resale prices (i.e., a horizontal agreement to engage in vertical price fixing)

13. Agreements to use a delivered pricing system

Once a price-fixing agreement has been proved, it is no defense that the parties had not established a mechanism for enforcing the agreement or that the parties to the agreement cheated on each other by departing from the agreed-on prices.

PRICE FIXING BY BUYERS

The term price fixing generally conjures visions of sellers meeting in a smoke-filled room to fix prices but it is also possible for buyers to fix prices. A number of activities engaged in by purchasers have been condemned as direct or indirect price fixing. Unlawful buyer price fixing includes the following:

1. Agreements among distributors to fix the prices at which they will purchase from producers

2. An agreement by members of a trade association to use centralized purchasing power and price lists to force artificially lower prices from suppliers

3. Agreements to limit buying to force prices lower

4. Agreements to divide supplies up for auction

JOINT BUYING AND SELLING

Joint selling arrangements between or among competitors may violate section 1 of the Sherman Act as price fixing. For example, a joint venture formed by several competitors to sell their collective output at an agreed-on price was unlawful. Similarly, an agreement between the two leading domestic lead producers to appoint each other as their exclusive sales agent in their respective areas of operation was unlawful. Joint selling arrangements have a high potential for collusion and anticompetitive results. Accordingly such arrangements are presumptively unlawful.

However, not all joint selling arrangements are unlawful price-fixing schemes. A joint selling arrangement may greatly reduce transaction costs, achieve efficiencies of integration, or even create a new market. Such an arrangement would be procompetitive. For example, the Department of Justice found a proposed arrangement in which independent distributors of USD corporation would make joint bids on national accounts which had multiple locations to be procompetitive. The independent dealers were confined to exclusive service territories and therefore were not competitors with each other for the sale of USD products. Through joint bidding for national accounts, the distributors could compete for those accounts which they would otherwise be unable to do.

Joint purchasing arrangements are much less likely to violate section 1 of the Sherman Act. Cooperative purchasing or group buying is generally considered to be procompetitive and efficiency creating. They are not a form of concerted activity which is characteristically thought to result in predominantly anticompetitive effects. Among the procompetitive attributes of a joint purchasing arrangement are the following:

1. They permit purchasers to achieve economies of scale in purchasing.
2. They permit purchasers to achieve economies of scale in warehousing.
3. They permit small purchasers to obtain an inventory of goods available on short notice.

Key Point: Before joining any joint purchasing group be sure to document anticipated efficiencies to be obtained by the group.

Red Flag: Joint purchasing may also raise problems under the Robinson-Patman Act (see Chapter 10).

In deciding whether a group buying agreement is unlawful, it is necessary to consider the degree of market power aggregated by the buying group. When competition in the market is restrained by group purchasing because of the aggregation of market power, the Department of Justice is likely to challenge the arrangement. The Department of Justice has announced guidelines it will follow in deciding whether to challenge a purchasing group. These guidelines or rules of thumb are:

1. Whether the group's purchases account for 35 percent or more of the quantity of the good purchased in the market
2. Whether group purchasing of an input to a final product will facilitate price fixing in the final product market. In this regard, the Department will usually assume that there is no anticompetitive effect if the input product accounts for no more than 20 percent of the price of the final product
3. Whether the purchasing group will facilitate collusion among competitors

Key Point: In order to ensure that the formation of a purchasing group does not facilitate collusion, the group should establish the following procedures:

1. Permit members of the group to negotiate and deal independently with suppliers
2. Permit members of the group to participate in other purchasing groups
3. Require that all communications between a member and the group be kept confidential
4. Require that all negotiations on behalf of the group be conducted by an employee of the group who is not an employee of any member; moreover, no member should participate in the negotiations on behalf of the group

Red Flag: Buyer's groups which function as cartels to force the prices suppliers charge group members below the competitive level are unlawful per se.

EXCHANGES OF PRICE INFORMATION

Exchanges of price information among competitors is a price-fixing threat. The possibility that the exchange of price information will have an effect on ultimate prices and will facilitate tacit price collusion is particularly present when the market is oligopolistic, the product is homogeneous, and the demand is inelastic. In such a market the exchange of price data will result in a tendency to price uniformity.

An exchange of price information can result in a price-fixing charge if it is clear that the agreement, in fact, had stabilized prices and no other controlling circumstances could explain the price stabilization. The requirement for joint action—i.e. contract, combination, or conspiracy—is readily satisfied by a showing that a competitor furnished pricing data to another with the understanding that the other would in turn furnish data on its prices.

Once it is established that there has been an exchange of current price data a per se price-fixing violation will be found if the following two elements are present:

1. The exchange of price data had an effect on prices.

2. There was no justification for the exchange of data or effect on prices.

Key Point: The need to verify a competitor's price to meet the competition and thereby avoid a charge of price discrimination under the Robinson-Patman Act will not justify an exchange of price data.

If there is an exchange of price data followed by price uniformity or restraints on production, it is not necessary that there be an express agreement to fix prices. A "knowing wink" is sufficient.

Key Point: It is not unlawful to consider the prices charged by one's competitors in setting the price to be charged for one's product. Indeed, this is the essence of price competition. However, the price decision must be made unilaterally and not in consultation with competitors. Moreover, knowledge of a competitors prices should be obtained from independent third-party sources such as newspapers, trade papers, or advertising materials. It is not unlawful to "shop" a competitor so long as it is not done in a collusive, reciprocal fashion.

Key Point: The exchange of data regarding past prices is less dangerous than the exchange of data concerning current or future prices. Also exchanges of other trade data which only indirectly implicates price such as cost and production statistics is less likely to result in a price-fixing charge than is the exchange of current pricing data.

Key Point: It is unlikely that a firm will be found guilty of price fixing merely as a result of membership in a trade association that openly and fairly gathers and disseminates information as to product costs, volume of production, actual prices of past transactions, stock of goods on hand, approximate cost of goods on hand, and approximate transportation costs.

_____ BID RIGGING _____

Collusive bidding practices that restrain free competitive bidding is price fixing in violation of section 1 of the Sherman Act and section 5 of the Federal Trade Commission Act. A large portion of the Department of Justice antitrust enforcement activity is directed at ferreting out and prosecuting persons engaged in bid rigging. Collusive bidding is generally intended to permit competitors to share contract awards and maintain artificially high prices.

Typically unlawful collusive bidding schemes fall into one of the following three categories:

1. Comparison of bids prior to their submission to the contracting authority

2. Agreements to make identical bids, complementary bids, or bids higher than another bid

3. The use of a bid depository to permit bid comparisons and to facilitate fixing prices or splitting profits

An agreement between competitors to submit identical bids is the equivalent of price fixing and is illegal. Less direct means of fixing the price of bids have also been held to be illegal price fixing. For example, an agreement by competitors to use a common estimator to calculate and submit bids was held unlawful. So too was an agreement between competitors to limit their purchases to a certain percentage of the tobacco offered at tobacco auctions.

An agreement *not* to submit competitive pricing bids but to limit competition to nonprice items has been held to be unlawful by the Supreme Court. In a case involving the National Society of Professional Engineers, the court struck down a canon of ethics which prohibited the submission of competitive bids for engineering services. The court held that the canon "on its face" suppressed price competition in violation of section 1 of the Sherman Act. The court rejected the Society's defense that the canon was a reasonable effort to minimize the risk that price competition would produce inferior engineering work which would endanger public health and safety.

The Department of Justice has identified ten factors as evidence of collusive bidding. These factors include:

1. The failure of qualified bidders to participate

2. The successful bidder repeatedly uses unsuccessful bidders as subcontractors

3. Certain contractors repeatedly fail to bid against each other

4. Small groups of contractors who limit their work to federal, state or local jobs

5. Unusual bid disparities

6. Bids consistently awarded to contractors by geographic areas

7. Contractors who never win but frequently bid

8. Joint bids where both contractors could have bid separately

9. During re-bids the failure of original bidders to re-bid

10. A single firm bidding differently on a particular line item on two contemporaneous bids

Bid rigging is so clearly wrong and so easily understood that it does not happen by accident, neglect, or failure to understand legal technicalities. Participation in bid rigging is more likely to result in a jail term than in any other form of price fixing.

SPLITS

An activity related to bid rigging and which has been most common in the distribution of motion pictures is the use of splits. A split occurs when exhibitors negotiate among themselves for the right to bid on certain films. Usually the exhibitors agree not to bid or negotiate for the right to exhibit a film until the exhibitors have negotiated their splits.

For many years splits were thought to have some beneficial aspects and were tested under a rule of reason. However, since the late 1970s it has been recognized that splits are a form of price fixing and should be condemned as unlawful per se.

Price Uniformity, Price Leadership, and Conscious Parallelism

Price uniformity, price leadership, and consciously parallel pricing behavior all produce an end result in the market that looks like price fixing. That does not mean that these activities are illegal. Quite the contrary, if they result from the unilateral pricing decision of each firm in the market these activities are lawful. Price leadership is a pricing pattern in which the participants in a market follow or track the pricing decisions of an industry leader.

Key Point: Price uniformity, price leadership, and consciously parallel pricing are lawful only if they are the result of unilateral decision making.

Antitrust questions arise whenever there is evidence of price uniformity, price leadership, and conscious parallelism plus evidence of concerted behavior. Mere proof of parallel pricing behavior is not sufficient to establish a price-fixing violation. Rather, additional facts which tend to negate the idea of unilateral decision making are required.

Key Point: Consciously parallel pricing which is interdependent gives rise to an inference of price fixing.

The Supreme Court said in the landmark *Interstate Circuit* case that:

> It was enough that, knowing that concerted action was contemplated and invited, the distributors gave their adherence to the scheme and participated in it. Each distributor was advised that the others were asked to participate; each knew that cooperation was essential to successful operation of the plan. They knew that the plan, if carried out, would result in a restraint of commerce. . . . It is elementary that an unlawful conspiracy may be and often is formed without simultaneous action or agreement on the part of conspirators.

When evidence of a price-fixing conspiracy is predicated on conscious parallelism, the courts have required that there also be evidence of a "plus" factor. Such "plus" factors include:

1. Parties acted in contradiction to their own economic interest
2. Parties had a motive to agree
3. Parties had no reason to reach the same result unilaterally
4. Parties had meetings, corresponded, or communicated otherwise
5. There were simultaneous, identical pricing actions following meetings
6. Prices were raised in time of surplus
7. Products were artificially standardized
8. Terms and conditions of sale were uniform in a way not to be expected
9. High profit margins in an industry having homogeneous prices, identical prices and sharp competition

To permit a jury to find the concerted action necessary for a section 1 offense there must be evidence that tends to exclude the possibility of independent action. There must be direct and circumstantial evidence that reasonably tends to prove a conscious commitment to a common plan to fix prices.

Key Point: If you are in an industry in which uniform pricing or price leadership is common, you should build a document file of evidence showing legitimate independent business reasons for your pricing actions.

Red Flag: If you are in an industry in which uniform pricing or price leadership is common, you should ensure that you have no pricing discussions with competitors and that you do not exchange any pricing data with your competitors.

PRICE SIGNALING

Price signaling occurs when one firm in an industry publically announces an impending price increase and then watches to see if other firms in the industry follow the increase. If other firms do not follow the price increase, the increase can be rescinded. Price signaling is not unlawful per se. There are legitimate business reasons to preannounce a price increase—it permits customers to stock up at the old price and adjust to the new price.

However, if an industry develops a tacit understanding that price signaling will result in other industry firms adjusting their prices accordingly, a court could find that a price fixing conspiracy exists.

AGREEMENTS ON METHODS OF PRICING

A more subtle form of price fixing can occur when the parties agree to follow certain methods of setting price or set an element of the price. For example, agreements with respect to the offering of credit terms, down payments, discounts or trade-in allowances may be unlawful price fixing. Similarly agreements regarding methods of pricing such as agreements to utilize uniform mark-ups over costs and agreements specifying differentials among grades of products are price fixing. Cooperative advertising can result in price fixing when the price agreement is part of the promotion.

VERTICAL PRICE FIXING

Vertical price fixing like horizontal price fixing is unlawful per se. The Department of Justice is less interested in ferreting out vertical price-fixing schemes, however. Moreover, since other vertical market restraints are treated under a rule of reason, some courts may try to characterize the agreement as a nonprice vertical restraint thus bringing it within the rule of reason. At the same time, plaintiffs will try to characterize nonprice vertical restraints as vertical price restraints.

Vertical price restraints are lawful if they are imposed unilaterally. The law has long recognized that a seller has a right to choose those with whom he or she will deal (see Chapter 6). Moreover, a seller may announce pricing policies and refuse to deal with any retailer who does not abide by the announced pricing policy. A supplier may use suggestions or strong persuasion to convince a distributor to follow pricing policies.

Red Flag: Once a supplier has begun to supply a distributor, any conduct that would *force* a distributor to adhere to a price is illegal.

Efforts to force distributors to adhere to a suppliers' pricing policies will violate section 1 of the Sherman Act if the efforts result in an express, implied or inferred agreement to fix prices. For example, termination of a dealer for failure to adhere to the suppliers' price policy followed by reinstatement with a promise to adhere to the supplier's pricing policy is unlawful.

RESALE PRICE MAINTENANCE

Resale price maintenance is a system of vertical price fixing that occurs when a manufacturer sets the wholesaler's resale price or the final retail price or when a wholesaler sets the retailer price. Resale price maintenance is a per se violation of the antitrust laws despite the vocal criticism levied at it recently. While it may be unlikely that a vertical price-fixing scheme will trigger a criminal action, civil actions, particularly those brought by disgruntled or terminated dealers, remain a very real threat.

As in the case of other price-fixing violations it makes no difference whether the price is a maximum price or a minimum price and it is no defense that the price is reasonable. In the absence of an express agreement on prices between different persons in the distribution chain, an agreement may be inferred from conduct of the parties. Some examples of situations in which the required agreement may be inferred are:

1. Argument of persuasion approaching "coercion" to adhere to the price
2. "Policing" retailers through the use of wholesalers, or other retailers or special agents
3. Conditioning a price reduction or promotional pricing on the buyer's reducing his resale price
4. Increasing the wholesale price to follow the customer's resale price increase in an attempt to secure compliance with a suggested retail price program

A manufacturer is free to announce and implement a retail pricing policy and then refuse to deal with customers who do not abide by that policy. However this is a narrow path to tread. If the termination results from complaints of other retailers, it may be held to be unlawful resale price maintenance. Also if termination is threatened, or if the dealer is terminated and reinstated and then the dealer complies with the pricing program, there is an unlawful price fixing conspiracy.

HOW A MANUFACTURER CAN CONTROL RETAIL PRICES

There are a number of actions a manufacturer can take to control retail prices charged by independent distributors which are lawful.

First, a manufacturer can advertise its suggested retail price directly to the ultimate consumer. This will discourage retailers from charging more than the suggested price.

Second, the manufacturer can place the suggested retail price directly on the product packaging. This activity known as preticketing serves a function similar to advertising suggested retail prices.

Third, although the law is somewhat uncertain, a manufacturer may be able to require the pass-on of a price reduction to the ultimate consumer. Factory rebates or cents off coupons may be used to accomplish this result.

FAVORED NATIONS CLAUSE

A favored nations clause in a sales agreement guarantees a distributor that the supplier will not sell to a competing distributor at a lower price. Favored nations clauses can be either lawful or unlawful depending on how they are structured. If the clause permits the supplier to offer distributor B a lower price than that which was previously offered to distributor A but merely ensures that thereafter distributor A will also be charged the new lower price, the clause is lawful. On the other hand, if the favored nations clause precludes the supplier from offering a lower price to distributor B than was offered to distributor A, the clause is unlawful price fixing. Accordingly, the wording of a contract favored nations clause is a matter requiring great care. Here are examples of a lawful clause and an unlawful clause.

Lawful Clause: Supplier hereby agrees that it will at all times during the term of this agreement charge distributor the lowest price that supplier charges to any other distributor.

Unlawful Clause: Supplier hereby agrees that it will not offer or charge to any distributor a price for widgets which is lower than the price of widgets charged to distributor under this agreement.

CONSIGNMENT SALES

True consignment sales provide a means for a supplier to set the retail price of its product without being guilty of resale price maintenance. Genuine consignment contracts do not violate section 1 of the Sherman Act because the owner of a product is not prohibited from fixing the price at which the owner's agent sells the product to a third party. Courts will carefully examine claimed consignment sales to ensure that the arrangement is a true consignment and not merely a sham to cover that which is in reality an unlawful resale price fixing scheme.

Key Point: The most important indicia of a true consignment sale is that ownership and risk of loss remain with the supplier.

PROMOTIONAL PRICING

Promotional pricing is generally judged under a rule of reason standard and is lawful if the dealer remains free to charge whatever price market conditions and competition require. Promotions in which the manufacturer offers a price rebate directly to the consumer have been upheld because the distributor remains free to charge whatever prices are desired. Similarly, promotional price reductions offered to wholesalers are lawful so long as the wholesaler remains free to decide whether to pass the price reduction along to the retailer.

The law is unsettled regarding the extent to which a supplier who grants a discount to permit the retailer to charge competitive prices can require that the price reduction be passed on to the consumer. The tenth and seventh circuits have permitted the supplier to require flow through of the price reduction.

Dealer Assistance Programs

Dealer assistance programs typically involve a temporary price reduction designed to permit a retailer to meet interbrand price competition. Such temporary price reductions are not unlawful per se if the reduced price is available to the retailers regardless of whether the retailer makes a corresponding reduction in the retail price. However, it has been held that denying a distributor the right to participate in a dealer assistance program because the distributor failed to adhere to the manufacturer's suggested retail price was unlawful. The dealer assistance program was unlawfully made the quid pro quo for adhering to the suggested retail price.

Cooperative Advertising

It is unlawful to condition participation in a cooperative advertising program on adherence to a manufacturer's suggested retail price program.

Red Flag: Promotional programs must be offered to all distributors on a proportionally equal basis (see Chapter 11).

NATIONAL ACCOUNTS

Often a supplier will negotiate price terms with a large national purchaser on behalf of the supplier's independent distributors located throughout the nation. If a national accounts program requires the independent distributors to participate and requires them to observe the negotiated price, the program will be unlawful. However, when participation in the national accounts program is voluntary and the distributors are free to attempt to deal with purchaser outside of the national accounts program a rule of reason analysis is applied. The program can also be structured so that the manufacturer makes the sales to the national account with the independent distributors merely functioning as agents to deliver the product.

PRICING AND PATENT LICENSING

Under certain limited circumstances, the holder of a patent may fix the price at which the licensee sells the patented product. The patent holder must do so unilaterally and not in conjunction with holders of other patents. Moreover, the price fixing cannot be done as part of a cross-licensing scheme between patentees. Further, if a large percentage of the sellers in a market are involved in the patent price fixing, the price fixing is unlawful.

Red Flag: The law is very uncertain regarding the extent to which price limitations can be included in patent licensing. No price restraints should be used without first obtaining legal counsel.

It is probably lawful to fix the price at which the licensee sells the patented product if the following factors are present:

1. Both the patentee and the licensee must be engaged in manufacturing the patented product and selling it in competition.

2. The price must relate to the patented product and not merely a part of the product.

3. The price must be established and enforced unilaterally.

4. The price must apply to a product that is itself patented.

5. The price restraint must apply only to a single licensee.

PRICE SQUEEZE

A price squeeze occurs when a vertically integrated manufacturer which also sells at retail in competition with independent retailers sets its wholesale price at such a high level that the independent retailer can no longer meet the manufacturer's retail price. The resulting price squeeze drives the competing independent retailer out of the market. The manufacturer must control the market for the input whether it be raw materials or a finished product for the strategy to have any effect. A price squeeze is unlawful monopolization in violation of section 2 of the Sherman Act.

BELOW-COST PRICING

At least half of the states have statutes which specifically prohibit making sales below cost. Some state statutes include a statement of how the cost is to be determined and many vary greatly in their coverage. The Oklahoma statute defines costs and then makes it unlawful to use below-cost sales as loss leaders or to unfairly divert trade from a competitor. The statute then exempts certain sales such as sales made to meet a competitor's price, the forced sale of perishable goods, business liquidation sales, the sale of damaged or discontinued goods, clearance sales, and sales to charitable or governmental bodies. Wisconsin has a very similar statute. The Montana statute, on the other hand does not necessarily prohibit the use of loss leaders.

Key Point: Because of the wide variation in state laws dealing with sales below cost, legal counsel should be consulted before making below-cost sales.

PREDATORY PRICING

No conspiracy or agreement is required for unlawful predatory pricing. Rather, predatory pricing is a form of monopolization in violation of section 2 of the Sherman Act. Unfortunately the law is unsettled regarding a precise statement of just what constitutes predatory pricing. On the other hand, the courts have made it extremely difficult to prove a claim based on predatory pricing.

Predatory pricing is a pricing strategy that sets very low prices in the hopes of driving a competitor from the market. It depends for its success not only on the elimination of competition by suffering a loss in the short term but also on the ability to recoup that loss by charging more than a competitive price in the long term. The strategy will not be successful if there are low barriers to market entry because as soon as the predatory firm raises its price above a competitive level new competitors will enter the market.

Courts have been very sensitive to the difficulty in separating a predatory price from a low price which simply reflects the very competition that the Sherman Act is designed to promote. Condemnation of price reductions could chill the very behavior the antitrust laws are designed to promote.

Key Point: A predatory price directly harms a competitor. It does not increase efficiencies and in economic terms results in a net welfare loss.

Although the courts have not come to agreement on all points regarding the offense of predatory pricing, there is general agreement that a cost-based test should be used. Generally speaking, prices which equal or exceed the average total cost of the product will not be considered to be predatory. On the other hand, a price that is below marginal cost or below average total cost may be predatory.

As one might expect there is much room to argue over what is average total cost or the average variable cost of a product. In a very general sense the following definitions may be given:

1. *Fixed Costs.* Costs that do not vary with output. For example, the cost of the building in which a product is produced does not vary with the amount of product produced in the building.

2. *Variable Costs.* Costs that change with changes in the amount of output. For example, the cost of cloth used varies with the number of T-shirts that are produced.

3. *Average Total Cost.* The sum of all fixed and variable costs divided by the quantity produced.

4. *Average Variable Cost.* The sum of all variable costs divided by the quantity produced.

There is no definitive determination as to whether an otherwise unlawful predatory price can be defended on grounds that it was necessary to meet the prices being charged by other sellers. Any use of a price below average variable cost should be documented as being established to meet competitive prices.

LIMIT PRICING

Limit pricing is anticompetitive pricing behavior designed to exclude new entrants from the market. It clearly evidences a monopolistic intent. Limit pricing entails the pricing of a firm's product at a level just below that which a prospective market entrant would need to charge in order to sustain a successful entry into the market. Unlike predatory pricing, a limit price is set somewhere above the firm's costs.

AVOIDING PRICING VIOLATIONS

A number of steps can be taken to minimize the likelihood of becoming involved in a pricing violation of the antitrust laws. The most important step is to create a general business atmosphere of abiding by all applicable laws. The virtues of good corporate citizenship should be stressed in employee handbooks, periodic memoranda from the CEO, by lectures at company retreats, in employee newsletters and through formal antitrust compliance seminars. This atmosphere reduces the likelihood that employees will conspire with their competitive counterparts to fix prices.

The second important step is to demonstrate a commitment by top management to comply with antitrust laws.

A number of business strategies can be adopted to reduce the danger of pricing violations. These include:

1. Standardizing operating procedures—this has the effect of limiting the decision-making responsibilities of lower lever employees
2. Dismissal of employees involved in antitrust violations
3. Changing the company's reward system—for example, placing salespersons on salary rather than on commission
4. Moving decision making, especially price decision making, to a higher level of management
5. Using antitrust audits to identify potential trouble
6. Encouraging employees to report suspicious conduct directly to corporate counsel

Some companies require sales employees each year to answer a short questionnaire designed to ferret out potential antitrust problems. Typical questions might be:

- Has any competitor approached you or an employee you supervise to discuss prices or other competitive information?

- Have you had any contacts with competitors at business meetings, trade associations, or other occasions that might cause antitrust concern?

- Has the Product Development Department asked you to obtain knowledge of the prospective price actions of competitors?

- Are you aware of any attempts by our competitors to get advanced information of our prospective price actions?

- Have you been involved in any situation in which our pricing or other business practices have been the subject of complaint by our customers, competitors or the government?

- Has any customer attempted to persuade you not to quote a price to or to refrain from selling to another customer?

A particular danger area is trade association meetings. When competitors meet informally at trade association gatherings it is easy for shop talk to drift into a discussion of industry pricing problems. Participation in such conversations, however innocent at the time, can lead to an inference of an agreement to fix prices if price uniformity later develops. Therefore all personnel attending trade association gatherings should be strongly instructed not to participate in any discussions dealing with prices. Moreover, they should not even remain in the room during such discussions because some witness will surely remember their presence but forget their refusal to participate. Rather, the employee should create quite a scene in announcing disapproval of the discussion and in withdrawing from the scene.

It is helpful to carefully document both costs and any other basis for a change in prices. This provides evidence of unilateral pricing and also assists in defending against a charge of predatory pricing.

chapter ten

AVOIDING PRICE DISCRIMINATION

Price discrimination may violate both the Sherman Act and the Clayton Act. In very simple terms, it occurs when a supplier sells its product to competing purchasers at different prices. Price discrimination issues are often complex with fine distinctions and judically created exceptions. Marketing personnel should be alert to the need to seek antitrust counsel when price discrimination problems arise. Although the Department of Justice has the authority to enforce the price discrimination provisions of the Robinson-Patman Act, it has generally stood aside to let the Federal Trade Commission take enforcement action. Private enforcement action is also available. The Robinson-Patman Act impacts more business decisions than does any other antitrust law.

Federal Trade Commission enforcement action is most likely to occur in any of three situations:

1. When price discrimination has been used as a tool for attempted monopolization or predatory conduct

2. Where a distributor with market power has forced the manufacturer or wholesaler to give it a price discount not available to others

3. Where a manufacturer has tried to confer market power on a favored dealer in exchange for preferential treatment in the future

On the other hand, the commission is unlikely to bring enforcement action

1. Where price differences merely reflect the actual differences in the costs of servicing dealers

2. Where a price differential results from a good faith effort to meet the price of a competitor

3. Where the differential is small and is likely to be short lived

4. Where alternative sources of supply are readily available at a discounted price

5. Where action by the commission would tend to stabilize prices among members of an oligopoly

Price discriminations in violation of the Robinson-Patman Act occurs when the following factors are present:

1. There are at least two completed sales

2. At least one of the sales crosses a state line

3. The sales involve commodities rather than services

4. The commodities in each of the sales are of like grade and quality

5. The sales must be for the use, consumption, or resale of the commodity within the United States or any of its territories.

6. Each sale is made by the same seller.

7. Sales are made to at least two different purchasers.

8. The sales must be reasonably contemporaneous.

9. At least one sale must have been at a discriminatory price.

10. The discrimination in price must be harmful to competition.

DISCRIMINATION IN PRICE

The Supreme Court has held that price discrimination "is merely a price difference." To determine whether there is a price difference courts will consider the actual net prices paid after consideration has been given to discounts, rebates, surcharges, and other factors affecting price. Credit terms may be discriminatory if differences are large and not based on sound business judgment.

The prices being compared need not be simultaneous but must be contemporaneous.

The focus is on the price charged to the purchaser rather than on the cost to the seller. Accordingly, it is not price discrimination under Robinson-Patman to charge all buyers a uniform price even though it costs the seller more to sell to some buyers than others. In other words, the Robinson-Patman Act does not require the seller to use cost-based pricing. For Robinson-Patman Act purposes price is the invoice price less any discounts, offsets, or allowances not reflected in the invoice price.

A seller many change a price from time to time without engaging in price discrimination so long as those purchasing at the same time are offered the same price.

Delivered Pricing

A seller may avoid Robinson-Patman price discrimination problems by quoting a price F.O.B. from the plant. However, price discrimination problems may arise if the seller quotes a delivered price. Delivered prices, the most common method of pricing in some industries, may take a wide variety of forms, but may be placed in four categories

Category I: The seller may offer a uniform delivered price to each purchaser regardless for location.

Category II: The geographic market is divided into various zones and uniform prices are charged within each zone but prices between zones differ.

Category III: The seller may quote prices which include the actual cost of transportation from an arbitrarily established base point or points which may or may not be an actual point of production.

Category IV: The seller may use a freight equalization pricing system in which prices are based on the price at the seller's actual points of production plus actual transportation.

It is sometimes argued that the use of a delivered price is discriminatory because it uses arbitrary shipping points or average transportation charges. When the transportation charge exceeds the actual transportation costs either because a uniform delivered price or a zone price or a base-point price is quoted it is referred to as phantom freight. If the actual transportation cost is more than the price quoted, it is referred to as freight absorption.

The format of a delivered pricing system selected by the seller will reflect market conditions and the relationship of transportation costs to the value of the product sold. For example, if the cost of transportation is relatively small a uniform delivered price is advantageous to a seller because it facilitates national advertising and permits the seller to compete for sales to purchasers who are at a great distance from the seller. On the other hand, pricing by zones permits the seller to extend its sales to more distant markets even when transportation costs are relatively high.

A pricing system utilizing freight equalization is useful in permitting a seller to improve its competitive position against competitors who are located in various places. The seller can compete for sales against a competitor who is situated more favorably vis-à-vis a particular purchaser.

Base-point pricing tends to be used by dominant firms in an industry to maintain market position. To be effective, such a system requires collaboration between the dominant firms thus creating antitrust risks.

Since no price differential is created by a uniform delivered price, there is no Robinson-Patman section 2(a) violation. Charging uniform prices within zones does not create a price discrimination problem unless purchasers within one zone are actual competitors of customers in another zone. Also prices quoted for a base-point or freight equalization method are discriminatory since the price varies depending on the location of the customer.

Discrimination Caused by Discounts, Offsets, and Allowances

Even when invoice prices are uniform, price discrimination may be created by the use of various discounts, offsets, or allowances. Because discounts and offsets result in an actual reduction in the invoice price they can result in direct price discrimination. Allowances, on the other hand, cause indirect price discrimination. Both direct and indirect price discrimination are unlawful.

Typical offsets or discounts that have created direct price discrimination are:

1. Cash payments for prompt payment or for cash payment
2. Quantity discounts
3. Rebates

However, the use of discounts or offsets are not unlawful if they are reasonably available to all competing purchasers.

Types of allowances that may result in indirect price discrimination include:

1. Preferential credit terms
2. Allowances for freight
3. Special booking practices
4. Gifts of goods or bonus merchandise

5. Guarantees against price declines

6. Preferred warehousing terms

7. Special merchandise return privileges

HOW TO AVOID PRICE DISCRIMINATION WHEN USING DISCOUNTS, OFFSETS, OR ALLOWANCES

The use of discounts, offsets, and allowances will not create unlawful price discrimination if the seller offers the same price and the same discount, offset, or allowances to all customers. If the offer is the same to all customers, it does not matter that some customers fail to take advantage of the discount, offset, or allowance made available or that the uniform prices do not recognize the functional role of the purchaser as wholesaler or retailer.

Indirect price discrimination will generally utilize methods that may also be illegal under other sections of the Robinson-Patman Act. (These are discussed in detail in Chapter 11.) A reader planning to use allowances in a marketing program should consult Chapter 11.

TWO PURCHASERS

There must be sales to two different purchasers. Accordingly, there is no violation if one purchaser refused to buy because of the discriminatory price that was offered. Moreover, courts have refused to apply section 2(a) to such nonsale transactions as real estate leases, licenses, agency agreements, or consignments.

COMMODITIES

Section 2(a) applies only to the sale of commodities rather than services or intangibles. Commodities may be thought of as synonymous with "goods," "products," or "wares."

LIKE GRADE AND QUALITY

Products subject to discriminatory pricing must be of like grade and quality. Brand names and titles in themselves do not determine whether products are of like grade and quality. Instead, the grade and quality of a product are determined by the characteristics of the product itself. The amount of difference between products to permit price differences is not subject to formulistic statement. However, bona fide physical differences affecting marketability should be sufficient even if they have little affect on the seller's costs.

_____ **COMPETITIVE INJURY—WHAT IT IS** _____

Only price discrimination having an adverse affect on competition is unlawful under section 2(a). The test is whether the price discrimination substantially can:

A. Lessen competition or tend to create a monopoly in any line of commerce

B. Injure, destroy, or prevent competition with any person who either grants or knowingly receives the benefit of such discrimination, or with the customers of either of them.

Three types of injury to competition, are recognized by the statute:

1. Lessening of competition in any line of commerce

2. Tending to create a monopoly

3. Injuring, destroying, or preventing competition

Any of these three types of competitive injury may occur at any of four levels of competition protected by the Robinson-Patman Act. The four levels are:

1. Injury to competitors of the seller, known as primary level.

2. Injury to competitors of the favored purchaser, known as second level.

3. Injury to competitors of the customers of the favored purchaser, known as third level

4. Injury to competitors of customers of customers of the favored purchaser, known as fourth level

If there is evidence that price discrimination was accompanied by a predatory intent, courts will presume that competitive injury occured. Similarly, when a discriminatory price has been offered to a favored customer in a substantial amount and for a lengthy time period, injury to second level competition will be assumed. In other cases, there must be evidence of a "reasonable possibility" that the discriminatory price will injure competition.

WHAT THE SELLER CAN DO

There are certain activities a seller can undertake even if the activity might otherwise be considered a violation of section 2(a) of the Clayton Act. These activities are often described as defenses.

Meeting the Competition

The central purpose of the antitrust law is to promote competition and especially price competition. Accordingly, the Robinson-Patman Act provides that a seller may offer an otherwise unlawfully discriminatory price "in good faith to meet an equally low price of a competitor." The Federal Trade Commission has said, "The standard of good faith is simply the standard of the prudent businessman responding fairly to what he reasonably believes is a situation of competitive necessity." The Supreme Court has stated that the seller must "show the existence of facts which would lead a reasonable and prudent person to believe that the granting of a lower price would, in fact, meet the equally low price of a competitor."

The seller must make some effort to verify the competitive price in order to show good faith. However, because of the danger of price fixing the seller should not contact the competing seller to verify the price. Rather when the buyer claims to have been offered a lower price elsewhere the seller should evaluate that claim in light of available documentary evidence and market data and its previous experience with the buyer.

The rule generally requires that the seller meet but not beat the competitive price. That is, the seller's good faith price reduction must be intended merely to meet the competitive offer. A reasonable leeway is accorded the seller who may not know the precise level of the competitive price.

The essential elements of a price reduction to meet competition justification are:

1. There must be a bona fide good faith effort to meet the competition.

2. The price being met must be a lawful price.

3. The price reduction to meet the competition may, in some competitive situations, be on an area basis rather than on a customer-by-customer basis.

4. The price reduction must only "meet" the competition rather than "beat" the competition.

5. The price reduction may be used to attract new customers and not merely to retain existing customers.

6. The price being met must be the price offered by the seller's competitor and not that of the purchaser's competitor.

Attempts to justify a price differential based on the meeting-the-competition defense have been rejected when the courts or the Federal Trade Commission believed that it was not done in good faith.

Example 1   The seller had sold goods below cost and had a strong ability to affect market prices.

Example 2   While seller's weaker rivals had made selected price cuts on a customer-by-customer basis, the seller made broad and deep price cuts on an area basis.

Example 3   Seller failed to verify a customer's report of a lower competitive price and failed to corroborate a different price reported by one of seller's experienced salesmen. Further, seller continued to offer the reduced price for three years without making efforts to determine whether the lower price was still offered by its competitors.

On the other hand, the meeting-the-competition defense has been recognized in the following instances.

Example 4   A sellers' quantity discount did not precisely meet the competition because of the realities of market conditions in the industry.

Example 5   Market conditions made exact price meeting impossible and seller did everything possible to find the right price level.

Example 6   The market was highly competitive and price reductions were made in response to individual situations over a three year period.

Example 7   The seller made good faith efforts to verify its competitor's prices but was unable to do so.

*Key Point:*When a prospective purchaser reports that seller's competitor has offered a lower price, seller should make good faith efforts to verify that the lower price was in fact offered for goods of like quantity and quality. Such good faith efforts might include conversations with other customers or reviewing written documentation of the competitor's offer.

Red Flag: Contacting a competitor to verify that a lower price had been offered raises a substantial likelihood of generating price-fixing claims. In the event of price-fixing allegation, it is no defense that price information was exchanged in order to verify a meeting-the-competition price.

Note: Appendix B, the Antitrust Compliance Program includes a sample form for use in documenting price reductions made to meet-the-competition.

Red Flag: A seller of a premium grade product who lowers the price to meet the price offered for a nonpremium product will not merely meet the competition but will beat the competition.

Cost Justification

Price differentials may be maintained if they only make "due allowance for differences in the cost of manufacture, sale, or delivery resulting from different methods or quantities." To justify a price differential on grounds of cost, a seller need not show its costs on a customer-by-customer basis but rather may show cost for groups or classes of customers so long as the customers are properly grouped.

The grouping of customers for cost justification must include only customers who are homogeneous. In the language of the Supreme Court, the customer group must be

> composed of members of such self-sameness as to make the averaging of the cost of dealing with the group a valid and reasonable indicium of the cost of dealing with any specific group member.

The costs that can justify a price differential must be of the type recgonized by the statute. Included are:

1. Differences in distribution costs
2. Selling and delivery costs
3. Manufacturing costs
4. Billing and credit losses
5. Advertising
6. Promotion and selling
7. Freight and delivery
8. Depreciation and amortization

A cost study prepared prior to the sale will be given more credence than a study made after the sale.

In practice the cost justification defense has been illusory. Although sellers have often raised the defense, they have seldom been successful.

The cost-justified price need not exactly equal the selling price if the difference is *de minimis*. In practice differences amounting to no more than 1 ½ percent have been regarded as *de minimis*.

Changed Conditions

When conditions change between sales, the change in conditions may justify different pricing of the sales. The law recognizes that prices may change because of the actual or imminent deterioration of perishable goods, obsolescence of seasonal goods, distress sales under court process, or sales in good faith due to discontinuance of business in the goods concerned.

OFFERING QUANTITY DISCOUNTS AND REBATES

An area of pricing worthy of some individual attention is the offering of quantity discounts and rebates. Quantity discounts or rebates may be lawful under the cost-justification defense. Thus, where the discount has no relationship to cost savings it may be held to be unlawful. Nor is it sufficient that the discount is only theoretically available on equal terms to all but in practice is not.

> *Example 8*   An annual unit volume plan was unlawful where there were only five purchases who could qualify for the largest discount.

> *Example 9*   A quantity discount plan was lawful where discounts were received by a great majority of the firm's customers and the dollar amount of differences was small.

The outcome of any quantity discount case will turn largely on the facts presented. The general rules are clear enough. The discount must be cost related and equally available to all. To obtain a good understanding of the application of the rule, it is helpful to consider some actual situations that have come before the courts or the Federal Trade Commission.

> *Example 10*   A cease and desist order was issued to stop discounting of padlocks sold to a jobber maintaining several branch offices. The discount was based on aggregate sales although all deliveries were not made to a single location.

Example 11   It is unlawful to base a discount on the aggregate total purchases from individual purchasers joined together in a purchasing group.

Example 12   A discount based on the container size of the purchase is lawful where the discount merely reflects the costs of the container.

Example 13   An offer of a uniform 5 percent discount on purchases in truck-lot quantities was not cost justified because the discount was an average cost saving. In some particular instances the actual savings would be less than the discount granted.

USING FUNCTIONAL DISCOUNTS

Price discounts based on the function performed by the purchaser are common in industry. For example, a lower price may be offered to a wholesaler than to a retailer. The justifying theory is that the wholesaler relieves the manufacturer of some of the burdens of distributing the product. In a very simple distribution scheme wholesalers would all be offered the discount and retailers would not compete with wholesalers.

In practice the distribution scheme is often more complex. Lines frequently are not cleanly drawn between wholesalers and retailers. Wholesalers establish their own retail outlets and retailers integrate upstream by forming buyers groups.

The Federal Trade Commission indentifies the controlling problem as whether resale competition actually exists between and among those receiving discounts. Another factor for consideration is whether the wholesaler is controlled by the retailer.

The fact that the favored purchaser performs services which would otherwise be performed by the seller does not always justify a discount in price. It is important that the opportunity to perform the services and thus obtain the discount is equally available to all purchasers. When factors such as the purchaser's credit rating, ability to serve, and ability to stock the goods are considered in making the functional discount available, it has been held that the discounts are not available to all on equal or proportionately equal terms.

On the other hand selling to all customers at the same price regardless of the customers place in the distribution chain is lawful. There is no price discrimination because all customers are charged the same price.

The Supreme Court has ruled that in determining whether two purchasers are competitors and therefore subject to price discrimination, it is important to consider actual competition rather than the nomenclature applied to the purchaser—i.e., wholesaler, jobber, distributor, and so on. In determining whether to purchasers are in actual competition, courts and the commission will look to see whether they sell to the same customers.

Example 14   A discount given to a wholesale grocer sponsoring a chain of stores was unlawful as a functional discount where deliveries were made to the individual stores rather than to the wholesaler. Only payments and orders were funneled through the wholesaler.

Example 15   The Federal Trade Commission has issued an advisory opinion in which it said that it would not approve any discount plan in which a wholesaler's eligibility for added discounts is contingent on the imposition by the wholesaler of specified restrictions on customers.

Example 16   In another Federal Trade Commission advisory letter, a trade group of household product manufacturers was told that a discount given to dealers who stocked the product was improper. The purpose of the plan was to increase sales of inventory. Discounts, if of sufficient magnitude to affect competition, would have to be justified by actual savings in the manufacture, sale, or delivery of the product or by meeting the competition. Alternatively, compensation for services rendered by the dealers must be offered to all on proportionately equal terms.

A seller may offer wholesale or functional price discounts without engaging in unlawful price discrimination. Thus a discount may be offered to wholesalers so long as it is made equally available to all purchasers operating on the functional level of wholesaler.

Now let's consider some examples of various pricing activities to determine whether they are permissible.

Example 17   The seller made price reductions in response to verbal information received from sales staff, brokers, and prospective buyers without other supporting evidence. Are the price reductions lawful efforts to meet the competition?

Answer: No. On similar facts the Federal Trade Commission held that the lack of evidence which would have led a reasonable and prudent person to believe that the granting of a lower price would in fact have been to meet the equally low price of the competitor prevented the seller from relying on the defense of meeting the competition. The seller should have made efforts to substantiate reports of the competitors lower price.

Example 18 Prior to offering a price discount, company officials personally contacted store owners who reported higher discount offers from others and thereby learned the price offered by the competitor and in some instances the name of the competitor. Is this bona fide meeting the competition?

Answer: Yes.

Example 19 Firm A offered a 10 percent price reduction on hearing that 10 of its 125 customers had reported that company B was offering a 10 percent price concession. Is firm A entitled to claim bona fide efforts to meet the competition?

Answer: No. There was no evidence that any of the customers had actually received the discount from firm B.

Example 20 A firm offered different prices for products of like grade and quality to customers depending on whether the customers were chain stores or independent. Can the differences be justified on these facts?

Answer: No. Differences in ownership do not create a cost justification for a price differential. In this particular case, there was evidence that some independents made larger volume purchases than did some of the chain stores.

Although the purported purpose of the law is to enhance price competition, the Robinson-Patman Act often works to reduce competition. For example, firm A can not offer a special low wholesale price to its retailers on condition that the retailers drop their prices to compete with neighboring retailers selling firm B's product. Such a discount has been held to be discriminatory against retailers who chose not to take advantage of it and against retailers not offered the same discount.

Similarly, it has been held to be unlawful to offer a special price to customers who enter exclusive dealing contracts unless the special price is cost justified.

By now it should be apparent that price discrimination can occur in an endless array of situations attesting to the inventiveness of the human mind. Courts and the Federal Trade Commission will look not merely to the form of the transactions, but also the effect. It may be helpful to consider some additional examples.

Example 21   A seller was enjoined from offering an advertising allowance on each case of merchandise sold. It was said that the allowance was not available on equal terms to all purchasers because some were not large enough to deal in case size quantities. No cost justification was established.

Example 22   The issuance of coupons redeemable for cash was illegal price discrimination when the coupon program was not made available to all of the seller's customers on proportionately equal terms.

Example 23   An advisory opinion was issued by the commission holding that for a manufacturer who sold at a delivered price to offer a discount to customers who picked up the merchandise at the factory would probably be illegal.

GEOGRAPHIC PRICE CUTTING

Cutting prices in a certain geographic area or region my violate Section 2(a) of the Clayton Act even when all customers in the area are given the discount. The greatest anticompetitive impact is at the primary line (sellers level). Therefore, geographic price cutting may also be challenged as being predatory under the Sherman Act because it is intended to injure competition from purely local competitors who cannot subsidize sales in the discount area with profits from full price sales made in other areas.

Even if the local competitor targeted by the geographic price cuts enjoys a market share of over 90 percent, such geographical price cuts are unlawful.

Example 24   It was held unlawful for a company to lower its prices in certain parts of the country where the company had an established business while maintaining higher prices in other localities where competition was not so strong.

Among the geographic pricing systems that have been attacked under section 2(a) of the Clayton Act are base-point pricing, delivered price systems, and zoning systems.

In a base-point pricing system, the seller quotes a price from some selected geographic location other than its plant or factory. Freight or delivery charges are quoted from the base point. Both single and multiple base points have been used. A freight equalization system under which the seller agrees to charge no more for transportation than is charged by a competitor is similar to a base-point pricing program.

Base-point pricing systems have been condemned as discriminatory because purchasers who are located closer to the point of manufacture than to the base point are required to pay phantom or nonexistent freight charges.

A system that charges a uniform price throughout the nation is not discriminatory. Also zone prices may be lawful if the zones are properly selected.

> *Example 25*   Is it lawful for a seller with uniform zone delivery charges to grant "backhaul" freight allowances to specific buyers equal to the seller's equal freight costs for each buyer?
>
> *Answer:*   No. According to an advisory opinion issued by the Federal Trade Commission. Discrimination would occur because "the freight factor included within the price is not the actual freight to any given point, but an average of the freight costs for all customers within the zone wherein the delivered price is quoted."

However, in a subsequent advisory opinion the commission stated that offering a uniform F. O. B. price available to all customers on a nondiscriminatory basis is permissible.

chapter eleven

DEALING WITH ADVERTISING AND PROMOTIONAL ALLOWANCES

Suppliers will often find it advantageous to provide their distributors with advertising or promotional materials or services. This is a legitimate and lawful marketing activity—but one that can be abused. For example, a Federal Trade Commission study, whose results were published in 1935, found that large chain stores were using their purchasing power to obtain discriminatory advertising and service allowances from suppliers. Accordingly, a portion of the Robinson-Patman Act was designed to prohibit discrimination disguised as promotional payments or allowances. The Robinson-Patman restraints on discriminatory advertising and promotional allowances are sometimes described as restraints on indirect price discrimination.

The Robinson-Patman Act makes it unlawful for suppliers to make payments to distributors for advertising or promotional services unless the payments are available to other competing distributors on proportionally equal terms. The act also makes it unlawful for a seller to furnish advertising or promotional material or services to a distributor unless the materials and services are available to competing distributors on proportionately equal terms. The two sections of the Robinson-Patman Act thus covers the use of advertising and promotional materials and services both when the supplier furnishes them and when the supplier pays the distributor to furnish them. These statutory provisions are absolute and a failure to comply with their requirements is a per se violation.

The provisions of the act apply to any advertising or promotional materials. In practice, however, they frequently involve some form of cooperative advertising activity, but other promotional activities are also covered. Promotional activities may include the payment for or furnishing of services or facilities for such items as:

1. Handbills
2. Window and floor displays
3. Demonstrators and demonstrations
4. The payment of "push money" to clerks and salespersons
5. Catalogs
6. Display and storage cabinets
7. Display materials
8. Special packaging or package sizes
9. Accepting returns for credit
10. Prizes or merchandise furnished for conducting promotional contests
11. Coupons redeemable for merchandise
12. Customer lists
13. Additional product lines
14. Poster advertising
15. Magazine and newspaper advertising
16. Warehouse service or discounts
17. Private label promotions
18. Free merchandise for consumers

Although there are minor language differences between the two Robinson-Patman Act sections, they have been interpreted as though those differences did not exist. The elements of the prohibitions found in the two Robinson-Patman Act sections are as follows:

Payment for Advertising 15 USC section 13(d)
It is unlawful for any person engaged in commerce, in the course of such commerce, to pay or contract to pay anything of value to a customer in compensation for facilities furnished by the customer in connection with the processing, handling, sale, or offering for sale of any product unless the payment is made available on proportionately equal terms to all other competing customers.

Furnishing Advertising 15 USC section 13(e)
It is unlawful for any person to discriminate in favor of one purchaser

and against another purchaser or purchasers of a commodity bought for resale, with or without processing by contracting to furnish or furnishing of, or by contributing to the furnishing of any services or facilities connected with the processing, handling, sale, or offering for sale of such commodity so purchased upon terms not accorded to all purchasers on proportionately equal terms.

By judicial interpretation, the courts have added the requirement that in order to find discrimination there must be (a) contemporaneous sales of (b) products of like grade and quality. Further, just as in the case of direct price discrimination, one of the sales must cross a state line. The requirements of contemporaneous sales, and that the sale be of goods of like grade and quality are discussed in Chapter 10. The requirements apply to the payment for or the furnishing of advertising or promotional materials and services.

Note: Sales do not include:

1. Agency or consignment transactions.

2. Refusals to deal

3. Leases and licensing transactions

4. Credit transactions

For sales to have been contemporaneous they must:

1. Provide for or anticipate reasonably simultaneous delivery of the goods

2. Have been entered into within a reasonably short time period. In determining what is a reasonably short time period, courts will consider:

   a. The character of the industry. If prices change rapidly, the relevant time period will be shorter.

   b. The nature of the product. For example, if the product depreciates rapidly, a sale made after substantial depreciation is not a sale of like quality. Therefore, contemporaneous sales must occur before there has been sufficient time for depreciation.

   c. The length of time between sales. As a rule of thumb, courts seems to hold that sales five months apart are not contemporaneous.

Like Grade and Quality

Since the sales must be of products of like grade and quality, genuine physical differentiations between the products take the sales outside the coverage of the Robinson-Patman Act. However, if the distinctions are not genuine but merely "decorative" or "fanciful" then the products are of like grade and quality.

> *Example 1*   A manufacturer produces many products. Must the manufacturer extend promotional allowances on all products if an allowance is made available on one product? No. However, the allowance made available on one product must be made available to all purchasers of the product who compete with the purchaser receiving the allowance.

Sales by a Single Seller

The contemporaneous sales must be made by a single seller. Occasionally some uncertainty may arise when a manufacturer and a subsidiary both make sales of the same commodity in the same market or when the subsidiary acts as a distributor for the manufacturer. In such cases, the manufacturer and the subsidiary will be deemed to be a single seller if the manufacturer controls the subsidiary's pricing and distribution activities. Indicia of control include:

1. Consultation regarding prices and distribution policies
2. Contractual arrangements binding the subsidiary to follow the manufacturer's prices
3. The manufacturer solicits customers for the subsidiary
4. The manufacturer has the right to accept or reject the subsidiary's customer
5. The manufacturer fixes the prices and terms of the subsidiary's sales agreements
6. The manufacturer engages in direct negotiations with customers of its subsidiary

SELLER'S DUTY TO MAKE ALLOWANCES AVAILABLE ON PROPORTIONATELY EQUAL TERMS

The statute imposes an affirmative duty on sellers who either pay for or furnish advertising or promotional materials and services to make the promotions available on proportionately equal terms to all competing customers. The promotional activities must be in connection with the resale of the commodity. Thus, a service supplied in connection with the initial sale rather than the resale is not covered by sections (d) and (e).

Red Flag: Services supplied in connection with the initial sale may be price discrimination under section (a).

HOW TO MAKE A PROMOTION AVAILABLE

A supplier desiring to use some form of cooperative advertising or promotional scheme must make it available to all of its competing customers which compete with each other. Making the promotional program available to all competing resalers becomes problematical when some or all of the competitors may be indirect purchasers.

The party making the promotional program available has an affirmative duty to notify all competing buyers of their eligiblity to participate in the promotional program. The notification must inform the competing purchasers of the terms of the promotional program. A failure to make known the availability and terms of a promotional program is concealment and as a practical matter means that the program is not available to the disfavored purchaser. An exception to the duty to notify exists in the rare situations in which notification would be a futile gesture. However, the safest practice is to make notification even when doing so is futile.

Key Point: Notification should be in writing and the promotional program should be a written program.

The Federal Trade Commission Guides for Advertising Allowances and Other Merchandising Payments and Services provide guidance for giving the required notification. The seller, according to the guides, "should take reasonable action in good faith, to inform all his competing customers of the availability of his promotional program." The notification should either contain all of the relevant details of the offer and be given in time to permit the customer to make an informed decision whether to participate, as an alternative the notice should include a summary of the essential features and identify a specific source who may be contacted for specific details.

If one-step notification is impracticable, the seller may maintain a continuing program of notifying all competing customers of the types of promotions offered by the seller and a specific source to be contacted in order to be placed on a list to receive full and timely notice of all relevant details of the promotions offered. This notice should also advise the customers that the promotions are designed to be practically useable by all competing customers regardless of size.

Notifications to Indirect Customers

A seller may provide notification of promotional programs to indirect customers in either of three ways. First, the seller may enter into contracts with wholesalers requiring them to perform all or a part of the seller's duties to make notification. Second, the seller may enclose notice of the promotional program in each shipping container and place a conspicuous notice of the enclosure on the outside of each container. Third, the seller may publish notice of the plan's availability and essential features in generally distributed trade publications.

Contracting with Wholesalers

A seller may satisfy its obligation to provide good faith notification to its indirect customers by contracting with the seller's wholesalers to provide the required notice. The contract must provide that the wholesaler will undertake the following obligations:

1. Give the notice required by the Federal Trade Commission guides to the indirect customers.
2. Check customer's use of the promotional allowance or materials as required by the Federal Trade Commission guides.
3. Implement the plan in a manner that will ensure its functional availability to the seller's indirect customers.
4. Provide written certification to the seller at reasonable intervals that the seller's indirect customers have been and are being treated in conformity with the agreement.

In addition the seller must take affirmative steps to verify that indirect customers are receiving the proportionally equal treatment to which they are entitled. This requires the seller to make spot checks, designed to reach a cross-section of indirect customers, at least every 90 days.

Other Notification

The Federal Trade Commission guides provide the following illustrative example.

> *Example 2*   A seller has a plan for the retail promotion of its product in Kansas City. It makes direct notification to its direct customers and may use any of the following methods to notify its indirect customers.

A. The seller may place on a shipping container or a product package that can reasonably be expected to come to the attention of the managerial personnel of all of the retail customers handling the product a conspicuous notice of the availability and essential features of the promotion and a source for obtaining specific details. This notice must reach the customer in time for the customer to make a decision whether to participate.

Instead of identifying a source to contact for specific details, the seller could include brochures describing the details of the program in the shipping containers.

If it is impracticable to include the essential features of the plan in such notices, the seller may substitute a summary of the types of promotions offered and a statement that such promotions are useable in a practicable business sense by retailers regardless of size.

In order to ensure that notice reaches the indirect customers' management, it may well be necessary for the seller to supplement shipping container notices with additional notices in trade journals, invoices, and envelope stuffers to be used by wholesalers.

B. If a promotional plan simply consists of providing retailers with display materials, the materials may be included in the product container.

C. Advising customers from accurate and reasonably complete mailing lists. If retailers must have a state license, notice to all license holders is sufficient.

D. Placing an announcement of the availability and essential features of promotional programs, and identifying a specific source for further particulars and details, at reasonable intervals in publications which have general and widespread distribution in the trade and which are recognized in the trade as means by which sellers announce the availability of such programs.

What Are Proportionately Equal Terms?

In addition to notifying both direct and indirect customers of the existence of a promotional program, a seller also has a duty to offer a plan that provides to all customers regardless of their size a meaningful opportunity to participate in the promotional program. This may require the seller to offer alternative programs. A plan which cannot practicably be used by some of the customers is tantamount to a failure to offer the program to those customers.

The promotional plan should be designed to permit participation by all types of competing customers. It must not discriminate against a particular customer or customer class. The seller must not utilize a plan that either directly or indirectly eliminates some competing consumers. If a seller offers alternative promotional plans, each plan must provide proportional equality. The Federal Trade Commission guides provide that:

> When a seller, in good faith, offers a basic plan, including alternatives, which is reasonably fair and nondiscriminatory, and refrains from taking any steps which would prevent any customer, or class of customers, from participating in his program, he makes his plan functionally available to all customers, and the failure of any customer or customers to participate in the program should not be deemed to place the seller in violation of the act.

> *Example 3*   A manufacturer offers a plan for cooperative advertising on radio, television, or general circulation newspapers. Purchases by some customers are in amounts which would not justify this type of advertising.
>
> Therefore, the promotional program is not "functionally available" to the small customers. The manufacturer may offer them a functionally available alternative on proportionally equal terms such as envelope stuffers or handbills.

> *Example 4*   A seller offers a cooperative advertising plan in which the seller pays 75 percent of advertising in large daily newspapers regularly used by chain-stores but only 50 percent of the cost of advertising in newspapers that are used by smaller stores. This promotional program discriminates against some customers and is unlawful.

Courts have held that a "proportionally equal" program is one in which the terms of the offer are fair and reasonable and offered in good faith. Proportionally equal does not require that there be an exact measure of proportionality.

Proportionality may be offered based on the quantity of goods purchased during a particular time period or on the dollar volume of purchases. Neither method can be used to discriminate in favor of high volume or high dollar purchases.

Example 5   A seller cannot give a higher percentage promotional allowance to a high volume customer than to a low volume customer.

Example 6   A seller cannot restrict participation to customers who purchase a minimum quantity.

Example 7   A seller may lawfully offer to pay a specific part (e.g., 50 percent) of the cost of local advertising up to an amount equal to a fixed percentage, (e.g., 5 percent) of the customers dollar volume of purchases over a specific time period.

Example 8   A seller should not select one or few customers to receive special allowances to promote the product while making allowances available in some lesser amount to those who compete with them.

Example 9   A seller should not identify or feature one or a few customers in his or her own advertising without making the same service available on proportionately equal terms to customers competing with the identified customers.

Example 10   A seller who makes employees available or arranges with a third party to furnish personnel for purposes of performing work for a customer should make the same offer available on proportionately equal terms to all other competing customers. In addition the seller should offer useable and suitable alternatives of equivalent measurable cost to those competing customers to whom such services are not useable and suitable.

Sales to Competing Buyers

The duty to offer proportionately equal promotional allowances applies only to competing buyers. Accordingly, a cooperative advertising program offered to a buyer who has no competing buyers need not be offered to noncompeting buyers. To be competitors, buyers must deal in goods of like grade and quality.

A. Geographic Competition. A promotion may be offered only to those competing buyers within a geographic area comprising a natural market.

Example 11   A national manufacturer sells to three retailers located in Roanoke, Virginia. It has no other customers reselling in Roanoke or vicinity. If the manufacturer offers a promotion to one customer in Roanoke it must offer the promotion to all. However, the promotion may be offered to the Roanoke retailers and no others.

Example 12   A national seller has direct buying retail customers which resell exclusively in the Baltimore trade area and other customers within that area that purchase through wholesalers. The seller may lawfully confine its promotional campaign to Baltimore provided he or she affords all retailing customers in the area the opportunity to participate including those who purchase through wholesalers.

B. Functional Competition. The requirements of the Robinson-Patman Act apply only when the buyers compete on the same functional level. For example, two wholesalers operate on the same functional level but a wholesaler and a retailer do not. If the buyers are at the same functional level, they may compete even if they do not engage in the same type of busines. Accordingly, a vending machine operator and an over-the-counter retailer might compete.

C. Direct and Indirect Purchasers. The seller must ensure that its promotional programs are available to competing buyers whether these buyers purchase directly from the seller or indirectly from a wholesaler.

MEETING THE COMPETITION

When allowances or services which are forbidden by the Robinson-Patman Act are granted or furnished, they are unlawful per se unless the defense of meeting the competition is applicable.

Red Flag: The defense of meeting the competition has rarely been successful.

Key Point: The defense of meeting the competition is strictly limited to those situations in which a seller grants a disproportionate allowance to individual customers as a good faith response to a competitive situation.

Red Flag: There is no cost justification defense to a claim of providing discriminatory advertising and promotional materials.

CUSTOMER'S USE OF ALLOWANCES

The Federal Trade Commission guides provide that the seller should take reasonable steps to ensure that the services being payed for are actually being furnished and that the seller is not overpaying for these services. The seller should also ensure that the buyer is using an advertising allowance for the purpose for which it is given.

Key Point: If a buyer is misusing an advertising allowance, the seller should discontinue the payments.

A seller who takes good faith and reasonable and prudent measures to verify the performance of customers will have satisified the seller's obligations under the act, even though a buyer has retained an allowance in excess of the cost or approximate cost of the services performed by the seller.

AVOIDING DISPUTES

Many disputes with distributors may be avoided if there is a written distribution agreement which describes the supplier's obligation to advertise and promote the product. A written agreement will be particularly helpful if cooperative advertising is offered. In such cases, the distributor's rights to participate in any cooperative advertising and promotional program should be clearly stated. Distribution agreements are discussed in detail in Appendix A.

PROMOTIONAL ALLOWANCE CHECKLIST

_____ Is the program in written form?

_____ Was written notification given in reasonable detail and in sufficient time to permit competing customers to decide whether to participate?

_____ If written notice was not given to a competing customer, does the file document the fact that giving notice would be a futile gesture?

_____ Does the file document the efforts made to ensure that notice was given to indirect customers?

_____ Have the Federal Trade Commission guides for notice to indirect customers been observed?

_____ Does the file include copies of all notices mailed or published?

_____ Is the promotional program particularly useable in a business sense by all competing customers?

_____ Is the promotion available to all competing buyers?

_____ Is the promotional program monitored by the seller?

chapter twelve

HOW TO AVOID ADVERTISING PITFALLS

Nearly every marketing program involves the use of advertising. How little or how much advertising to use is a matter of managerial judgment. However, selecting the type and content of advertising displays can raise legal issues that can be a trap for the unwary. For example, the simple use of the name or picture of an employee without first obtaining the written permission of the employee may violate the employee's right of privacy. Moreover, the Federal Trade Commission has adapted a myriad of regulations aimed at safeguarding the public from deceptive advertising. This chapter will discuss some of the more common and more important advertising pitfalls.

HOW NOT TO VIOLATE RIGHTS OF PRIVACY

Claims for the violation of a person's right of privacy may arise from the following actions:

1. Commercial appropriation
2. Intrusion on one's personal solitude
3. Portraying a person in a false light

While the elements of a claim for commercial appropriation vary from state to state, in general terms, it is the unauthorized use of the name, picture, likeness, or voice for purposes of advertising or trade.

Key Point: The Supreme Court has held that there is no First Amendment prohibition against claims for violation of private rights against commercial appropriation. First Amendment protection in such situations is limited to situations involving information about matters of public conern. The use of a person's name, picture, likeness, or voice for purposes of trade is a much broader classification than simply advertising. Trade would include the use of a person's picture by its sale or commercial publication for purposes other than a matter of public interest.

Key Point: Specific written consent should be obtained for any use of a person's name, picture, likeness, or voice for commercial purposes.

Commercial use of a person's identity is subject to regulation by statute in some states. For example, in New York claims for commercial appropriation are governed by the state's privacy statute which requires written consent for the use of a person's identity (see the sample consent and release form). The consent must be specific and not merely implied. Thus it was an invasion of privacy for a bank to use a photograph of its employees in a display at a trade fair.

Unless the name of an individual used obviously refers to a particular person of that name, the consent of any person with that name is sufficient. Accordingly, the safe course is to use the name of a real person from whom consent has been obtained rather than use a fictitious name which may just happen to be the name of a real person who has not consented.

Since it is the identity of the person that is protected, the use of a picture may give rise to a lawsuit even if it does not show the person's face. It is sufficient that the individual "is capable of identification from the objectionable matter itself" if "someone familiar with the person in the photograph could identify them by looking at the advertisement." It may be sufficient that the individual depicted can identify the photograph.

> *Example 1* When the photograph of the back of a woman who was skinny-dipping was used in an advertisement without her consent, the court held that it was sufficient for her to claim that she could be identified from her long and slender back, slim waist, bony elbows, short free-flowing hair, and two dimples above the buttocks.

The use of the "likeness" of a person includes the use of drawing, sketches, cartoons, and other representations. A more difficult question is raised by the use of look-alikes. It has been held that in a lawsuit charging commercial appropriation through the use of look-alikes the essential test is whether people who could identify an actual picture of the suing celebrity would believe that the advertisement contained a picture of the celebrity. Further, the look-alike may have a right to sue if the written consent to use the look-alike's photograph in that manner was not authorized.

Sample Consent and Release Form

For good and valuable consideration, receipt of which is hereby acknowledged, on behalf of myself and any business entity of which I am an officer, director, partner, or employee and my successors, heirs, and assignor, I agree and represent to _____ and its advertising media, publishers, and interested media that:

1. I am of legal age and sound mind.

2. I hereby give my permission irrevocably and in perpetuity to use my name, picture, likeness, voice, and identity or any material based on or derived therefrom, and to reproduce, copy, publish, broadcast, or otherwise use the same, or to refrain from so using them, in any manner or media whatsoever, throughout the world, including, for any and all advertising, promotion and other trade purposes.

3. I further agree that I shall retain no right of approval and I shall have no claim to additional compensation or benefit arising from the commercial use of my identity.

4. I shall have no claim and I hereby waive any claim based on invasion of privacy, defamation, or right of publicity nor shall I have any claim arising out of any blurring, alteration, optical illusion, or use in composite form.

_____

Name

Sworn to before me this_____day of_____19_____.

_____

Notary Public

Note: The sample release form is written to give broad protection to the advertiser. The model may insist on a more limited release. This release is intended only to provide protection from lawsuits based on invasion of privacy. It is not intended to substitute for a contract with a model or an advertising agency. Such a contract would be the proper document to restrain the model from appearing in advertisements for competing products.

___ FIRST AMENDMENT PROTECTION FOR COMMERCIAL SPEECH ___

It was not until 1976 that the Supreme Court accorded a measure of first amendment protection to commercial speech. Commercial speech includes advertising and other speech proposing a commercial transaction. However, the first amendment protection of commercial speech is not as extensive as the protection of noncommercial speech. The protection of commercial speech extends beyond the informational content of the advertising material to encompass freedom of expression and creativity as well.

Red Flag: There is no first amendment protection for commercial speech which proposes an unlawful transaction or which is false, deceptive, or misleading.

Regulation of commercial speech must be limited to restraints justified by a substantial governmental interest and must directly advance the government interest with the minimum necessary restraint. Nondeceptive commercial speech may be regulated only when the government can show a compelling need for the regulation. A mere potential for abuse will not justify regulation of commercial speech.

First amendment protection of commercial speech extends to photographs, illustrations, parody, caricatures, and other creative art as well as to written material. Visual media can be regulated only if it is false or misleading or there is some other substantial governmental interest in regulating the media. Even then the regulation must vindicate the governmental interest through the least restrictive available means.

In extending first amendment protection to visual media the Supreme Court said:

> The use of illustrations or pictures in advertisements serves important communicative functions; it attracts the attention of the audience to the advertiser's message, and it may serve to impart information directly. Accordingly, commercial illustrations are entitled to the First Amendment protections afforded verbal commercial speech. . . .

Despite the extension of first amendment protection to commercial speech, there remains much room for legitimate regulation of advertising. For example, the Supreme Court upheld state regulation of the use of trade names by optometrists stating that trade names are "a form of commercial speech that has no intrinsic meaning." Most of the rest of this chapter will be given over to a discussion of the law regulating commercial speech.

HOW TO AVOID UNFAIR AND DECEPTIVE ADVERTISING

Unfair and deceptive acts and practices are declared unlawful by section 5 of the Federal Trade Commission Act. Additionally, section 12 of the Federal Trade Commission Act makes it unlawful to disseminate, or cause to be disseminated, any false advertisement inducing the purchase of food, drugs, devices, or cosmetics.

Unfairness and deception are disapproved whether wilful or inadvertent. Unfair business practices can result from a failure to include information, deceptive methods of packaging, the deceptive shape of a product, and even a deceptive corporate name. These actions can be the unintended result of an overly eager and flawed marketing program. Many unfair practices are discussed in Chapters 17 and 18. The Federal Trade Commission can enforce section 5 by seeking penal sanctions, cease and desist orders, and other injunctive relief. Section 12 proceedings involving food, drugs, and cosmetics are enforced by the Food and Drug Administration.

Deceptive advertising is generally defined as "having the capacity or tendency to deceive."

Single or occasional acts are unlawful as well as recurring acts or methods of doing business.

Since it is sufficient that the advertisement has a tendency to deceive, it is not necessary that any actual deception occur. In determining whether an advertisement is deceptive, the Federal Trade Commission will consider the entire representation of the product and its effect on the average or ordinary purchaser including the ignorant, unthinking, and credulous but not the stupid consumer. Things not said as well as things said may result in deception.

As a general policy matter the Federal Trade Commission supports truthful advertising because it spurs product innovation and cost competition. The commission has a history of opposing efforts by industry or professional groups to restrain advertising. In considering whether to bring an action against false or deceptive advertising the Federal Trade Commission will consider:

1. Effectiveness of industry self-regulation

2. Potential for injury to the consumer

3. Ability of consumers to evaluate the advertising claims

4. Likelihood of private enforcement actions

A great variety of activities can result in advertising which is unlawfully deceptive. Advertising can be deceptive because of what it fails to disclose as well as for what it does disclose. The definitions of deceptive advertising or false and misleading advertising are intentionally broad.

Liability for deceptive advertising can extend beyond those who actually disseminate the false advertising to the public. Thus, a manufacturer who contributes to the cost of a distributor's false advertising through a cooperative advertising program is liable. Also a manufacturer of a therapeutic device which supplied members of the healing professions with false, misleading, and deceptive advertising to be distributed by the healing professionals violated the Federal Trade Commission Act.

Advertising may be deceptive even if the statements made are literally true. Deception used to secure the first contact with a customer is unlawful even if the initial deception is later clarified. Further a higher standard may be required in labeling than in other advertising. Moreover, in an action brought by the Federal Trade Commission to enforce the act, the commission does not have to prove actual deception. It is sufficient that deception of consumers is a probable result.

For example, the false use of the word "mills" in a rug distributor's name created an opportunity for retailers to misrepresent to consumers that the distributor was a manufacturer of rugs. There was a reasonable probability that consumers would be deceived.

WHEN YOU CAN USE EXAGGERATION OR PUFFING IN ADVERTISING

Advertising may be lawful and not deceptive when the representations are merely exaggeration or permissible "puffing." Puffing is not considered to be a misrepresentation of fact. Puffing includes:

1. Fanciful sales talk which no reasonable person would take seriously such as a statement that a machine is "almost human"

2. Expressions of broad generality such as a claim that a toothpaste will "beautify the smile"

3. Statements that are largely a matter of personal opinion. For example, the words "easy," "perfect," "amazing," "prime," "wonderful," and "excellent" are often regarded as mere dealer's talk or puffing which entails no misrepresentation or deception.

Red Flag: Although words like "easy" are often considered permissible puffing, they must be judged in the context of the entire advertisement. For example, misrepresentation of the "ease" with which a product may be used has often been found misleading.

Not all exaggeration falls within the category of permissible puffing. The following categories of puffing or exaggeration have held to be misleading.

1. Advertisements for treatments or prevention of illness or disease. Puffing with respect to health products obviously creates a high risk to the consumer and the consumer is unlikely to be able to judge the claims.

2. Misrepresentations which could place the consumer in danger if relied on—for example, a misrepresentation regarding the use or effectiveness of a water safety floatation device.

3. Statements designed to frighten a consumer into purchasing a product.

4. Statements which attribute nonexistent characteristics to a product.

Examples of product puffing which have been held impermissible include:

1. A claim that yogurt is nature's perfect food

2. A television commercial for shaving cream purporting to be used to shave sandpaper when the actual object being shaved was plexiglas

3. Claims that a cigarette was "milder", "smoother," and left "no unpleasant after taste"

4. A claimed guarantee of "first-class workmanship and materials"

Closely related to permissible puffing is advertising that uses "spoofing" of "fanciful" presentations to startle or amuse the viewer. However, fanciful or spoofing representations are unlawful when they depict a product in use and exaggerate the results achieved from its use. For example, a television commercial showing an actor wearing a stained garment who is then immersed in water shown rising from the bottom of the screen to his chin with soap being added and the actor emerging in a clean garment was unlawful when the garment was actually cleaned by normal machine washing.

MATTERS THAT MUST BE DISCLOSED

Failure to disclose certain material facts is an unfair trade practice under section 5 of the Federal Trade Commission Act. A material fact is one which is important to a consumer in making a decision to buy a product. One material fact that must be disclosed is a change in the nature or composition of an existing product. Thus, the publication of a book in an abridged form must disclose the abridgment in advertising. If a new ingredient is substituted for one previously advertised extensively, the substitution must be disclosed.

> *Example 2*   A reduction in the quality of tires offered for sale without a change in the trade name was unlawful unless the quality reduction was disclosed.

Note: See Chapter 17 for a discussion of the deceptive use of trademarks and trade names.

Another material fact that may require disclosure is the composition of the product. If the appearance of a product is deceptively similar to the appearance of products made with other materials, the product's composition must be disclosed. For example, articles made with rayon must disclose the rayon content to ensure that consumers are not deceived into believing that the product is made of silk. Similarly, the use of base metals treated to resemble stainless steel, gold, or other precious metals must be disclosed. Use of materials that are imitations of other materials must be disclosed. Accordingly disclosure has been required for the use of "imitation leather" and "imitation turquoise,"

Dangers inherent in the use of a product are material facts that must be disclosed. The disclosure of danger is particularly sensistive in advertisements for food, drugs, and cosmetics. Advertisement of these items is subject to the overlapping regulation of the Federal Trade Commission and the Food and Drug Administration. Therefore, advertisers of these products must become familiar with the regulation by both agencies.

Red Flag: Warnings of danger may be required on product labels even when not required in advertising material. For example, the dangers in the use of laxatives by persons showing symptoms of appendicitis must be revealed in the label but need not be disclosed in advertising. See Chapter 15, Product Labeling.

The Federal Trade Commission has ruled that potential product dangers should be disclosed for products that are injurious if they come in contact with the skin or are inhaled or are poisonous if eaten. Disclosure of electrical shock danger has been required for electrical appliances. Dangers from products containing flammable preparation must also be disclosed.

Red Flag: The Flammable Fabrics Act has outlawed the sale of most flammable fabrics.

Red Flag: Hazardous substances sold in containers for household use must contain specific warnings on the label (see the Federal Hazardous Substances Act).

The Federal Trade Commission has required the disclosure of the danger of injury from toys that are constructed in such a way as to be likely to break and cause serious injury to a child.

DISCLOSURE OF FOREIGN ORIGIN

It has been held that a prospective customer's concern for the origin of a product is the most compelling reason for requiring disclosing the foreign origin of a product. Therefore, an unfair trade practice claim based on a failure to disclose a foreign origin may be defended against by evidence that the consuming public has no preference for a domestic manufacturer. If the product has no domestic competitor, disclosure of foreign origin is not required under the Federal Trade Act. However, as a general rule, it is an unfair trade practice to offer to sell a product of foreign origin without disclosure of the country of origin.

Red Flag: Disclosure of foreign origin may be required by the Tariff Act even when not required by the Federal Trade Commission Act.

The disclosure of foreign origin may be required on both the product and the packaging, or only on the product, or only on the packaging. The key is that the consumer be made aware of the disclosure. Thus, if the product itself discloses the foreign origin and that disclosure is not obscured by the packaging, it may not be necessary to make a disclosure on the packaging.

If the nature of the product makes it impractical to place the disclosure on the product, disclosure on the packaging is sufficient.

If the sale is made on the basis of a product sample, the disclosure must be made on the sample.

Disclosure of foreign origin is frequently required on point-of-sale advertising. Disclosure must also be made in mail-order catalogs and other mail-order solicitations. Mail-order disclosure is necessary because the consumer does not have the opportunity to inspect the product itself prior to purchase.

Concealment or obliteration of material disclosing foreign origin may be an unfair trade practice when disclosure of foreign origin is required.

For the disclosure requirement pertaining to a specific product, legal counsel should be consulted.

DISCLOSURE OF IMPERFECTIONS

When sale is made of products that contain imperfections or were rejected or classified as "seconds," this fact must be disclosed. Depending on the circumstances, disclosure has been required on the product, the container, the advertising, invoices, and shipping memoranda.

DISCLOSURE OF LIMITED AVAILABILITY

The fact that only limited quantities of the advertised product are available must be disclosed in the advertising. Disclosure is required when an advertised product is available in only limited quantity or is not stocked in quantities sufficient to meet the reasonbly anticipated demand. Further, if the item is available at only certain outlets or "participating dealers" that fact must also be disclosed. Failure to disclose the limited availability may be treated as evidence of unlawful "bait" advertising discussed later in this chapter.

A specific Federal Trade Commission ruling (found at 16 CFR section 424) declares it to be an unfair trade practice to advertise the sale of any food and grocery products for sale at a stated price when the stores covered by the advertisement do not have the products in stock and readily available to customers during the period of the advertisement. It is a defense to show that quantities sufficient to meet the reasonably anticipated demand were ordered in timely fashion.

Key Point: Adequate records should be retained showing the derivation of the reasonably anticipated demand for the product and the timeliness of the product order.

Red Flag: General disclaimers such as "not all items available at all stores" or "available at most stores," are not sufficient. Rather a disclaimer used in advertising should be specific such as "available only at stores featuring delicatessen departments."

Key Point: While the Federal Trade Commission declined to extend its rule to other retail establishments, the commission said that the legal principles involved are of general applicability and in the future the commission will consider matters involving mispricing and unavailability of other advertised commodities in that spirit.

WHAT IS UNLAWFUL "BAIT" ADVERTISING?

Bait advertising is an alluring but insincere offer to sell a product or service which the advertiser in truth does not intend or want to sell. Its purpose is to switch customers from the advertised product (bait) to another higher priced product. No advertisement containing an offer to sell a product should be published when the offer is not a bona fide effort to sell the advertised product.

The initial offer should not misrepresent the product. Thus, no statement or illustration should be used in an advertisement which misrepresents or creates a false impression of the grade, quality, make, value, currency of model, size, color, useability, or origin of the product which, on disclosure of the true facts, might lead the purchaser to switch from the advertised product to another. Apprising the buyer of the true facts subsequent to the deceptive advertisement will not cure the illegality.

Under the Federal Trade Commission advertising guidelines, an advertiser should engage in no act to discourage the purchaser from purchasing the advertised product. Among the acts which will be viewed as discouraging the purchase of the advertised product are the following:

1. The refusal to show, demonstrate, or sell the product in accordance with advertised offer

2. Disparagement of the advertised product or of the guarantee, credit terms, availability of service, repairs, or parts in connection with the product

3. The failure to have available at all outlets listed in the advertisement a sufficient quantity of the advertised product to meet reasonably anticipated product demands, unless the advertisement clearly and adequately discloses that supply is limited and/or the merchandise is available only at designated outlets

4. The refusal to take orders for delivery of the advertised product within a reasonable period of time

5. Showing or demonstrating a product which is defective, unuseable or impractical for the purpose represented or implied in the advertisement

6. Use of a plan of compensating salespersons designed to prevent or discourage them from selling the advertised product

Certain after-sale practices may also be part of a bait and switch scheme. These practices constitute the "unselling" of the advertised product. Practices which the Federal Trade Commission will consider in determining whether there was a bona fide intent to sell the advertised product include:

1. Accepting a deposit for the advertised product, then switching the purchaser to a higher-priced product

2. Failure to make a delivery of the advertised product within a reasonable time or to make a refund

3. Disparagement by acts or words of the advertised product, or the disparagement of the guarantee, credit terms, availability of service, repairs, or in any other respect, in connection with it

4. The delivery of the advertised product which is defective, unuseable or impractical for the purpose represented or implied in the advertisement.

State Bait-and-Switch Statutes

Some states have statutes which specifically outlaw bait-and-switch practices. Frequently state courts look to Federal Trade Commission decisions for guidance in interpreting and applying the state statute. The best defense against bait-and-switch problems is a well-trained sales staff.

WHAT TO DO WHEN DEMAND FOR AN ADVERTISED PRODUCT EXCEEDS SUPPLY

Occasionally it will happen that a marketer will advertise a product which it believes it has available in adequate amounts but the demand exceeds the supply. It is clear from the proceeding section that it is an unlawful trade practice to advertise a product without disclosure of limited availability. However, it is not unlawful to underestimate the demand for an advertised product when the estimate was reasonable. Accordingly, when demand unexpectedly exceeds the supply, the retailer should take immediate steps to preserve documents showing the reasonableness of the demand estimated. If no such documents exist, an after-the-fact memorandum to the file should be prepared explaining how the quantity to be ordered was determined and why the quantity was sufficient to meet any reasonably anticipated demand. This memorandum can become an invaluable aid in remembering what happened when the distributor is asked to explain its actions weeks, months, or even years later.

Another mitigating action the distributor can take, and one which will preserve good will, is the issuance of "rainchecks." Of course, if the product was available to the distributor at a special low price for only a short period and that price is no longer available, it may not be economically feasible to provide "rainchecks." Any circumstances which preclude the issuance of "rainchecks" should be recorded in a memorandum to the file.

HOW TO USE ENDORSEMENTS AND TESTIMONIALS IN ADVERTISING

It is widely recognized that word-of-mouth advertising is extremely valuable. Consumers are likely to rely on the product or service recommendation of a relative, neighbor, friend, or trusted figure. To capitalize on this consumer propensity, advertisers make use of endorsements and testimonials. Moreover, the testimonial or endorsement of a celebrity figure will focus consumer attention on the product message. The lawful use of endorsements and testimonials requires an understanding of the Federal Trade Commission's guides of their use.

In its guidelines for the use of endorsements and testimonials in advertising, the Federal Trade Commission considers testimonials to be a subset of endorsements. Accordingly the commission's final guidelines generally refer only to endorsements but also apply to testimonials. The term endorsements is broadly defined to mean any advertising message which consumers are likely to believe reflects the opinions, beliefs, findings, or experience of a party other than the sponsoring advertiser. This definition is broad enough to include, for example, the use of an excerpt from a film critics review in an advertisement for a motion picture. However, not all verbalized statements about a product are endorsements made by unidentified persons whose identity is not generally known.

> *Example 3* A fictionalized dramatization of two women in a supermarket discussing the virtues of a laundry detergent is not an endorsement when the women are not identified.

> *Example 4* An unidentified announcer used to extol the virtues of a pain reliever is not an endorsement when the announcer does not purport to express his or her own opinions but rather appears as a spokesperson for the drug company.

On the other hand an endorsement may occur by indirection.

> *Example 5* In a television announcement for golf balls, a recognized professional golfer is shown hitting the golf balls. This would be considered an endorsement even though the golfer makes no verbal statement.

> *Example 6* When a well-known professional race car driver is shown in a television advertisement for automobile tires, speaking of the smooth ride, strength, and long life of the tires, the commission would say there was an endorsement even though the driver did not state the facts as a matter of personal opinion. In the view of the commission, the public is likely to treat the statement as one of the driver's opinion rather than considering the driver to be a mere spokesperson for the manufacturer.

In using an endorsement it is necessary to ensure that the advertising statement reflects the honest opinions, findings, beliefs, or experience of the endorser. If the endorsement is that of a celebrity or an expert, it can be used only as long as the advertiser has good reason to believe that the endorsement continues to reflect the opinions of the celebrity or expert.

Key Point: When using a celebrity or expert endorsement, at periodic intervals the advertiser should obtain from the celebrity or expert a reaffirmation of the endorsement.

Similarly, when the advertisement states that the endorser actually uses the product, the endorser must have been a bona fide user of the product at the time the endorsement was made. Further, the endorsement can continue to be used only so long as the advertiser has good reason to believe that the endorser remains a bona fide product user.

Consumer Endorsements

Advertisements which purport to present endorsements by actual consumers should in fact use actual consumers or clearly and conspicuously disclose that the persons in the advertisements are not actual consumers of the product.

If the advertisement uses a consumer endorsement focusing on a key or central attribute of the product, the endorsement must be representative of what consumers may generally expect from the product.

Red Flag: Claims concerning the effectiveness of any drug should not be made in advertising directed to the general consumer unless:

1. The advertiser has adequate scientific substantiation for such claims
2. The claims are not inconsistent with any determination that has been made by the Food and Drug Admininstration with respect to the drug.

Expert Endorsements

Advertising which utilizes the endorsement of an expert should do so only when the endorser actually possesses the expert qualifications being represented. Further, the expert's endorsement must be supported by an actual exercise of the expert's expertise in evaluating the product's features or characteristics. The expert's product evaluation must have included testing or examination of the product typical of that used by experts in the field making such an evaluation. If the advertisement states or implies that the expert compared various products, the expert must have done so. Finally, the expertise of the endorser must be relevant to the subject matter of the endorsement.

Endorsements by Organization

Endorsements by expert organizations are viewed by the Federal Trade Commission as representing a group judgment based on collective experience and free from the subjective influences that may affect individual evaluations. Such endorsements must be obtained by a process that fairly reflects the collective judgment of the organization. If the organization is an expert organization, its collective judgment must be based on the examination of the product by experts recognized by the organization or on the conformance by the product to standards previously adopted by the organization.

CHECKLIST FOR USE OF ENDORSEMENTS AND TESTIMONIALS

_____ Does the advertisement reflect the opinions, beliefs, findings, or experience of someone other than the sponsoring advertiser. If so, it is likely to be an endorsement or testimonial.

_____ The advertisement must reflect the honest opinions, beliefs or findings of the endorser.

_____ Celebrity or expert endorsement can be used only so long as it continues to reflect the view of the celebrity or expert.

_____ If the advertisement claims that the endorser actually uses the product, the endorser must have been a bona fide user of the product at the time the endorsement was made.

_____ If the advertisement purports to use consumer testimonials but in fact uses actors, the use of actors must be conspicuously disclosed.

_____ Experts making endorsements must possess relevant expertise and must have exercised that expertise in making the endorsement.

HOW TO MAKE LAWFUL USE OF COMPARATIVE ADVERTISING

The Federal Trade Commission encourages comparative advertising. The commission issued a policy statement in 1979 stating that industry self-regulation standards should not restrain the use of truthful comparative advertising. The Federal Trade Commission defines comparative advertising as advertising that compares alternative brands on objectively measurable attributes or price and identifies the alternative brand by name, illustration, or other distinctive information.

The commission believes that truthful comparative advertising is a source of important information to consumers and assists them in making rational purchase decisions. Moreover, comparative advertising encourages product improvement and innovation and can lead to lower prices.

Product Disparagement

Comparative advertising which disparages another product is not unlawful if it is truthful and not deceptive. However, it is unlawful if it makes use of false or misleading pictures, depictions, or demonstrations.

Advertising Substantiation

The commission has opposed efforts to require greater substantiation of advertising claims made in the context of comparative advertising than in other advertising.

Red Flag: Competitors may respond to a comparative advertising campaign by filing suit for trademark infringement under the Lanham Act.

The use of a trademark in comparative advertising is not an infringing use of the trademark in the absence of misrepresentation or the likelihood that the consumers will be confused. In determining whether the use of the trademark in comparative advertising is deceptive the courts focus on the meaning conveyed by the advertisement and whether it is false. Generally, proof of a Lanham Act trademark infringement claim will require the use of a customer survey to demonstrate confusion. The advertiser does not have the burden of proving whether advertising claims were truthful. Rather the complaining party must prove the advertising claims are false.

Red Flag: If in its advertisement, the advertisor claims to have studies substantiating its claims, these facts must be substantiated or its advertising is false.

USE OF SUCH WORDS AS "HALF-PRICE," "CENTS OFF," IN ADVERTISING

It is common for marketers to promote a product by offering "free" merchandise or two-for-one sales. Such offers are effective and valuable merchandising tools. However, the use of such terms lead the consumer to believe that a bargain is being offered and care must be taken to avoid misleading the consumer. To provide guidance to advertisers for the use of such offers, the Federal Trade Commission issued guidelines in 1971.

Note: See also the discussion of deceptive pricing in Chapter 9.

The Federal Trade Commission guidelines are based on the assumption that a consumer views an offer of a free item, as in a buy-one-get-one-free offer, to mean that the consumer can purchase one product at the usual price and get another at no cost. Therefore, the purchaser has the right to believe that the seller is not recovering any part of the cost of the free item directly by marking up the price of the purchased article or indirectly by substituting a product of inferior quality.

The Federal Trade Commission defines "regular" to mean the price at which articles of the same quantity and quality were sold with the same accompanying prices in the same general market area within the preceding 30 days. If the price fluctuated in the preceding 30 days, then the "regular" price is the lowest price at which substantial sales were made in the previous 30 days.

Key Point: A "free" offer cannot be made when the price of the product is customarily set by negotiation.

In making a "free" offer, all of the terms and conditions for receiving the free item must be set forth at the outset of the offer in a clear and conspicuous manner. Disclosure of the qualifying terms and conditions in a footnote is not sufficient.

However, it is lawful to make mere notice of a "free" offer on the main display panel of a label or offer so long as the following conditions are met:

1. The notice does not constitute an offer or identify the item being offered as "free."

2. The notice informs the customer of the location, elsewhere on the package or label, where the required disclosures may be found.

3. No purchase or other such material act is required before the consumer can discover the terms and conditions of the offer.

4. The notice and the offer are not otherwise deceptive.

Supplier's Free Offer Responsibilities

While a supplier cannot lawfully engage in resale price maintenance, it does have a responsibility to act if it learns that a retailer is not passing on the "free" offer. If the supplier learns that the retailer is utilizing the "free" offer for deceptive purposes, the supplier should take appropriate steps to stop the deception including, if necessary, withdrawal of the "free" offer.

The supplier must make the "free" offer promotion available on reasonably proportional terms to all of its retailers. See Chapter 11, Advertising and Promotional Allowances.

In advertising the promotion the supplier should clearly state in which geographic areas the promotion is available and whether it is available from all dealers or only from participating dealers.

Key Point: Within any trade area, a "free" offer should not be made for more than six months of any 12-month period. At least 30 days should elapse between the close of one "free" offer and the start of another "free" offer for the same product.

Key Point: Sales under a "free" offer promotion should not exceed 50 percent of the total volume of sales of the product within a given trade area.

CHECKLIST FOR "FREE" OFFERS

_____ Seller cannot recoup the cost of the "free" item either directly or indirectly.

_____ "Regular" price used in conjunction with a free offer must be the prevailing price for the item in the market within the preceding 30 days.

_____ Terms and conditions of the "free" offer must be set forth clearly and conspicuously.

_____ "Free" offer must be available to all retailers on proportionately equal terms.

_____ Advertising for the "free" offer must clearly state whether the offer is limited only to participating dealers or is available in only limited geographic areas.

ADVERTISING SUBSTANTIATION

The Federal Trade Commission has reaffirmed its commitment to the belief that section 5 of the Federal Trade Commission Act requires both advertisers and advertising agencies to have a reasonable basis for any advertising claims before the claims are made. The requirement that substantiation exists before the claims are made applies to express or implied claims of objective assertions about the product or service advertised.

Example 7 An advertisement stating that a product removes stains from all rugs is an objective assertion.

Red Flag: A failure to have a reasonable basis for objective claims constitutes an unfair and deceptive practice in violation of section 5 of the Federal Trade Commission Act.

If the advertisement itself contains a statement indicating the type and amount of substantiation for the statement, the advertiser must have at least that level of substantiation.

> *Example 8*   Language that states the degree of substantiation available includes
>
> 1. "Tests prove"
> 2. "Nine out of ten doctors recommend"
> 3. "Studies show"

When the advertisement itself does not indicate the level of substantiation, the commission assumes that consumers expect a "reasonable basis" for the claims. Whether a reasonable basis for the claim exists depends on a number of factors relevant to weighing the benefits to consumers from requiring substantiation against the costs of substantiation. Among the factors to be considered are:

1. Type of claim made
2. Product
3. Consequences of a false claim
4. Benefits of a truthful claim
5. Cost of developing substantiation
6. Amount of substantiation experts in the field believe is reasonable

Red Flag: Substantiation may be required for reasonably implied claims as well as for express claims.

SPECIAL INDUSTRY ADVERTISING REQUIREMENTS

The Federal Trade Commission has issued a number of industry specific advertising guidelines that should be consulted as appropriate. These guidelines relate directly to advertising or indirectly through the definition of practices deemed to be misrepresentation:

> Advertising Fallout Shelters
> Advertising Radiation Monitoring Instruments
> Advertising Shell Homes

Avoiding Deceptive Use of the Word "Mill" In the Textile Industry

Cigarette Advertising Guides

Deception in the Use of the Word "Free" in Connection with Sale of Photographic Film and Film Processing Service

Deceptive Labeling in Advertising Adhesive Compositions

Decorative Wall Paneling

Dog and Cat Food Industry

Feather and Down Products Industry

Fuel Economy Advertising for New Automobiles

Hosiery Industry

Household Furniture Industry

Jewelry Industry

Labeling, Advertising, and Sale of Wigs and other Hairpieces

Ladies Handbag Industry

Law Book Industry

Luggage and Related Products Industry

Mail-Order Insurance Industry

Metallic Watch Band Industry

Mirror Industry

Private Vocational and Home Study Schools

Rebuilt Reconditioned and Other Used Automobile Parts Industry

Shoe Content Labeling and Advertising

Tile (Ceramic) Administrative Interpretation

Tire Advertising and Labeling

Watch Industry

HOW TO AVOID DECEPTIVE PRICE ADVERTISING

Price is the most sensitive matter for marketing most products in a competitive environment. Therefore, it is only natural that efforts are made to market a product by describing the price in terms that lead the purchaser to believe that a bargain is being offered. Offering bargain prices is a lawful activity and price competition is one of the primary goals of the Sherman, Clayton and Federal Trade Commission Acts. However, because price is such a sensitive factor in consumer decision making, the opportunities for deceptive use of price signals are abundant. Therefore, the Federal Trade Commission has issued guides covering deceptive pricing practices.

Reductions from Previous Prices

A common form of bargain pricing is to offer the consumer a reduction from the previous price for the item. This form of bargain pricing is lawful if the markdown is from a bona fide previous price at which the article was offered for sale to the public for a reasonably substantial period of time. On the other hand, the bargain price is deceptive if the previous price was not bona fide but rather was an artifically inflated price established for the purpose of enabling the subsequent offer of a price reduction.

A former price is not fictitious solely because no sales were made at that price if the product was openly and actively offered for sale at that price for a reasonably substantial period in the recent and regular course of business. In such cases the seller must not advertise the former price as a selling price but as an offered price.

> *Example 9* It would be deceptive to advertise a product as "formerly sold at $_____" unless substantial sales had actually been made at that price. When substantial sales have not been made at the previous price, the advertisement should contain language such as "previously offered at $_____".

Typical of previous prices which are fictitious are the following:

1. A price at which the article had never been offered for sale
2. A price never used in the ordinary course of business
3. A price used in the remote past but not in the recent past
4. A price that was not openly offered to the public
5. A price that was not maintained for a reasonable length of time before the advertised price reduction

Even when the former price is not advertised but instead the advertisement merely uses the words "sale," "price slashed," or "reduced prices," the advertisers must take care that the amount of price reduction is not so small as to be meaningless. The price reduction must be sufficiently large enough that if it were openly stated in the advertisement, the consumer would believe that a genuine bargain was being offered.

> *Example 10*   An advertisement for an item at a price "reduced to $9.99" when the former price was $10 is misleading and deceptive.

Price Comparisons

Another common form of bargain price marketing is to advertise goods for sale at prices lower than those charged by other merchants in the trade area. Such bargain prices may be offered on a short-term basis or may be a permanent method of operation. The Federal Trade Commission is generally supportive of comparison advertising believing that it will stimulate product innovation and price competition. Nonetheless, it is possible to use such pricing or price advertising in a deceptive manner. Thus, an advertiser who claims to be selling at prices below those charged by others in the trade area for a particular article should be reasonably certain that the higher prices it is claimed that competitors charge is a price at which substantial sales have been made.

> *Example 11*   *(Lawful Price Advertisements)* When a number of the principal retail outlets in the trade area are regularly selling Brand X for $10, it is lawful to advertise "Brand X sold elsewhere for $10, our price $7.50."
>
> *Example 12*   *(Deceptive Price Advertisement)* It would be misleading to advertise "Brand X retail value $15, my price $7.50" when only a few suburban stores price Brand X at $15 while all of the principal retail outlets offer Brand X for about $7.50. The advertisement is deceptive in suggesting that $15 is the prevailing price for Brand X.

A marketer might wish to use price comparisons in which the comparison price is not for the same product but for a product which is a substitute of like grade and quality. For example, when both products X and Y can be used interchangeably, the advertiser may want to compare the prices of X and Y. This type of advertising serves a useful purpose when it is made clear to a consumer that a comparison is being made with other merchandise which is in fact of similar quality and is available in the trade area. The advertiser is responsible for ensuring that the advertised price of the comparable product does not exceed the price at which such product is actually being offered by representative retail outlets in the area.

Manufacturer's Suggested Retail Price

Another form of bargain price advertising is to advertise a price reduction from the manufacturer's suggested retail price. Many consumers believe that the manufacturer's list price or suggested retail price is the prevailing price. Accordingly, these consumers will assume that a price advertised as below the manufacturer's list price or suggested retail price represents a bargain price. If in fact, a substantial number of sales are not made at the manufacturer's price, an advertisement of a price below the manufacturer's price may mislead the consumer.

Frequently the manufacturer's price will be the price at which the product is sold for at the principal retail outlets for the product. At the same time the product may be offered at below the manufacturer's price in discount stores. The manufacturer's list price or suggested retail price will not be deemed to be fictitious if it is a price at which a substantial number of sales are being made in the advertiser's trade area. While this general principle applies both to national advertisers and to local advertisers, their duties to ensure that the advertising is not deceptive are somewhat different.

A local advertiser is expected to have at least a general idea of the prices being charged in his trade area. Therefore, before advertising his price as a reduction from the manufacturer's list price, he should ascertain whether the manufacturer's price is in fact the price regularly charged by the principal retail outlets in his trade area. However, if the manufacturer's price is being followed only by small suburban stores, house-to-house canvassers and credit houses accounting for an insubstantial volume of sales in the trade area, it would be deceptive to advertise a reduction from the manufacturer's price.

On the other hand, a national advertiser cannot reasonably be required to investigate the prevailing prices of its articles in each local trade area. Thus a manufacturer's advertised list price nationally should not exceed the highest price at which substantial sales are made in the trade area. However, the manufacturer must act in good faith in advertising a list price and may not affix an inflated preticketed price to the product to facilitate the offering of phony price reductions.

Example 13 *(Lawful Advertising)* The manufacturer of Brand X advertises Brand X in a national magazine as having a "suggested retail price $10." The price is determined by a market survey which establishes that in a substantial number of representative communities, the principal retail outlets make a substantial number of sales of Brand X at $10 in the regular course of business. The manufacturer has not advertised a fictitious price. A retailer in one of these communities may advertise "Brand X, manufacturer's suggested retail price, $10, our price $7.50."

Buy-One-Get-One-Free

Frequently a product will be marketed by offering additional merchandise if the consumer purchases a product at a certain price. Typical of the language used in advertising such bargains follows:

1. Buy-One-Get-One-Free
2. Free
3. Two-for-One-Sale
4. Half-Price Sale
5. Now 50% More
6. 1 Cent Sale
7. 50% Off

When such terms are used in advertising care must be taken not to mislead the consumer. All of the terms of the offer must be made clear at the outset.

In making such an offer, by increasing the regular price of the article required to be purchased, or decreasing the quantity or quality of the product the seller may unlawfully deceive the consumer.

Advertising "Wholesale" or "Factory" Prices

It is deceptive advertising for a retailer to offer goods for sale at "wholesale" prices when in fact a "retail" price is charged. Similarly, it is deceptive to advertise "factory" price, unless the price is that which is actually paid by those purchasing directly from the manufacturer.

Advertising Fur Products

The Fur Products Labeling Act (see Chapter 15) requires that all advertisements, representations, public announcements, or notices intended to aid and promote the sale of fur products reveal the following information:

1. The name of the animal that produced the fur in accordance with the fur products name guide
2. The country of origin of imported furs
3. Disclosure of the use of used, bleached, dyed or artifically colored fur

4. Disclosure of the use of waste furs.

Red Flag: Misleading illustrations of a fur product in advertising is unlawful.

Mail Fraud

Sending false advertising through the U.S. Mail can in some instances constitute a federal crime of mail fraud (see Chapter 16).

Advertising Credit Terms

Regulation Z implementing the federal Truth-in-Lending Act establishes certain requirements for advertising credit terms. Please consult Regulation Z found in Appendix C.

chapter thirteen

DEVELOPING A CONSUMER CREDIT AND COLLECTION PROGRAM

Providing credit to purchasers is an important part of many marketing programs. Because abuses have occurred both in the offering of credit and in the collection of debt a substantial body of law now regulates these activities. As with so many areas this book cannot substitute for the advice of a qualified attorney. Nonetheless, this chapter will provide the initial guidance necessary to develop a credit and collection program that can then be submitted to legal counsel for final review. It will provide a ready reference for dealing with day-to-day problems that will arise in administering a credit and collection program.

This chapter deals with consumer credit rather than commercial credit extended to a business. Business-to-business credit is covered largely by state enactments of the Uniform Commercial Code.

OFFERING CREDIT

A good starting point in establishing a credit program or in reviewing an existing program is to develop an awareness of the requirements of the Equal Credit Opportunity Act. The purpose of the act is, as its name suggests, to ensure that applicants for credit are not subject to discrimination because of race, color, religion, national origin, sex, age, marital status, because all or part of the applicant's income is derived from a public assistance program, or because the applicant has in good faith exercised rights granted by the Consumer Credit Protection Act.

175

Laws precluding discrimination are now a well-accepted part of the public policy of our nation. Discrimination may result from the offering of different credit terms depending on the applicants' status as well as by simple denials of credit. Failure to comply with the requirements of the Equal Credit Opportunity Act (ECOA) can result in civil liability and result in actual damages sustained plus punitive damages up to $10,000 plus attorney's fees (see Table 1).

In addition to legal actions brought by disappointed credit applicants individually or as a class, administrative enforcement may be brought by various government agencies as shown on Table 1.

What You Can Ask Under the Equal Credit Opportunity Act

A particularly troublesome area is obtaining background information to determine credit worthiness. Asking the wrong questions can inadvertently provide a disappointed credit applicant with a basis for making a discrimination claim. Employees involved in taking credit applications must be trained carefully to ensure compliance with the Equal Credit Opportunity Act.

The following good faith inquiries are not unlawful if not used for the purpose of discrimination.

1. Citizenship of applicant.
2. Marital status to determine the creditor's rights and remedies if credit is granted.
3. Inquiries regarding age and amount of public assistance received for the purpose of determining the amount and probable continuance of income levels.
4. Inquiries regarding the credit history of the applicant.
5. Other inquiries pertinent to determination of credit worthiness.

Key Point: Age can be considered as part of an empirically designed credit rating system if it is soundly designed. Age can be used to favor a creditor.

Actions Which Do Not Constitute Discrimination

By law certain actions taken by a creditor do not constitute discrimination. These actions are:

1. Requesting both parties to a marriage to sign a lien as long as the creditor does not consider sex or marital status in evaluating credit worthiness

2. Considering state property laws in determining credit worthiness

3. Extending credit to each party to a marriage separately when each party voluntarily applies separately, even if state law prohibits the separate extension of credit; federal law preempts state law in this regard

Key Point: When each party to a marriage voluntarily applies for and receives credit, the accounts cannot be combined for purposes of determining finance charges or loan ceilings.

What to Do When Credit Is Denied

Within 30 days of an application for credit, the creditor must notify the applicant of the action taken. When the action taken is adverse to the applicant, the notification must either set forth the reasons for the adverse action or notify the applicant that they have a right to receive a statement of the reasons for the adverse action. An adverse action is either a denial or revocation of credit or an unfavorable change in the terms of credit. In the latter case, the applicant must be informed that they have 60 days in which to request a statement of reasons. Upon receipt of a statement of reasons the creditor has 30 days in which to respond.

TIME CHART FOR ADVERSE NOTICE

Date of Application	
30 Days	Notice of Action. Action may contain statement of reasons for adverse action.
60 Days	Applicant may request statement of reasons.
30 Days	Creditor must supply statement of reasons.

Thus a total of 120 days may elapse between the initial credit application and the statement of reasons for the adverse action.

Key Point: The statement of reasons for an adverse action on a request for credit must contain specific reasons for the action.

Important Point: The Board of Governors for the Federal Reserve system has issued regulations governing the implementation of the act. The board is also authorized to exempt certain classes of credit in particular states if the state law provides protection equal to or greater than that provided by federal law. Legal counsel should be consulted regarding state law requirements.

FAIR CREDIT BILLING ACT

The informed use of credit promotes a stable economy. To promote an informed use of credit, Congress has determined that it is necessary to ensure that consumers understand the cost of the credit they obtain. Therefore Congress passed the Fair Credit Billing Act (FCBA). The FCBA is intended to assure that there is a meaningful disclosure of credit terms in consumer credit transactions and protects consumers from inaccurate and unfair billing practices. The act also applies to leases of consumer goods where leases are used as alternatives to installment credit sales. One thrust of the FCBA is to require that certain material facts be disclosed. The act is administered by the Board of Governors of the Federal Reserve System which has issued regulations implementing the act.

FCBA and State Laws

Many states have enacted laws covering the same matters covered by the FCBA. To the extent state laws are inconsistent with the FCBA, the FCBA governs. Where there is no inconsistency, the state law remains applicable. If the Federal Reserve Board determines that the state disclosure requirements are consistent with the FCBA a creditor may use the state disclosures rather than the federal disclosures. However, even when state disclosures are used the finance charges and the annual percentage rate (APR) charged must be disclosed in accordance with the federal disclosure requirements.

The FCBA does not annul or alter state laws concerning the types, amounts or rates of charges, or elements of charges allowed under state laws.

Key Point: It is important to consult legal counsel to ensure that credit forms used comply with applicable state and federal law.

Disclosures Required by the FCBA

The board is charged with providing by regulation for the form and data which must be disclosed. The disclosures must be clear and conspicuous with the APR and finance charges more conspicuous than the other data. The disclosure must be made to the party principally obligated by the extension of credit. A creditor or lessor may add additional information or explanation to the material required by law to be disclosed.

Open-End Consumer Credit Plans

Before opening an open-end consumer credit plan (OECCP), the creditor must disclose the following items:

1. When the finance charge may be imposed

2. Time period the credit is extended without imposition of a finance charge

3. The method for determining the balance which is subject to the finance charge

4. The method used to determine the amount of the finance charge including any minimum or fixed amount imposed as a finance charge

5. Each periodic rate that may be used to compute the finance charge, including the range of balances to which the rate is applicable and the corresponding nominal APR determined by multiplying the periodic rate by the number of periods in the year

6. Identification of any other charges that might be imposed as part of the plan or method of computation in accordance with the board's regulations

7. Whether a security interest will be taken in either

   a. Property purchased as part of the credit transaction

   b. Property not purchased as part of the credit transaction (such property must be identified by item or type)

8. A board proscribed statement of the protection given to the person obligated by the extension of credit and stating certain of the creditor's obligations under the act and regulations

Billing for OECCP

For each billing cycle in an open-end credit account where a finance charge is imposed or where there is an outstanding balance, the creditor must furnish a statement to the obligor showing:

1. Outstanding balance at the beginning of the statement period

2. Amount and date of each credit extension during the period and a brief identification of each credit transaction

   Key Point: A failure to provide the foregoing billing information is not a violation of the act if the creditor maintains reasonable procedures to provide such information and treats inquiries in accordance with the procedures for handling billing errors which are discussed below.

3. Total amount paid on the account during the billing cycle

4. Amount of any finance charge added to the account during the period, itemized to show amounts due to the application of percentage rates and amounts imposed as a minimum or fixed charge

5. Each rate and range of balances applicable where one or more periodic rates are used to compute a finance charge

6. APR

7. Balance on which the finance charge is computed and a statement showing how the balance is determined

8. Outstanding balance at the end of the period

9. Date by which payment must be made to avoid additional finance charges

10. Creditor's address for receiving billing inquiries

Handling Billing Errors

The board has established certain procedures and time periods for dealing with billing errors or claimed billing errors in open-end consumer credit plans. For purposes of the billing error regulations a billing error consists of any of the following items.

1. A statement showing a credit extension in a wrong amount or for a transaction not engaged in by the obligor

2. A transaction for which the obligor requests clarification or documentary evidence

3. A statement showing an extension of credit for goods not accepted by the obligor or undelivered to the obligor

4. Failure of the statement to properly reflect a payment made by the obligor or a credit issued to the obligor

5. A computation or accounting error

6. Failure to mail the statement to the last address the obligor has given to the creditor. However, mailing to an address given less than 20 days before the end of a billing cycle is sufficient

7. Any additional form or error that the board may identify by regulation

To bring an error to the attention of the creditor, the obligor must provide written notice to the creditor. The written notice must be sufficient to enable the creditor to identify the name and account number of the obligor, set forth the amount of the claimed billing error, and give reasons why the obligor believes there is an error.

Responding to an Alleged Billing Error

If the creditor receives notice of an alleged billing error within 60 days of having transmitted the required billing statement, the creditor must take one of the following courses of action.

1. The creditor can make the appropriate corrections in the account including crediting any finance charges or amounts erroneously billed and transmit to the obligor a notice of such corrections. Creditor shall also provide an explanation for any changes made in the charges to the account.

2. When the creditor does not agree that there is a billing error, the creditor shall send a written explanation to the obligor stating why the creditor believes the billing is correct. If obligor has requested documentation of the credit transaction, the creditor shall provide such documentation.

Key Point: When the alleged billing error is that the goods were not received, a creditor cannot consider the billing statement to be correct unless such goods were actually delivered or sent to the obligor.

BILLING ERROR TIMETABLE

Bill Sent	
60 days after bill sent	Last day for obligor to claim error
30 days after notice of error	Creditor sends written acknowledgement of claim of error or takes responsive action
2 billing cycles or no more than 90 days after notice of error	Creditor takes action in response to claim of billing error

Key Point: Even when a portion of a credit debt is subject to the error procedures, the creditor may take action to recover and collect any undisputed amounts.

Key Point: An amount subject to the error procedure cannot be reported as delinquent to a credit reporting agency until the error procedures have been completed. If the amount is still in dispute after the error procedures have been completed, the amount may be reported as a disputed amount but the creditor must provide the obligor with the name and address of each person to whom the disputed amount is reported.

Payment Without Incurring a Finance Charge

When the open-end consumer credit plan permits the obligor to make timely payments without incurring a finance charge, no finance charge may be imposed for late payments unless the billing statement is mailed at least 14 days prior to the date for payment to avoid finance charges.

Credit Balances in Consumer Credit Accounts

If a consumer credit account shows a credit balance of more than $1, the creditor must refund such amount on request of the obligor on the account. If no refund request is made but the credit balance remains for six months, the creditor must make a good faith effort to make a refund by cash, check, or money order.

What to Do When Goods Purchased by a Credit Card Are Returned

In a credit card sale, on acceptance of a return of the goods sold, the seller must promptly transmit a credit statement to the card issuer. The card issuers must then credit the purchaser's account.

Cash Discount

A credit card issuer cannot prevent a seller from offering buyers a discount for cash purchases. A cash discount does not constitute a finance charge if the discount is offered to all prospective buyers and the availabilty of the discount is clearly and conspicuously disclosed.

THE DEBT COLLECTION PROCESS

The debt collection process has been subject to great abuse over the years. Creditors have resorted to deceptive and unfair practices in an effort to collect debt. Abusive debt collection practices contribute to personal bankruptcy, marital instability, job loss, and invasion of privacy. To eliminate abusive debt collection practices Congress enacted the Fair Debt Collection Practices Act (FDCPA). The FDCPA applies generally to the actions of third-party debt collections. It does not apply to the creditor's actions in trying to collect its own debt unless the creditor uses a name other than its own indicating to the consumer/obligor that a third-party collection agency is involved. Moreover, the act does not apply to the efforts of an officer or employee of the creditor collecting debts owed to the creditor in the creditor's name.

Since a seller can easily avoid having to worry about the Fair Debt Collection Practices Act by simply acting in its own name, the details of the act will not be discussed here.

Key Point: Many states have enacted statutes regulating debt collection. Federal law does not invalidate these state laws unless the state law is inconsistent with the FDCPA. Even then the state law is invalid only to the extent of the inconsistency. Therefore, counsel should be consulted to determine the applicability of any state statute.

USURY LAWS

State laws prohibiting usury must be consulted since variation exists. Usury may be defined as a bargain in which the debtor agrees to pay a rate of interest which is greater than the legal rate of interest. State statutes typically describe how the rate of interest is to be calculated and then set limits for the rate of interest that can be charged. For example, the Colorado Consumer Credit Code states that for nonrevolving credit interest may not exceed:

1. 25 percent per year on a balance of $600 or less, 20 percent per year on amounts of more than $600 or less than $2100 and 15 percent per year on amounts of $2100 or more; or
2. 21 percent per year on the unpaid balance of the amount financed.

For revolving credit, in Colorado the interest billed monthly cannot exceed 1¾ percent of the average daily balance.

Red Flag: Contracts which include a usurious interest rate are illegal and unenforceable.

Key Point: State usury laws are generally designed to protect consumers rather than merchants and do not apply to the extension of credit to businesses.

FAIR CREDIT REPORTING ACT

The widespread use of credit has become a cornerstone of our consumer economy. Congress has determined that the American banking system depends on fair and accurate credit reports. Consumer reporting agencies have assumed a vital role in assembling and evaluating consumer credit and other information on consumers. It is important that consumer reporting agencies exercise their responsibilities fairly and impartially and with respect for the consumer's right of privacy. Accordingly, Congress enacted the Fair Credit Reporting Act to ensure that information is gathered and disseminated with due regard for confidentiality, accuracy, relevancy, and proper use.

The Fair Credit Reporting Act can be violated by users of credit information as well as by consumer reporting agencies which gather and disseminate credit information. For that reason it is important that marketers who extend credit have a passing familiarity with the requirements of the act.

How to Comply with the Fair Credit Reporting Act

The act imposes certain requirements on users of information supplied by a consumer reporting agency. When credit or insurance is denied or the charge for credit is increased to a consumer based on a report by a comsumer reporting agency, the user of the information must advise the consumer of the action taken and must supply the consumer with the name and address of the consumer reporting agency that furnished the credit report.

If credit is denied or the charge for credit is increased based on information obtained from a source other than a consumer reporting agency, the information relied on must be disclosed to the consumer if the consumer makes a written request for such information within 60 days after learning of the adverse action. The user must clearly and conspicuously disclose to the consumer his or her right to request such information at the time the consumer is notified of the adverse credit action.

Key Point: The user of such credit information will not be liable for a violation of these requirements if the user can establish by a preponderance of evidence that the user maintains reasonable procedures to ensure compliance.

State Laws

The Fair Credit Reporting Act does not preclude the operation of state laws relating to the collection, distribution, or use of credit information unless the state law is inconsistent with the federal law.

FEDERAL TRUTH-IN-LENDING ACT

The Federal Truth-in-Lending Act is intended to assure a meaningful disclosure of credit terms so that the consumer will be able to compare various credit terms available. The Board of Governors of the Federal Reserve Bank has issued Regulation Z to implement the Truth-in-Lending Act and the Fair Credit Billing Act. Regulation Z is lengthy and complex and a copy should be obtained and kept at hand for guidance in consumer lending. This book provides an overview for quick reference and guidance to the provisions of the Regulation Z. An abridged copy of Regulation Z may be found in Appendix C.

Regulation Z is divided into four subparts.

Subpart A

Subpart A provides general information regarding the regulation's coverage and organization. It also contains definitions, defines exempt transactions, and describes methods of determining what finance charges are.

Subpart B

Subpart B contains rules applicable to open-end credit transactions. Included are the disclosure requirements and the provision for periodic billing statements. Also covered are rules applicable to credits and account transactions, treatment of payments and credit balances, procedures for resolving billing errors, annual percentage rate, rescission requirements, and advertising. (*Note:* Certain requirements regarding billing practices are discussed above under the Fair Credit Billing Act.)

Subpart C

Subpart C contains regulations relating to disclosure, treatment of credit balances, annual percentage rate calculations, and rescission requirements for closed-end credit.

Subpart D

Subpart D includes miscellaneous regulations relating to such matters as oral disclosures, the effect of state laws, and Spanish language disclosures.

SUBPART A

For purposes of Regulation Z a credit sale is one in which the seller is a creditor and the consumer:

i. Agrees to pay as compensation for the use of the credit a sum substantially equivalent to, or in excess of, the total value of the property and services involved

ii. Will become or has the option to become the owner of the property on compliance of the agreement for no additional consideration or for only a nominal consideration

A creditor is any of the following persons:

1. A person who regularly extends consumer credit subject to a finance charge or payable by more than four installments and to whom the obligation is initially payable

2. An arranger of credit

3. A person that honors a credit card

4. For Subpart B, a credit card issuer that extends either open-end credit or credit that is not subject to a finance charge and is not payable by written agreement in more than four installments

5. For Subparts B and C, a credit card issuer that extends closed-end credit that is subject to a finance charge or is payable by written agreement in more than four installments

Finance charges are defined as the cost of consumer credit in a dollar amount paid by the consumer as an incident to or condition of the extension of credit. It does not include any charge that would be payable in a comparable cash transaction. Examples of items possibly included in finance charges are listed in Table 2. Charges which are excluded from finance charges are listed in Table 3. Certain security interest charges may be excluded from finance charges if they are itemized and disclosed. These charges are listed in Table 4. Premiums for credit life, accident, health, or loss of income insurance may be excluded from the finance charge if the following conditions are met.

A. Premiums for credit life, accident, health or loss of income may be excluded from finance charge if:

1. The insurance coverage is not required by the creditor and that fact is disclosed.

2. The premium for the initial term of the coverage disclosed. If the term is less than the term of the transaction the insurance term shall also be disclosed. The premium may be disclosed on a unit cost basis only in open-end credit transactions, closed-end credit transactions by mail or telephone under §226.17(g) and certain closed-end credit transactions involving an insurance plan limiting the total amount of indebtedness subject to coverage.

3. The consumer signs or initials an affirmation of written request for the insurance after receiving the disclosures. Any consumer may sign or initial the request.

B. Insurance premiums for loss of or for damage to property or liability arising out of used or property ownership may be excluded if:

1. The insurance coverage can be obtained from a person of the consumer's choice and that fact is disclosed.

2. If coverage is obtained through the creditor, the premium for the initial term shall be disclosed. If the term of the insurance is less than the term of the transaction, the term of the insurance shall also be disclosed. The premium may be disclosed on a unit cost basis only in open-end credit transactions.

SUBPART B

The general disclosure requirements contained in Subpart B of Regulation Z are discussed above under the Fair Credit Billing Act.

Subpart B also provides rules pertaining to a consumer's right to rescind when a security interest is or will be taken in the consumer's principal dwelling. In any credit transaction giving rise to a right to rescind, the creditor is required to provide the obligor with two copies of the notice of the right to rescind. The notice of the right to rescind must identify the credit transaction and must clearly disclose:

1. Retention or acquisition of a security interest in the consumer's principal dwelling

2. Existence of the consumer's right to rescind

3. Method for exercising the right to rescind together with a form for that purpose designating the creditor's place of business

4. Effects of recession

5. Date the recession period expires

The right to rescind is to be exercised in writing prior to midnight of the third business day following the credit transaction giving rise to the security interest. If the writing is sent by U. S. mail, it is given when mailed. If notice is given by telegraph, it is given when filed for transmission. If the notice is sent by any other means, it is deemed to be given when received at the creditor's place of business.

A consumer may give a written waiver of the right to rescind when credit is deemed necessary by the consumer to meet a bona fide personal financial emergency. Unless the consumer waives the right to rescind, no moneys are to be disbursed except to an escrow account and no goods or services provided until expiration of the rescission period and the creditor is reasonably satisfied that the consumer has not rescinded.

This chapter merely alerts the reader to the type of problems encountered in providing credit. Regulation Z should be consulted along with legal counsel prior to establishing a credit program. Of course when credit is extended by a third party as it is in credit card transactions, the obligations of the seller are substantially reduced. Most of the burden is shifted from the seller to the third party who extends the credit. The ability to shift much of the burden of complying with the laws governing credit transactions to third parties makes it practicable for small business to sell on credit.

Key Point: This chapter deals with consumer credit. It does not deal with various forms of financing offered by manufacturers to wholesalers or distributors.

TABLE 1

ECOA Agency Enforcement

• Under Federal Deposit Insurance Act (12 U.S.C.S. 1818) by Comptroller of Currency, Federal Reserve Banks by the Federal Reserve Board, FDIC insured banks by Board of Directors of FDIC

- Under 12 U.S.C.S. §146d, 12 U.S.C.S. §1730, 12 U.S.C.S. §1426i, §1437 (Home owner and housing statutes) by Federal Home Loan Bank Board acting directly or through FSLIC in case of institutions subject to those provisions
- Under Federal Credit Union Act enforced by Administrator of Nation Credit Union Administration for any Federal Credit Union
- Acts regulating commerce enforced by Interstate Commerce Commission
- Under Federal Aviation Act of 1958 by Civil Aeronautics Board with respect to any air carrier of foreign air carrier subject to the act
- Under Packers and Stockyards Act by Secretary of Agriculture
- Under Farm Credit Act of 1971 by Farm Credit Administration
- Under Securities Exchange Act of 134 by SEC
- Under Small Business Investment Act by the Small Business Administration

  Any violation of the ECOA shall be deemed a violation of the Federal Statutes granting the agencies listed above enforcement powers
- If the enforcement agency is not specifically listed above, then the Federal Trade Commission is the enforcing agency

---

TABLE 2

Items Included in Finance Charges

- Interest, time price differential, amount payable under an add on, or discount system of charges
- Service, transaction, activity, and carry charges
- Loan fee, finders fee, assumption fees, and similar charges
- Appraisal, investigation, and credit report fees
- Premiums or other charges for any guarantee of insurance protecting creditor against consumer's default
- Charges imposed on a creditor by another for accepting or purchasing a consumer's obligation if the consumer is required to pay charges in cash as an addition to the obligation
- Premiums or other charges for life, accident, and so on, insurance

- Premiums or other insurance charges against property loss or damages
- Discounts for purposes of inducing payment by means other than use of credit

---

TABLE 3

Items Excluded from Finance Charges

- Credit application fees
- Charges for actual unanticipated late payment for exceeding credit limit delinquency, default, or similar acts
- Fees for participating in a credit plan
- Charges imposed by financial institutions for payment for overdraw, unless payment previously agreed on in writing
- Sellers points
- Interest forfeited by law on time deposit used as security for an extension of credit
- Fees related to getting a real property mortgage if they are bona fide and reasonable: (i) title examination, (ii) deed preparation, mortgages and reconveyance, settlement and similar documents, (iii) notary appraisal and credit report fees, (iv) amounts required to be paid in escrow or trustee accounts if the amounts could not otherwise be included in the finance charges.

TABLE 4

Security Interest Charges
Which May Be Excluded from Finance Charges

- Taxes and fees prescribed by law that are or will be paid to public officials for determining existence of or perfecting, releasing, or satisfying a security interest
- Premium for insurance in lieu of perfecting security interest to extent that premium does not exceed the fee in (e) (1) or section 226.4(e)(1) of Regulation Z

chapter fourteen

WHAT YOU SHOULD KNOW ABOUT WARRANTIES AND PRODUCT RECALLS

In the past 20 years, the rise of the consumer movement has made the public more aware of the value, terms, and conditions of warranties. As a result, more companies are using warranties as a marketing tool. Warranties often contain complex provisions that may confuse and deceive consumers. The use of warranties is subject to regulation by both state and federal statutes. Moreover, the use of common warranties by competitors may violate the antitrust laws by restraining competition in the provision of warranty terms. Thus competitors should not agree to offer certain warranty provisions. Rather, each firm should design its own warranty program unilaterally. In discussing warranties, it is useful to distinguish between warranties attached to sales between merchants which are subject to the Uniform Commercial Code and warranties attached to sales to ultimate consumers which are subject to federal law as well as state law. The focus of this chapter is consumer warranties.

CONSUMER WARRANTIES

In addition to any state remedies that may be available to consumers under warranties, Congress has enacted the Magnuson-Moss Warranty/Federal Trade Commission Improvement Act to impose certain restrictions governing the use of warranties. The federal act covers tangible personal property which is distributed in commerce and normally used for personal, family, or household purposes. The act deals with three problem areas associated with consumer warranties.

The first is disclosure. The act requires the disclosure of certain information to the consumer if the seller makes use of a written warranty. The matters which must be disclosed are set forth in regulations promulgated by the Federal Trade Commission.

The second problem area treated by the Magnuson-Moss Act is the definition of the scope of the warranty. Warranties are divided into limited warranties and full warranties. If a written warranty is used, the warranty must state whether it is full or limited.

The third area covered by the act is the extent and nature of the remedies of the consumer under the warranty. The statute and the Federal Trade Commission regulations encourage the development of informal, exclusive, objective, and fair procedures for the resolution of warranty disputes. However, the statute does not require the seller to provide any procedures for the resolution of warranty disputes. The supplier may simply leave resolution of such disputes to the courts.

Warranties covered by the act are defined as promises or affirmations of fact made in connection with the sale of a consumer product which affirm or promise that the material or workmanship sold is defect free or will meet a specified level of performance over a specified period of time or that the supplier will refund, repair, replace, or otherwise remedy the situation if the product fails to meet certain specifications.

MAGNUSON-MOSS WRITTEN WARRANTIES

Written warranties under the Magnuson-Moss Act are divided into full warranties and limited warranties. The act sets forth standards that the warranty must meet if it is to be designated as a full warranty. On the sale of any consumer good worth more than $10 in which the warranty does not meet the standards for a full warranty, it must be conspicuously designated a limited warranty. If the statutory standards are met, then the warranty must be designated as a full warranty. Both full and limited warranties may be offered with respect to various parts of a product. In such cases the warranties must be clearly and conspicuously differentiated. (Sample warranties are given on pages 206 through 207.) The minimum standards for a full warranty are:

1. The warrantor must remedy the defect, malfunction or failure within a reasonable time and without charge.

2. No limitation may be placed on the duration of any implied warranties.

3. The warrantor may not exclude or limit consequential damages for breach of any written or implied warranty, unless the exclusion or limitation is conspicuous on the face of the warranty.

4. If the warrantor is not able to remedy the defects in the product within a reasonable number of tries, the warrantor must permit the consumer to select either a refund or a replacement without charge.

5. The warrantor can not require the consumer to perform any duty other than notification as a condition for securing a remedy for any product malfunctions, defects or failures to conform to the written warranty. (Unless the warrantor can prove that the imposition of some additional duty is reasonable.)

Any warranty designated a full warranty will bind the warrantor to the requirements for full warranties under the act. For example, use of the term "full five-year warranty" cannot be used to describe a limited warranty that lasts a full five years. Rather it will be construed to mean a statutory full warranty. Any warranty not intended to meet the statutory requirements for a full warranty must be clearly described as a "limited warranty," e. g. "limited five-year warranty." The Federal Trade Commission discourages use of the words "guaranty" or "guarantee." Entitling a warranty as "manufacturer's warranty and limitation of liability" is unlawful because the statute requires that only the terms "full warranty" or "limited warranty" be used.

Who Is Liable on Warranty?

Ordinarily only the supplier making the warranty is liable to action by the Federal Trade Commission or private civil suit. A retailer who merely sells a product subject to a manufacturer's warranty is not liable on the warranty. However, the retailer's actions under the laws of some states may be deemed to be an adoption of the supplier's warranty making the retailer liable.

A written distribution agreement should include provisions dealing with the respective warranty obligations of the manufacturer and the distributor. For example, the agreement should state whether the distributor has any duty to make warranty repairs and the obligation of the supplier or manufacturer to reimburse the distributor for warranty repairs. A more detailed discussion of distribution agreements is found in Appendix A.

Expressions of Policy Which Are Not Warranties

General expressions of company policy concerning customers satisfaction which are not subject to any specific limitations need not be designated as full or limited warranties. However, Section 5 of the Federal Trade Commission Act relating to unfair and deceptive practices is applicable as are the enforcement provisions of the Magnuson-Moss Act.

Examples of such general policy statements are:

>"satisfaction guaranteed"
>
>"money back guaranty"
>
>"free trial offer"

Such phrases should only be used in advertising a product if the seller or manufacturer refunds the full purchase price of the product at the buyer's request.

Under the Federal Trade Commission guides the following advertising language is permissible:

> We guarantee your satisfaction. If not completely satisfied with Acme Spot Remover, return the unused portion within 30 days for a full refund.

> Money Back Guarantee! Just return the ABC watch in its original package and ABC will fully refund your money.

Who May Claim Performance of a Warranty?

Under the Magnuson-Moss Act the warranty must extend to any consumer to whom the product is transferred during the duration of the warranty. Thus a full five-year warranty must extend to John who purchases the product originally, to Mary who buys it from John two years later, and to Joe who buys it from Mary one year later. It does not extend to Harry who buys it from Joe four years later because the original five-year term of the warranty has expired. A full warranty may not restrict the warranty rights of a transferee of the purchaser during the term of the warranty. However, a warranty may be limited in duration by its terms to the initial purchaser. For example, an automobile battery may be sold with a warranty designated as a "full warranty for as long as you own your car." Subsequent purchasers of the car would have no rights under the warranty.

When "life" or "lifetime" warranties are advertised the advertising must make it clear what "life" is used to measure the duration of the guarantee. The Federal Trade Commission guidelines provide the following examples of permissible "lifetime" warranty advertisements.

> Our lifetime guarantee on the Whisper Muffler protects you as long as your car runs—even if you sell it, trade it, or give it away.

> Our battery is backed by our lifetime guarantee. Good for as long as you own the car.

When a product is sold with a warranty limited to the first owner, the

Federal Trade Commission rules preclude the manufacturer from requiring the purchaser to present documentary proof that the purchaser was the first owner. However, the manufacturer can ask consumers to affirm that they are the first owner of the warranted product.

Warranty Registration Cards

Manufacturers frequently want to use warranty registration cards as a means of gathering marketing data. In order to ensure return of the warranty registration cards the manufacturer may desire to condition warranty coverage on return of the registration card.

Key Point: Return of a warranty registration card cannot be made a condition of warranty coverage under a full warranty. However, under a full warranty limited to a fixed time such as "full five-year warranty," return of a warranty registration card may be used as a nonexclusive means of proving date of purchase.

Service Contracts Distinguished

A service contract is distinguished from warranty under the Magnuson-Moss Act under the following circumstances:

1. It calls for some payment by the purchaser in addition to the purchase price of the product.
2. It relates to inspection, cleaning, or maintenance of the product but does not include a promise of a level of performance or an affirmation that the product is free of defects in materials or workmanship.

Insurance Policies Distinguished

Some contracts between manufacturers and purchasers may meet the statutory standards for a warranty or service contract but under state law are treated as insurance policies. When such contracts are in fact regulated by the state as insurance they are not subject to the Magnuson-Moss Act.

Red Flag: If the agreement departs from simple warranty language and thus may be treated as a policy of insurance under state law, consult legal counsel.

> *Example.*   Policies of automobile breakdown insurance are regulated by the insurance laws of many states.

WHEN THE TERMS OF THE WARRANTY MUST BE MADE AVAILABLE TO THE PURCHASER

The Federal Trade Commission rules place different duties on sellers and manufacturers to make known the terms of a warranty prior to the time of sale.

1. *Duties of Manufacturer or Warrantor.* The Federal Trade Commission requires warrantors of products costing more than $15 to do the following:

   a. Provide sellers of the product with sufficient warranty material to satisfy the duties placed upon sellers by doing any of the following:

      i. Providing a copy of the warranty with each warranted product

      ii. Providing a tag, sign, sticker, label, decal, or other attachment to the product which contains the full text of the written warranty

      iii. Printing or attaching the full written text of the warranty on the carton, container or case, used to display the product

      iv. Providing a notice, sign or poster disclosing the text of the warranty

   b. Providing a notice, sign or poster disclosing the text of the warranty

2. *Duties of Sellers.* The seller of a warranted product has a duty to make the text of the written warranty readily available for examination by the buyer. For in-store sellers this duty may be satisfied by either of the following methods:

   a. Displaying a copy of the text of the written warranty in close proximity to the display of the warranted product

   b. Furnishing a copy of the text of the written warranty to prospective purchasers upon request and by placing prominent signs in the store or department advising prospective purchasers of the availability of warranties for inspection

Duties of Catalog and Mail-Order Sellers

Catalog and mail-order sales include all offers for sale of a consumer product covered by a written warranty including instructions for ordering the product without a personal visit to the seller's establishment. Persons making sales of warranted products by catalog or mail-order sales must do either

1. Inform the prospective purchaser that a copy of the written warranty may be obtained free by writing to a specified address

2. Displaying the full text of the warranty either on the page on which the product is displaced or on the facing page or in an information section of the catalog which is referenced on the page or facing page on which the product is displayed

Duties of Door-To-Door Sellers

Door-to-door sales of consumer products include all personal solicitations for sales made at a location other than the seller's place of business. Persons making door-to-door sales of warranted consumer products must notify prospective purchasers both orally and in any written materials that the seller has copies of the written warranty available for inspection by the prospective buyer at any time during the sales presentation.

Limitations on Implied Warranties

Implied warranties are described in more detail. A full warranty may not place any limitation on the duration of implied warranties. On the other hand, if only a limited warranty is offered, implied warranties may be limited to the duration of the limited warranty.

If limitations are placed on the duration of implied warranties, they must be accompanied by the following statement:

> Some states do not allow limitations on how long an implied warranty lasts, so the above limitation may not apply to you.

What Warranty Terms Must Be Disclosed

Under rules adopted by the Federal Trade Commission to implement the Magnuson-Moss Act, any warrantor of a consumer product costing more than $15 must clearly and conspicuously disclose in a single document the following items:

- The identity of the persons entitled to the protection provided by the warranty

- A clear description of the parts, products or components covered by the warranty

- A statement of what the warrantor will do in the event of a defect, malfunction, or failure to conform to the written warranty

- The date on which the warranty commences if different than the purchase date and any limitation on the duration of the warranty

- A step-by-step explanation of the procedure required for the purchaser to obtain performance of the warrantor's obligation under the warranty

- Information respecting any informal dispute mechanism available to settle disputes arising from the warranty

- Any limitation on the duration of implied warranties

- Any exclusions or limitations on relief such as restrictions on the recovery of consequential damages. Any such limitation must be accompanied by the following statement:

  > Some states do not allow the exclusion or limitation of incidental or consequential damages, so the above limitation or exclusion may not apply to you.

- The following statement must also be included in any written warranty:

  > This warranty gives you specific legal rights, and you may also have other rights which vary from state to state.

How to Establish an Informal Dispute Mechanism

The Magnuson-Moss Act does not require a warrantor to adopt an informal mechanism for resolving disputes arising under warranties although warrantors are encouraged to do so. If an informal dispute mechanism is created by the warrantor, the consumer may be required to resort to informal dispute resolution prior to commencing any legal action for violation of the warranty.

Any informal mechanism adopted by the warrantor must conform to the Federal Trade Commission's Informal Dispute Settlement Mechanism rules. If the warrantor utilizes an informal dispute settlement mechanism, the warrantor must make certain disclosures regarding the mechanism *on the face of the warranty*. The following items must be disclosed:

1. Statement that the dispute mechanism is available

2. Name and address or telephone number of the dispute settlement organization

3. Statement as to whether a consumer must first resort to the dispute settlement organization before seeking a remedy under the Magnuson-Moss Act

4. Statement that the consumer does *not* have to resort to the dispute mechanism before pursuing any legal remedies outside of those created by the Magnuson-Moss Act

5. Statement as to whether additional information relating to the informal dispute settlement mechanism is included in the materials accompanying the product

The warrantor must also include in the written warranty or in separate materials accompanying the product either

1. A form addressed to the dispute settlement organization containing spaces for the information required for a prompt resolution of the dispute

2. A toll-free telephone number for the dispute settlement organization.

In addition, the warrantor must include the following information either somewhere on the warranty or in other materials accompanying the product:

a. The name and address of the dispute settlement organization

b. A brief description of the settlement procedures

c. The time limits adhered to by the settlement organization

d. The types of information which the settlement organization may require for prompt resolution of warranty disputes

Warrantor's Duties to Cooperate

The warrantor has a duty to act in good faith both to fulfill its responsibilities under the warranty and if a dispute settlement organization is used to cooperate with the settlement process. If the dispute is submitted directly to the warrantor, the warrantor has a reasonable amount of time to determine whether and to what extent it will act to satisfy the consumer. The warrantor must then notify the consumer of its decision. In notifying the consumer of its decision, the warrantor must also provide the consumer with information regarding the informal dispute settlement organization unless, of course, the warrantor has decided to fully satisfy the consumer.

Once a dispute has been referred to a dispute settlement organization, the statute places additional duties on the warrantor to cooperate with the organization. These duties are to:

1. Respond fully and promptly to any reasonable requests for information relating to disputes

2. Comply with any reasonable requirements imposed by the settlement organization to fairly and expeditiously resolve warranty disputes

3. On notification by the organization of any decision that would require action by the warrantor to immediately notify the organization whether and to what extent it will abide by the decision

4. Act in good faith in determining whether it will abide by the decision of the settlement organization

5. Perform any obligations it has agreed to perform

Eleven Required Settlement Organization Procedures

In order to ensure fairness to the consumer in dispute settlements, the Federal Trade Commission Rules establish minimum procedure requirements that must be observed by the settlement organization.

Red Flag: The warrantor must ensure that the settlement organization is adequately funded and competently staffed to ensure fair and expeditious dispute resolution. Further, the warrantor is responsible for making certain that the settlement organization meets the minimum, requirements of the act. Therefore, prior to selecting a settlement organization, the warrantor must investigate the organization for compliance with the act.

The minimum procedural requirements which a dispute settlement organization must meet are:

1. On notification of a dispute the organization must immediately inform both the warrantor and the consumer of the receipt of the dispute.

2. Investigate, gather, and organize all information necessary for a fair and expeditious decision in each dispute.

3. When contradictory evidence is presented, the organization must notify both parties and provide them the opportunity to explain, rebut or submit additional evidence.

4. If the dispute has not been settled, the organization must render its decision within 40 days unless the decision is delayed:

   a. For up to seven days because the consumer had made no attempt to obtain a remedy directly from the warrantor

   b. Where the delay in issuing the decision is due *solely* to the failure of the consumer to provide promptly name, address, the brand name, product number, and a statement of the nature of complaint.

5. Include in its decision any remedies appropriate under the circumstances, including repair, replacement, refund, reimbursement for expenses, compensation for damages, or any other remedy available under the written warranty or under the act. Further, the decision shall state a reasonable time for performance by the warrantor.

6. Disclose the decision to the warrantor including its reasons for the decision.

7. Determine whether and to what extent the warrantor will abide by the decision.

8. Disclose to the consumer its decision, the reasons for its decision, and the warrantor's intended actions.

9. At the time of disclosing its decision to the consumer, the organization must also inform the consumer that:

   a. If the consumer is dissatisfied with the decision or the warrantor's intended or eventual performance, the consumer may pursue legal remedies including small claims court

   b. The organization's decision is admissible in evidence in a court proceeding

   c. The consumer may obtain copies of the organization's records of the dispute for a reasonable cost.

10. Ascertain from the consumer whether the warrantor has performed within ten working days of the date for performance.

11. Oral presentations will be heard by the organization only if both parties agree to an oral presentation.

Key Point: Neither party is bound by the decision of the settlement organization. However, the decision of the organization is admissible in evidence in any action brought under the Magnuson-Moss Act.

Record Keeping

The Federal Trade Commission rules impose extensive record keeping requirements on settlement organizations. The records must be retained for four years; an audit of the settlement organization must be conducted annually, and the results reported to the Federal Trade Commission. The audit is mainly to determine whether the organization and its activities are in compliance with the Federal Trade Commission rules. Among the items covered by the audit is an evaluation of the warrantor's efforts to make consumers aware of the informal dispute mechanism.

Why Use an Informal Dispute Settlement Mechanism?

Review of the extensive and detailed regulations governing the use of an informal dispute resolution mechanism may lead one to question whether it is worth the effort to use such a mechanism. In deciding whether to utilize a settlement mechanism the following points should be considered:

1. The complexities of establishing a mechanism are only encountered during the set up period.

2. Without the informal mechanism, the warrantor may be called on to defend itself in courts all over the country far from its principal place of business rather than at one centralized place.

3. A corporation frequently is not allowed to appear in court without an attorney. That is, a local employee of the warrantor cannot represent the corporation in court. On the other hand, most disputes subject to an informal mechanism will not require use of a lawyer.

4. The informal process will be less expensive and will require a great deal less of management's time.

5. Adoption of an informal dispute resolution mechanism provides the warrantor with one last chance to head-off litigation and satisfy the customer. There is often a chance that if a disgruntled consumer does go to court, he or she will bring a class action suit rather than just suing for self injuries.

Warranty Remedies Under the Magnuson-Moss Act

Private parties may not bring a civil action under the Magnuson-Moss Act until they have first resorted to an informal dispute resolution mechanism established by the warrantor. Consumers may bring an action under the act in either state or federal court for damages plus costs and attorneys fees. Consumers may also obtain injunctive relief.

The statute makes it a violation of the Federal Trade Commission Act for any person to fail to comply with the provisions of the Magnuson-Moss Act or the Federal Trade Commission rules and regulations implementing the act. Therefore, the Federal Trade Commission and the U. S. Attorney General can bring proceedings in U. S. District Courts to restrain

1. Any warrantor from making a deceptive warranty

2. Any person from failing to comply with the statute or the Federal Trade Commission rules and regulations.

Product Specific Warranty Regulations

From time to time the Federal Trade Commission has adopted regulations relating to the use of warranties for the sale of specific types of consumer products. Legal counsel should be consulted to determine the precise requirements for warranties for these products. Particular note should be taken of the following.

Sales of Used Motor Vehicles. It is declared to be a deceptive practice to sell a used car without a warranty when representing that there is a warranty or misrepresent the terms of a warranty. A Buyer's Guide form must be displayed on the side window of the car.

Textile Labeling. The commission has approved the use of invoice statements which also serve as warranty statements for the proper labeling of textiles. The warrantor warrants "that the merchandise is properly labeled as to content as required by the applicable Federal Trade Commission trade practice rules." For parties with products subject to more than one labeling act, the commission suggests use of the following language on the invoice:

> The undersigned hereby guarantees that the merchandise covered and delivered under this invoice is not misbranded, falsely invoiced, or falsely advertised under the Fur Products Labeling Act, and that reasonable and representative tests of such merchandise made under the procedures provided in Section 4 of the Flammable Fabrics Act show that it is not so highly flammable as to be dangerous when worn by individuals. The undersigned further warrants that the merchandise is properly labeled as to content as required by applicable Federal Trade Commission trade practice rules.
>
> John Doe Company
> Address_____

Other more specific language may also be used. The regulations regarding the Fur Products Labeling Act, Wool Products Labeling Act, Flammable Fabrics Act, and the Textile Fiber Products Identification Act should be consulted.

Antitrust Problems Arising from Warranties

In most instances the use of warranties will not raise any antitrust concerns. One area which the Federal Trade Commission has recognized as creating potential antitrust problems involved the circulation by a trade association among its members of a proposed warranty plan. The Federal Trade Commission noted that the most probable result of circulation of the proposed warranty would be the adoption of anticompetitive uniform terms and conditions by the members of the association.

Another antitrust problem with warranty use is the potential for coercing tie-in sales. Tie-in sales are discussed in detail in Chapter 8. Moreover the Magnuson-Moss Act specifically prohibits arrangements that condition coverage under a written warranty on the consumer's use of an article or service identified by brand, trade, or corporate name unless the article or service is provided to the consumer free of charge.

Key Point: The continued validity of a written warranty can not be conditioned on the use of only authorized parts or services for items not covered by the warranty.

Under a limited warranty providing only for the replacement of defective parts and which does not cover labor charges, the warrantor cannot require that the consumer use only labor approved by the warrantor. This would unlawfully tie the warranty to the labor used to replace the defective part.

IMPLIED WARRANTIES

Unless expressly excluded or modified when a manufacturer sells its product, there is an implied warranty that the product is of merchantable quality. To be of merchantable quality goods must meet the following requirements:

1. They must pass without objection in the trade as fitting the description under which they are sold.

2. In the case of fungible goods, they must be of fair average quality.

3. They must be fit for the ordinary purposes for which such goods are used.

4. The goods must be of even quality, kind and quantity within each unit and among all units involved.

5. The goods must be adequately contained, packaged, and labeled as the sales agreement may require.

6. They must conform to the promises or affirmations of fact made on the container or label.

The implied warranty simply establishes a minimum level of warranty and the parties remain free to set a higher level by contract. Implied warranties exist regardless of any intent by the seller and without any showing of reliance by the buyer.

If at the time a sale is made, the seller has reason to know the particular purpose for which the goods are desired and knows that the buyers are relying on the seller's skill or judgment to select or furnish suitable goods, there is an implied warranty that the goods are fit for the intended purpose. This implied warranty of fitness for a particular purpose may be excluded or modified by an express agreement of the buyer and seller.

Key Point: The seller must know that the buyer is relying upon the seller's skill and judgment to select the appropriate good.

Note: Implied warranties of merchantability and fitness for a particular purpose are not mutually exclusive. Accordingly, both implied warranties may be created by a single sale.

SALE BY SAMPLE OR DESCRIPTION

An express warranty of conformity attaches to a sale by sample when the sample is a part of the basis of the bargain. A sale by sample is made, where the sale is made on the basis of a sample of the goods sold. When the sale is made both by an express warranty and by sample or model, the goods must conform to the express warranty.

The significance of a sale by sample warranty is similar to that of a sale by description. Any description of the goods sold is an express warranty if it is part of the basis of the bargain. Thus, if certain specifications for the good are a part of the basis of the bargain, the goods must conform to the specifications.

WARRANTY OF TITLE

Unless the circumstances put the buyer on notice that a third party claims an interest in the goods, a contract for sale of goods implies a warranty by the seller that:

1. Title to the goods conveyed is good title and the transfer of title to the buyer is lawful.

2. The goods are delivered free from any lien, encumbrance or security interest.

3. If the sale is made by a merchant regularly dealing in goods of the kind sold that the goods are delivered free of any rightful claim by a third party of infringement.

LIMITED WARRANTY EXAMPLE

——————————— LIMITED WARRANTY ———————————

This product is warranted against defects for one year from the date of purchase. During the warranty period, the product will be repaired without charge for parts and labor. Simply bring your sales slip as proof of the date of purchase. This warranty does not cover transportation costs nor does it cover a product subjected to accident or misuse.

Except AS PROVIDED HEREIN, XYZ COMPANY MAKES NO WAR-RANTIES, EXPRESS OR IMPLIED, INCLUDING WARRANTIES OF MER-CHANTABILITY AND FITNESS FOR A PARTICULAR PURPOSE. Some states do not permit limitation or exclusion of implied warranties; therefore, the aforesaid limitations of exclusions may not apply.

This warranty gives you specific legal rights and you may also have other rights which vary from state to state.

FULL WARRANTY EXAMPLE

——————————— FULL LIFETIME WARRANTY ———————————

If this product should ever prove defective in workmanship or material, it will be replaced by XYZ Corporation. To obtain a replacement under this warranty, return the product to __(address)__ . SUCH REPLACE-MENT SHALL BE THE EXCLUSIVE REMEDY OF THE CONSUMER. XYZ SHALL NOT BE LIABLE FOR ANY LOSS OR DAMAGE, DIRECT OR CONSEQUENTIAL, ARISING OUT OF THE USE OF, OR INABILITY TO USE THIS PRODUCT. Some states do not allow the exclusion of incidental or consequential damages, so the above exclusion may not apply to you. This warranty gives you specific legal rights and you may also have other rights which vary from state to state.

FULL AND LIMITED WARRANTY EXAMPLES

——————————— FULL ONE-YEAR WARRANTY ———————————

For the first year after purchase and use within the continental United States by the original consumer XYZ Corporation will, at its option, repair or replace any part of this product which proves to be defective in material or workmanship under normal use.

During this period XYZ Corporation will provide all parts and labor necessary to correct such defects, free of charge, so long as the product has been installed and operated in accordance with the written instructions furnished with the product.

The customer will be responsible for cost of service calls resulting from problems considered Normal Responsibilities of User. To obtain service on your product, call the dealer from whom the product was purchased. The dealer will contact or direct you to the nearest authorized XYZ Service Station or local service company for inspection and repair of the product under the terms of this warranty. This product must be brought or sent to the applicable service shop for repair.

LIMITED SECOND- THROUGH FIFTH-YEAR WARRANTY

For the second through the fifth years of use, XYZ Corporation will make available a replacement compressor as may be required due to failure. Any and all labor charges for determination of cause of failure, installation of the replacement compressor and handling and postage charges for shipment of the replacement compressor will be the responsibility of the user.

Cartage charges for moving the appliance to a service shop (as may be required) and back to the user's home will also be the user's responsibility.

PRODUCT RECALLS

From time to time manufacturers find it necessary or expedient to recall a product for repairs. Recalls may be initiated voluntarily by the manufacturer or they may be made pursuant to federal statute. Federal statutes which may require product recalls are:

1. National Traffic and Motor Vehicle Safety Act of 1966, 15 U. S. C. §1391 et. seq.

2. Consumer Product Safety Act, 15 U. S. C. §2051 et. seq.

3. Federal Boat Safety Act, 46 U. S. C. §4310

4. Food, Drug, and Cosmetic Act, 21 U. S. C. §360h

5. National Mobile Home Construction and Safety Standards Act of 1974, 42 U. S. C. §5414

Nonstatutory Recalls

Even when not required by a statute a manufacturer may discover that a product that it has sold has a safety related defect. In such circumstances there is presently no common law duty on the manufacturer to recall the product for correction of the safety defect.

Red Flag: The law of products liability is rapidly evolving and courts may soon begin to impose a nonstatutory common law duty to recall.

Even without a common law recall duty, a manufacturer may find it beneficial to recall a product for repair. By recalling an unsafe product a manufacturer may reduce or eliminate potential liability from having sold an unsafe product.

Red Flag: If the safety defect was known or knowable at the time the product was sold or manufactured, then at least some courts would say that the manufacturer does have a duty to either remedy the defect, or if the defect cannot be feasibly remedied, then to give product users adequate warnings and instructions on how to minimize the danger.

To absolve itself of potential liability the manufacturer of the defective product should take the following actions at a minimum:

1. Offer to repair the product at no cost to the purchaser.
2. Communicate the offer of free repairs in time to prevent the accident.
3. Warn the purchaser of the risks and damages involved in continuing to use the product without repair.

As a general proposition, a manufacturer who has taken all reasonable steps to correct the product defect may succeed in freeing itself from future liability. If actual recall and repair of the product is not feasible, some measure less than recall which clearly puts the owner of the product on notice of the defect and informs the owner of methods of reducing the risk may provide a defense to a lawsuit by an injured party who has ignored the warning and has failed to take the risk-reducing steps recommended by the manufacturer.

Key Point: Even if the manufacturer voluntarily issues a warning, a court may permit a jury to determine whether

1. The language of the warning letter minimized the danger presented by the defect
2. The manufacturer was negligent in following up on its initial warning letter
3. The manufacturer was negligent in not making the repairs itself

4. The warning letter did not make the defect "open and obvious"

Therefore, drafting a recall letter requires great care and should involve legal counsel familiar with product liability law.

Use of Recall Letters in Litigation

Recall letters, even those issued in terms required by a federal statute, may be used against a manufacturer in a subsequent product liability case. Recall letters have been used by plaintiffs to show that the product was defective at the time of an accident, or because all motor vehicles covered by a recall were defective. Recall letters have also been treated by the courts as admissions by the manufacturer despite the fact that the language used in the letter is dictated by statute and the manufacturer is prohibited by law from including any language which would minimize the risk or suggest that it did not affect the particular consumer.

On the other hand a manufacturer may be able to use a recall letter to defend itself in subsequent litigation over injuries sustained in using the product. For example, the manufacturer may argue that the owner's failure to take action recommended by the recall letter is intervening negligence which insulates the manufacturer from liability. The manufacturer might also argue that after having received the recall letter and failing to take the recommended remedial action, the owner of the product assumed the risk of any subsequent injury.

Statutory Recalls

The discussion of statutory recall provisions is based on the provisions of the Consumer Product Safety Act. Substantially similar provisions are found in the other federal statutes providing for recalls. The Consumer Product Safety Act is used by way of example because of its broad coverage. The act applies generally to any product or component of a product for sale to a consumer for use around or in a household, in school, in recreation, or otherwise for the personal use or consumption or enjoyment of a consumer in or around a residence, a school, or in recreation. However certain products exempt from the act include tobacco, motor vehicles, pesticides, aircraft, boats, drugs or cosmetics, and food. Many exempt articles are of course subject to other statutory safety provisions.

The first issue relating to statutory recalls is determining whether a recall is required. The initial determination may be made either by the manufacturer or by the governmental agency charged with administering the law requiring the recall. Under the Consumer Product Safety Act the product recall procedure is invoked if the product either

1. Fails to comply with an applicable consumer product safety rule

2. Contains a defect which would create a substantial product hazard—i. e., a product which creates a substantial risk of injury to the public because of the pattern of defect, the number of defective products distributed in commerce, or the severity of risk.

If the Consumer Product Safety Commission determines that a substantial product hazard exists and that notification is required in order to adequately protect the public from that hazard, the commission may order a manufacturer, distributor or retailer to do one or more of the following:

1. Give the public notice of the defect.

2. Mail a notice of the defect to each person who manufactures, distributes, or retails the product.

3. Mail a notice of the defect to each person known to have purchased the product presenting the substantial safety hazard.

Key Point: Manufacturers, consumers and consumer organizations are entitled to a hearing before the commission regarding whether a notice or recall is required.

In addition to ordering notices of the defect, the Consumer Product Safety Commission can also order the manufacturer, distributor or retailer to:

1. Bring the product into conformity with the applicable consumer product safety rule or to repair the defect in the product.

2. Replace the product with a like or equivalent product which complies with the applicable consumer product safety rule or which does not contain the defect.

3. Refund the purchase price of the product (less a reasonable allowance for use if the product has been owned by the consumer for a year or more).

No charge can be made to a consumer who takes advantage of the remedies provided by the act.

ADMINISTERING A PRODUCT RECALL

After determining that a product recall is required, it is necessary to determine which products or product lines must be included in the recall. The recall notice must then be carefully drafted. The manufacturer must determine whether repairs can be made, and if repair is feasible, the manufacturer must design, develop, and test the repair. Any repaired parts must be purchased or manufactured and distributed to those who will make the repair. The party recalling the product must monitor the recall program, ensure that any required repairs are properly made, and determine how long the recall should remain in effect.

A table of consumer product safety standards and a list of related statutes is given below.

Table of Consumer Product Safety Standards

Standards for Architectural Glazing Materials, 16 CFR Part 1201

Safety Standards for Matchbooks, 16 CFR Part 1202

Walk-behind Power Lawn Mowers, 16 CFR Part 1205

Swimming Pool Slides, 16 CFR Part 1207

CB Base Station Antennas and Supporting Structures, 16 CFR Part 1402

Self Pressurized Consumer Products Containing Cholorofluoro-carbins, 16 CFR Part 1401

Related Statutes

Flammable Fabrics Act, 15 U. S. C. S. §§1191 et. seq.

Refrigerator Safety Act, 15 U. S. C. S. §§1211 et. seq.

Federal Hazardous Substances Act, 15 U. S. C. S. §1261 et. seq.

National Traffic and Motor Vehicle Safety Act, 15 U. S. C. S. §§1381 et. seq.

Poison Prevention Packaging Act, 15 U. S. C. S. §§1471 et. seq.

chapter fifteen

HOW TO HANDLE PRODUCT LABELING ISSUES

More than 8000 consumer products compete for the consumer's dollar. To a large extent, packaging has replaced the salesperson's spiel for these products. Packaging products in different sizes and quantity makes it exceedingly difficult for consumers to compare values. Accordingly, the Fair Packaging and Labeling Act imposes some mandatory requirements that apply to all consumer products and empowers regulatory agencies to impose additional requirements on other products.

In 1966, Congress identified certain marketing practices which it considered to be unfair or deceptive to consumers. These practices were prohibited by the Fair Packaging and Labeling Act. Practices which violate the Fair Packaging and Labeling Act are also declared to be unfair and deceptive acts in violation of section 5 of the Federal Trade Commission Act. While this chapter describes labeling requirements in detail, it does not exhaust the intricacies of federal regulation. This chapter is not a substitute for legal counsel.

The purposes of the Fair Packaging and Labeling Act are to enable consumers to obtain accurate information as to the quantity of the contents of the package and to facilitate value comparisons by consumers. The law applies to those who distribute goods across state lines rather than to those who merely sell the goods at retail. (See Tables 1 and 2).

The Secretary of Health and Welfare is charged with establishing regulations covering the packaging of foods, drugs, devices, and cosmetics while the Federal Trade Commission is charged with regulating all other consumer products. These two agencies are authorized to issue regulations on a product-by-product basis on finding need for regulations which cover:

1. Characterizations of package size
2. Sale price representations or implications
3. Statements listing ingredients
4. Slackfill packaging
5. Package size standards

Note: This chapter does not contain a detailed discussion of labeling requirements for food, drugs, and cosmetics.

See Table 4 for a listing of commodities for which specific regulations have been issued.

WHAT YOU MUST DO TO COMPLY WITH THE FAIR PACKAGING AND LABELING ACT MANDATORY REQUIREMENTS

The statute requires all products intended for sale at retail to ultimate consumers for consumption or use in households must specify on the product label:

1. Identity of the product
2. Name and place of business of the manufacturer, packer, or distributor
3. Net quantity of the contents
4. When the number of servings is represented, the net quantity per serving

While the statute itself does not further specify what a manufacturer, packer, or distributor must do to comply with these mandatory labeling requirements, the Federal Trade Commission has adopted regulations that provide specific details. The Federal Trade Commission regulations are discussed in the following pages.

Statement of Identity

The statement of the identity of the product shall be a principal feature of the principal display panel. It must be of such type size and so positioned as to be easily read and understood by the consumer. The statement of identity shall be written in lines generally parallel to the base of the package. The specification of identity shall be in terms of:

1. The name specified or required by any federal law or regulation, or if not so required

2. The common or usual name of the product, or

3. If there is no common or usual name of the product, then the generic name or other appropriate descriptive terms such as a statement of the product's function.

The specification of identity must not be false, misleading or deceptive in any respect.

Name and Place of Business

The label must conspicuously specify the name and place of business of the manufacturer, packer, or distributor. If the product is not manufactured by the party designated in the labeling material, the relationship of the parties must be revealed by the use of phrases such as

Manufactured for _____

Distributed by _____

Bottled by _____

A corporation must be identified by its actual corporate name which may be preceded or followed by the name of a particular division of the corporation. If the business is a sole proprietorship, partnership, or association, the name under which the business is conducted must be used.

The statement of the place of business must include the street address, city, state, and zip code. However, the street address may be omitted if it is shown in a current city directory or telephone directory. Standard abbreviations may be used.

If the product is manufactured, packaged, or distributed at other than the usual place of business, the label need only identify the principal place of business.

Net Quantity of Contents

A statement of the net quantity of the contents must be separately and accurately stated on the principal display panel. The statement shall not include any term qualifying a unit of weight, measure, or count such as "jumbo quart," "full gallon," "when packed," "minimum," or words of similar import.

The quantity statement shall be separated from the matter printed above and below by a space at least equal to the height of the lettering used in the declaration. It shall be separated from material to the right and left by a space at least equal to twice the width of the letter "N" of the style of type used in the net quantity statement.

The quantity shall be placed on the principal display panel within the bottom 30 percent of the area of the label panel in lines generally parallel to the base on which the package or commodity rests as it is designed to be displayed. The 30 percent rule does not apply if the package has a display panel of 5 square inches or less.

The net quantity may be expressed in terms of weight, measure, numerical count, or a combination which gives accurate information and facilitates value comparisons by consumers (see Table 3). If the commodity is a liquid, a liquid measure must be used. Weight must be used if the commodity is solid, semisolid, viscous, or a mixture of solid and liquid. An exception is made if there is a contrary consumer use or trade custom for expression of quantity.

The units of weight and measure which shall be used are:

1. For weight, avoirdupois pound and ounce
2. Fluids, a U. S. gallon of 231 cubic inches or quart, pint, or fluid ounce subdivisions thereof measured at 68 degrees Fahrenheit or 20 degrees Celsius
3. Linear measure, yards, feet, and inches
4. Area, square yards, square feet, or square inches
5. Dry measure, a bushel of 2,150.42 cubic inches and peck, dry quart, and dry pint subdivisions
6. Cubic measure, cubic yards, cubic foot, or cubic inch

In stating the weight of the contents the term "net weight" must be used. The net weight is to be expressed in pounds, ounces or fractions of pounds as follows:

1. If less than one pound, the net weight must be expressed in ounces.
   Example: Net weight 12 oz.
2. If between 1 and 4 pounds the net weight must be expressed in ounces followed in parentheses by a declaration in whole pounds with any remainder in terms of ounces, or common or decimal fractions of the pound.
   Example: "Net Weight 24 oz. (1 lb., 8 oz.)"
   Example: "Net Weight 24 oz. (1½ lbs.)"
   Example: "Net Weight 24 oz. (1.5 lbs.)"
3. If the net weight is 4 pounds or more, the net weight must be expressed in terms of whole pounds and ounces or common or decimal fractions of a pound.

Example: "Net Weight 5 pounds, 4 ounces"

Example: "Net Weight 5¼ pounds"

Example: "Net Weight 5.25 pounds"

When a fluid measure is involved use of the terms "net" or "net contents" is optional. The declaration of the net quantity for liquids should be expressed as follows:

1. If less than one pint, in terms of fluid ounces.

    Example: Net contents 8 fl. oz.

2. If at least one pint but less than one gallon, in terms of fluid ounces followed in parenthesis by a declaration of the largest whole unit (quarts, quarts and pints, or pints, as appropriate) with any remainder in terms of fluid ounces or common or decimal fractions of the pint or quart.

    Example: "Net 32 fl. oz. (1 qt.)"

    Example: "Net contents 56 fluid oz. (1 qt., 1½ pints)"

    Example: "Net 56 fluid oz. (1 qt., 1 pt., 8 oz.)"

    Example: It is not in terms of quart and ounces such as "Net 56 fluid oz. (1 quart, 24 ounces)"

3. If one gallon or more, in terms of the largest whole unit (gallons followed by common or decimal fractions of a gallon or by the next smaller whole unit or units such as quarts and pints) with any remainder in terms of fluid ounces or common or decimal fractions of the pint or quart.

    Example: "Net contents 2½ gal."

    Example: "Contents 2.5 gal."

    Example: "Net contents 2 gallons, 2 quarts"

For commodities whose quantity is expressed in length the terms used shall be as follows:

1. If less than one foot, the net quantity shall be expressed in terms of inches and fractions thereof.

2. If between 1 and 4 feet, the quantity shall be expressed in terms of inches followed in parenthesis by a declaration in the largest whole unit (a yard or foot) with any remainder in terms of inches or common or decimal fractions of the foot or yard.

Example: 40 inches (1 yd., 4 inches)

3. If 4 feet or more, in terms of feet followed in parenthesis by a declaration of yards and common or decimal fractions of the yard, or in terms of feet and inches.

For bidirectional commodities (including roll type commodities such as wrapping materials) the quantity shall be expressed as follows:

1. If the bidirectional commodity has a width greater than 4 inches but an area of less than 1 square foot, the quantity shall be expressed in terms of length and width in linear inches and fractions thereof.

2. If the bidirectional commodity has a width of more than 4 inches and has an area of 1 to 4 square feet, the net content shall be expressed in terms of square inches, followed in parenthesis by the length and width in the largest whole unit (yard or foot) with an remainder in inches or common decimal fractions of the yard or foot.

   Key Point: For commodities such as paper napkins consisting of useable individual units, the label must specify the unit area for an individual item but need not declare the total area of all such.

3. For a commodity with an area of 4 square feet or more, the contents shall be stated in terms of square feet followed in parenthesis by the length and width in the largest whole units (yards or feet) with any remainder in terms of inches or common decimal fractions of the foot or yard except that a dimension of less than 2 feet may be stated in inches within the parenthetical.

   Key Point: For commodities for which the area must be stated in terms of square inches, feet, or yards, the linear measurements may also be stated.

   Example: "25 sq. ft. (12 in. $\times$ 8.33 yd.) (12 in. $\times$ 300 in.)"

4. For commodities having a width of less than 4 inches the net quantity shall be expressed in terms of width in inches followed by the length in the largest whole unit (yard or foot) with any remainder expressed in terms of the common or decimal fractions of the yard or foot.

   Example: "2 inches $\times$ 10 yards"

   Example: "2 inches $\times$ 360 inches (10 yards):

The contents of commodities measured by area measure only shall be expressed as follows:

1. If less than one square foot, the area shall be expressed in terms of square inches and fractions thereof.

2. If the areas is between 1 and 4 square feet, the contents shall be expressed in terms of square inches followed in parenthesis by a declaration in square feet with any remainder stated in terms of square inches or common or decimal fractions of the square foot.

3. If the contents are 4 square feet or more, the contents must be expressed in terms of the largest appropriate whole unit (square yards, square yards and square feet, or square feet) with any remainder stated in terms of square inches or common or decimal fractions of the square foot or square yard.

For commodities made up of distinct useable units or of more than one ply the net quantity must include the number of ply or useable units in addition to the area of linear measurement.

Example: 100 two-ply facial tissues, 8½ inches by 10 inches

Key Point: Roll-type commodities such as paper towels are not considered to consist of individual useable units. They shall be labeled in terms of total area measurement and number of ply. However such measurement shall be supplemented by a statement of the number of perforated units and the dimensions of the individual units.

Conspicuousness

The statement of net quantity must appear in conspicuous and easily legible, boldface type or print in distinct contrast (by typography, layout, color, embossing, or molding).

Type Size for Statement of Net Contents

The Federal Trade Commission regulations also prescribe the type size that must be used for the statement of the net contents. The type size is established in relationship to the "area" of the principal display panel of the package or commodity. The "area" of the principal display panel means the areas of the side or surface that bears the principal display panel, not including the tops, bottoms, flanges at tops and bottoms of cans, and shoulders and necks of bottles.

The area of the principal display panel shall be calculated as follows:

1. For a rectangular package for which one entire side can properly be considered the principal display panel, the "area" of the principal display panel is the product of the height of the side times the width of the side.

2. For cylindrical or nearly cylindrical containers or commodities, the "area" is 40 percent of the product of the height of the cylinder times the circumference of the cylinder.

3. For other container shapes, the "area" shall be 40 percent of the total surface of the container or commodity.

Once the area of the principal display panel has been calculated, reference can be made to the Federal Trade Commission regulations to determine the type size required for the statement of the net contents. The full regulation is not reprinted here but in the main provides as follows.

1. For areas of 5 square inches or less, the type size must be at least 1/16 inch in height.

2. For areas of more than 5 inches but no more than 25 inches, the type size must be at least ⅛ inch in height.

3. For areas of more than 25 but no more than 100 square inches, the type size must be not less than 3/16 inches in height.

4. For areas of more than 100 square inches but no more than 400 square inches, the type size must be at least ¼ inch in height.

5. For an area of more than 400 square inches, the type size must be at least ½ inch in height.

Note: The letter heights given are for capital letters. If lower-case letters are used, the height is measured by the lower case letter "o". Letters shall not be more than three times as high as they are wide.

Variations in Quantity

Variations from the stated weight, measure, or numerical count are permitted when they result from unavoidable deviations in weighing, measuring, or counting the contents of individual packages which occur in good packaging practice.

Red Flag: Variations in weight, measure, or numerical count are not permitted to such an extent that the average of the quantities in the packages comprising a shipment or delivery is below the stated quantity. Nor are unreasonable shortages permitted even if they are balanced by overages in other packages.

Number of Servings

If the packaging bears a representation of the number of servings, uses, or applications of the commodity contained in the package, the package shall state, in immediate conjunction with representation of the number of servings, and in letters of the same size, a statement of the net quantity (in terms of weight, measure, or numerical count) of each serving, use or application.

Representations as to the total amount of objects to which the commodity may be applied or in which the commodity may be used is not a representation of the number of servings, uses, or applications, if it is stated in terms of standard units of weight, measure, size or count.

Key Point: If an industry has established a voluntary standard defining the meaning of the terms "serving," "use," or "application" for a particular consumer product, then any label representation as to the number of servings, uses, or applications shall correspond with the voluntary industry standard. Copies of published industry standards are available on request from the National Bureau of Standards, Department of Commerce, Washington, DC 20234.

Multiunit Packages

Marketers sometimes offer a package for retail sale containing two or more individually packaged or labeled units of an identical commodity in the same quantity. The declaration of the net quantity of a multiunit package is to be expressed as follows:

1. The number of individual packaged or labeled units
2. The quantity of each individual packaged or labeled unit including dual declarations when applicable
3. The total quantity of the multiunit package which may omit the parenthetical quantity statement of a dual quantity representation

   Example: Soap Bars: "6 Bars, Net Wt. 3.4 ozs. each, Total Wt. 20.4 ozs."

   Facial Tissue: "10 Packs, each 25 two-ply tissues, 9.7 in. × 8.2 in., Total 250 tissues."

Red Flag: If each of the packages of a multiunit package is intended for individual sale, each individual package must be labeled.

In the alternative, when each package of a multiunit package is not intended for separate sale, the multiunit package may carry a declaration of the quantity of the contents expressing the total quantity of the multiunit package without regard to inner packaging.

> *Example:* Deodorant Cakes: "5 cakes, Net Wt. 4 ozs. each, Total Net wt. 20 ozs." or "5 cakes, Total Net Wt. 20 ozs. (1 lb., 4 ozs.)"

> *Example:* Soap Packets: "10 packets, Net Wt. 2 ozs. each, Total Net Wt. 20 ozs." or "Net Wt. 20 ozs. (1 lb., 4 ozs.)" or "10 packets, Total Net Wt. 20 ozs. (1 lb., 4 ozs.)"

Variety Packages

Sometimes goods of different kinds are sold in one package. For example, a single package many contain plastic knives, forks, and spoons. Or a package may contain one item in a variety of sizes. Such packages are referred to as variety packages in the Federal Trade Commission regulations and have their own requirements for declaration of net quantity. Net quantity declarations for variety packs must conform to the following requirements:

1. The number of units for each identical commodity followed by the weight, volume, or measure of that commodity including dual declarations when applicable

2. The total quantity by weight, volume, measure, and count as appropriate of the variety pack; dual declarations may be omitted from the total quantity statement

The statement of total quantity must be the last item of the net quantity declaration.

> *Example:* "2 sponges 4½ ins. × 4 ins. × ⅜ in.
> 1 sponge 4½ ins. × 8 ins. × ¾ in.
> 4 sponges 2¼ ins. × 4 ins. × ½ in.
> Total 7 sponges"

> *Example:* "2 soap bars Net Wt. 3.2 ozs. each
> 1 soap bar Net Wt. 5 ozs.
> Total 3 soap bars Net Wt. 1¼ ozs."

> *Example:* (Liquid Shoe Polish) "1 Brown 3 fl. ozs.
> 1 Black 3 fl. ozs.
> 1 White 5 fl. ozs.
> Total 11 fl. ozs."

Example: (Picnic Ware) "34 spoons
                          33 forks
                          <u>33 knives</u>
                          Total 100 pieces"

Combination Packages

The Federal Trade Commission regulations refer to a package for retail sale consisting of two or more individual packages of dissimilar commodities as combination packages. For combination packages, the declaration of net quantity must contain an expression of weight, volume, measure, count, or a combination of them for each individual package or unit.

Examples:

Lighter fluid and flints: "2 cans—8 fl. ozs.; 1 package—8 flints"

Sponges and cleaner: "2 sponges each 4 in. × 6 in., 1 box cleaner—Net Wt. 6 ozs."

Picnic pack: "20 spoons, 10 knives and 10 forks, 10 2-ply napkins 10 ins. × 10 ins., 10 cups—6 fl. ozs."

WHEN CAN YOU ADVERTISE CENTS OFF, INTRODUCTORY OFFER OR ECONOMY SIZE?

The Federal Trade Commission has issued additional labeling regulations governing the use of terms such as "Cents Off," "Introductory Offer", and "Economy Size."

Cents Off

The Federal Trade Commission "cents off" regulations apply to the use of "cents off" which imply or state that the commodity is being offered for sale at a price lower than the ordinary and customary retail sale price. Under the regulations a label shall not contain a "cents off" representation unless the following conditions are met.

1. The commodity must have been sold by the packager or labeler in the trade area of the promotion at an ordinary and customary price in the recent and regular course of business.

2. The packager or labeler must sell the "cents off" labeled commodity at a reduction from its ordinary and customary price which is at least equal to the amount of the "cents off" representation imprinted on the commodity package or label.

3. Each "cents off" representation imprinted on the package or label must be limited to a phrase which reflects that the price marked by the retailer represents the savings in the amount of the reduction from the retailers regular price.

Example: Price marked is 5 cents off the regular price

Example: Price marked is 5 cents off the regular price of this package

4. A packager or labeler who sells at retail must display the regular price (designated as the regular price) clearly and conspicuously on the package or label of the commodity or on a sign, placard or shelf-marker placed in a position contiguous to the retail display of the "cents off" commodity.

A packager or retailer who does not sell directly to consumers must provide its retailers with the required sign, placard or shelf-marker.

5. The packager or labeler may not:

a. Initiate more than three "cents off" promotions for a single size commodity within the same trade area within a 12-month period.

b. Initiate a second "cents off" promotion for a single size commodity in the same trade area within 30 days of the last "cents off" promotion.

c. Maintain the "cents off" promotion for a single size item for more than six months in any 12-month period within a trade area.

6. Sales of a single size commodity within a trade area under a "cents off" promotion cannot exceed in volume 50 percent of the total sales of the commodity in the trade area in a 12-month period. The 50 percent limit may be based on sales projections but if sales are less than projected the 50 percent limit is determined by sales in the preceding year.

Key Point: A packager or labeler sponsoring a "cents off" promotion must prepare and maintain invoices or other records to show compliance with the Federal Trade Commission regulations. The records must be maintained for one year after the end of the promotion.

Introductory Offers

The Federal Trade Commission regulations define "introductory offers" as any printed matter containing the words "introductory offer" or the like used in labeling or packaging a new commodity implying that the commodity is being offered at a price below its anticipated ordinary and customary retail price. The following conditions apply to the use of introductory offers in labeling and packaging.

1. The commodity must be either new or changed in a functionally significant and substantial respect, or is being introduced into a trade area for the first time.

2. The label clearly and conspicuously qualifies each offer with the phrase "introductory offer".

3. The commodity is not sold as an introductory offer in any trade area for a duration of more than six months.

4. The packager or labeler intends in good faith to offer the commodity alone, at the anticipated ordinary and customary price for a reasonably substantial period of time following the end of the introductory offer.

Introductory Offer Coupled with Cents Off

An introductory offer coupled with a "cents off" promotion must also include the phrase "cents off the after introductory offer price".

The packager or labeler must sell the commodity at a reduction from the anticipated ordinary and customary price which is at least equal to the amount of the reduction from the after introductory offer price representation made on the commodity package or label.

Key Point: A packager or labeler sponsoring an introductory offer must prepare and maintain invoices or other records showing compliance with the Federal Trade Commission regulations. The records must be retained for one year following the end of the introductory offer.

Economy Size

The Federal Trade Commission economy size regulations apply to the use in packaging or labeling of the words "economy size," "economy pack," "budget pack," "bargain size," "value size," or similar words which state or imply that the retail sale price advantage is given to the purchaser because of the size of the package or the quantity of its contents.

An economy size representation cannot be made unless:

1. The packager or labeler also offers the same brand of the commodity in at least one other package size.

2. The packager or labeler offers only one packaged or labeled form of the brand with an economy size representation.

3. The packager or labeler sells the "economy size" package at a price per unit of weight, volume, measure, or count which is reduced by at least 5 percent from the actual price of all other packaged or labeled units of the same brand being offered at the same time.

Key Point: A packager or labeler sponsoring an "economy size" promotion must prepare and maintain invoices and other records showing compliance with the Federal Trade Commission regulations and maintain these for one year.

LABELING FOR TEXTILE, FUR, AND WOOL PRODUCTS

To protect consumers from deceptive acts in the sale of textiles, furs, and woolens, Congress has enacted the Textile Fiber Products Identification Act, the Fur Products Labeling Act, and the Wool Products Labeling Act. The Federal Trade Commission has enacted various rules, regulations, and guides to implement these acts.

Textiles

The Textile Fiber Products Identification Act is intended to prevent false advertising and deceptive labeling of textile fiber products. A product is misbranded if it does not bear a stamp, tag, label, or identification showing:

1. The constituent fiber or combination of fibers by generic name listed in order of weight

2. The percentage of each fiber by weight exclusive of ornamentation not exceeding 5 percent by weight.

3. The name or identification issued and registered by the Federal Trade Commission, of the manufacturer of the product.

4. The name of the country where the product was processed or manufactured if it was imported

Key Point: Use of a nondeceptive trademark is also permissible.

Key Point: Fibers not specifically identified because they are less than 5 percent by weight must be listed in aggregate as "other fibers."

Key Point: A person will not be guilty of a violation of the textile fiber act if he or she has received in good faith a written guarantee by a resident of the United States that the product is not misbranded or falsely invoiced.

The Federal Trade Commission has issued lengthy regulations governing the labeling and advertising of textile products. These regulations also include many helpful examples of suitable labels. Anyone marketing textile products should consult legal counsel to ensure that Federal Trade Commission requirements are met.

Fur Products Labeling Act

The Fur Products Labeling Act was enacted by Congress to protect consumers from deception and unfair competition resulting from misbranding, false or deceptive advertising, or false invoicing. Another purpose is to protect domestic fur producers against unfair competition. For purposes of the act, a fur product is any article of wearing apparel made in whole or in part of fur or used fur.

Under the act, it is an unfair and unlawful method of competition to (a) introduce or manufacture for introduction into commerce or (b) to sell, offer to sell, advertise, transport, or distribute in commerce any fur product that is:

1. Misbranded
2. Falsely or deceptively labeled or invoiced

Label Requirements

In general terms, a fur product is misbranded if the label affixed to the product does not state:

1. The name of the animal producing the fur in accordance with the Fur Products Name Guide (a copy of the Name Guide may be found in the Code of Federal Regulations 16 CFR, section 301.0)
2. The name or identification of the manufacturer
3. The person who introduced the product into interstate commerce
4. The name of the seller, transporter, or distributor
5. If imported, the country of origin
6. If the product contains used, bleached, dyed, artificially colored fur or is composed in whole or in substantial part of paws, tails, bellies or waste fur, the label must so state

A label is false or deceptive if the label misrepresents any of the required label information.

Key Point: Invoices for fur products must contain the same information as do labels.

Red Flag: No trade names, coined names, nor other words describing a fur product as containing the fur of a nonexistent or fictitious animal may be used in labeling a fur product.

Imported Fur

The following examples illustrate proper forms of disclosing the country of origin for imported furs.

> *Example:* Dyed Muskrat
> Fur Origin: Russia

> *Example:* Dyed China Mink
> Fur Origin: China

> *Example:* Tip-dyed Canadian American sable
> Fur Origin: Canada

> *Example:* Russian Sable
> Fur Origin: Russia

When the country of origin of the fur is unknown, the label must so state.

> *Example:* Fur Origin: Unknown

For domestic furs, the label may name the section of the country where the fur was produced.

> *Example:* Dyed Fur Seal
> Fur Origin: Alaska

Red Flag: When the name of the fur connotates a country of origin, but the true origin is the United States, the label must state the place of origin.

> *Example:* Dyed Persian Lamb
> Fur Origin: United States

> *Example:* Mexican Raccoon
> Fur Origin: United States

Examples of other required labeling disclosures are given below.

Example: Leopard
             Used Fur

Example: Dyed Muskrat
             Contains Used Fur

Example: Mink
             Fur Origin: Canada
             Contains Damaged Fur

Labeling Size and Type Size

The label itself must have minimum dimensions of 1¾ inches by 2¾ inches and be conspicuously and securely fastened to the fur product. The type size must be at least pica or 12 point and all of the required information must be set out in letters of equal size and conspicuousness.

The foregoing discussion merely highlights the law pertaining to the labeling of fur products. Legal counsel should review any labeling program before it is placed in use.

Red Flag: Certain record keeping requirements are imposed on manufacturers or dressers of fur products. Legal counsel should be consulted to ensure compliance with record keeping requirements.

WOOL PRODUCTS LABELING ACT

The purpose of the Wool Products Labeling Act is to protect producers, manufacturers, distributors, and consumers from the unrevealed presences in a product of substitute materials in wool products. The term wool under the act also includes the hair of camel, alpaca, llama, and vicuna. Misbranding of a wool product is an unfair and deceptive act or practice under the Federal Trade Commission Act.

A label must be attached to a wool product which discloses the name of woolen and nonwoolen fibers contained in the product and the percentage of each of them by total fiber weight. The woolen fiber must be identified as "wool", "reprocessed wool," or "reused wool."

Key Point: Understatement of the percentage of wool fiber is not unlawful.

Key Point: A deviation in wool fiber content from that stated on the label is not unlawful if it results from unavoidable variations in manufacturing despite the exercise of due care.

Imported wool products must contain the same label information as domestic wool products.

Key Point: Carpets, rugs, mats, and upholsteries are exempt from the Wool Products Labeling Act.

When at least 95 percent of the fiber content is wool, the label may use the term "all" or 100%" as follows.

> *Example:*   All wool—exclusive of ornamentation
>
> *Example:*   100% wool—exclusive of ornamentation

Specialty fibers (camel, llama, vicuna, or alpaca) may be specifically identified rather than using the word "wool."

> *Examples:*   55% Alpaca—45% Camel Hair
> 50% Recycled Camel Hair—50% Wool
> 60% Recycled Alpaca—40% Rayon
> 35% Recycled Llama—35% Recycled Vicuna—30% Cotton
> 60% Cotton—40% Recycled Llama

The words "mohair" and "cashmere" may also be used in lieu of the word "wool."

> *Examples:*   50% Mohair—50% Wool
> 60% Cotton—40% Cashmere

Country Where Processed or Manufactured

The label of each imported wool product must state the country in which the product was processed or manufactured. Products made completely in the United States must be labeled "Made in U.S.A." or contain some other clear and equivalent designation. Wool products made in the United States in whole or in part of imported materials must be labeled as:

> Made in U.S.A. of imported fabric
>
> Knitted in U.S.A. of imported yarn

The foregoing discussion merely highlights labeling requirements for wool products. Legal counsel should be consulted for specific labels.

AUTOMOBILE LABELS

Federal statute requires the manufacturer of any new automobile to affix to the windshield or side window a label containing the following information:

1. Make, model, and serial or identification number or numbers
2. Final assembly point
3. Name, and the location of the place of business, of the dealer to whom it is to be delivered
4. Name of the city or town at which it is to be delivered to such dealer
5. Method of transportation used in making delivery of such automobile, if driven or towed from final assembly point to place of delivery
6. The following information:
    a. Retail price of such automobile suggested by the manufacturer
    b. The retail delivered price suggested by the manufacturer for each accessory or item of optional equipment, physically attached to such automobile at the time of its delivery to such dealer, which is not included within the price of such automobile as stated pursuant to paragraph (a)
    c. The amount charged, if any, to such dealer for the transportation of such automobile to the location at which it is delivered to such dealer
    d. The total of the amounts specified pursuant to paragraphs (a), (b), and (c)

HAZARDOUS SUBSTANCES

Congress has enacted special legislation relating to the sale of hazardous substances. This section highlights labeling requirements for hazardous substances. No program for marketing hazardous substances should be implemented without prior review by legal counsel. In general terms hazardous substances include any substance or mixture of substances which may cause substantial personal injury or illness as a proximate result of any customary or reasonably foreseeable handling or use including foreseeable ingestion by children and is

1. Toxic
2. Corrosive

3. An irritant
4. A strong sensitizer
5. Flammable or combustible
6. Generates pressure through decomposition or other means

A product containing a hazardous substance is misbranded if it is not labeled in accordance with the Poison Prevention Packaging Act of 1970 or the Federal Hazardous Substance Act.

The Hazardous Substance Act requires the product label to contain the following information conspicuously stated:

A. Name and place of business of the manufacturer, packer, distributor, or seller
B. Common or usual name or the chemical name (if there be no common or usual name) of the hazardous substance or each component which contributes substantially to its hazard, unless the Secretary by regulation permits or requires the use of a recognized generic name
C. Signal word "DANGER" on substances which are extremely flammable, corrosive, or highly toxic
D. Signal word "WARNING" or "CAUTION" on all other hazardous substances;
E. An affirmative statement of the principal hazard or hazards, such as "Flammable," "Combustible," "Vapor Harmful," "Causes Burns," "Absorbed Through Skin," or similar wording descriptive of the hazard
F. Precautionary measures describing the action to be followed or avoided, except when modified by regulation of the Secretary pursuant to section 3 (15 USCS section 1262)
G. Instruction, when necessary or appropriate, for first-aid treatment
H. The word "poison" for any hazardous substance which is defined as "highly toxic" by subsection (h)
I. Instructions for handling and storage of packages which require special care in handling or storage
J. The statement
   i. "Keep out of the reach of children" or its practical equivalent
   ii. If the article is intended for use by children and is not a banned hazardous substance, adequate directions for the protection of children from the hazard

The required information must be prominently located and in conspicuous and legible type. The information must contrast by typography, layout, or color with other printed matter on the label.

<hr>

POISON PREVENTION PACKAGING ACT

<hr>

The Poison Prevention Packaging Act authorizes the Consumer Product Safety Commission to issue regulations requiring special packaging of products intended for household use if it finds that special packaging is required to protect children from serious personal injury or illness. In order to make such substances available to elderly or handicapped persons, those products may be sold in noncomplying packaging which bears the label:

> This package is for households without small children.

or some similar wording approved by the commission.

Legal counsel should be consulted prior to marketing products subject to the Poison Prevention Packaging Act.

<hr>

FLAMMABLE FABRICS ACT

<hr>

The federal Flammable Fabrics Act provides that the Consumer Products Safety Commission may promulgate flammability standards including labeling requirements for articles of wearing apparel and fabrics for use in wearing apparel and for interior furnishings.

Legal counsel should be consulted for detailed information regarding flammability standards.

Red Flag: Some states may impose flammability standards in excess of those imposed by the Consumer Product Safety Commission.

Under the act, the manufacture for sale, the sale, or the offering for sale of any product or fabric in interstate commerce that does not conform to an applicable flammability standard or regulation is unlawful and is an unfair and deceptive practice under the Federal Trade Commission Act.

Key Point: A seller who has received a guarantee from the person from whom the seller received the product or fabric guaranteeing that reasonable and representative tests made in accordance with commission standards show that the product or fabric conforms to applicability standards and who has not done further processing affecting flammability is immune from prosecution under the act.

The Consumer Product Safety Commission has published form guarantees that can be used under the Flammable Fabrics Act. Persons may rely on guarantees in the form provided for by the commission. Where the form guarantees are used as part of an invoice or other paper relating to the marketing or handling of products, fabrics or related materials subject to the act, wording of the guarantee may be varied from the commission form to limit the guarantee to specific items covered by the invoice or other paper. The name, address of the guarantor, and the date on the invoice or other paper will satisfy the requirement for those items in the commission guarantee forms.

General Guaranty Form

The undersigned hereby guarantees that reasonable and representative tests, made in accordance with procedures prescribed and applicable standards or regulations issued, amended, or continued in effect under the Flammable Fabrics Act, as amended, show that the product, fabric, or related material covered and identified by, and in the form delivered under this document conforms to the applicable standard or regulation issued, amended, or continued in effect.

Date: _____

Name _____

Address _____

A form of continuing guarantee renewable every three years may be filed with the Consumer Products Safety Commission. Forms for filing the continuing guarantee may be obtained from the Secretary to the Commission. When a continuing guarantee is on file with the commission, the guarantor may simply give notice of that fact by setting forth a statement on the invoice or other paper as follows:

Continuing guaranty under the Flammable Fabrics Act filed with the Consumer Product Safety Commission.

The form for filing a continuing guarantee with the commission is shown below.

The undersigned, _____ , a _____ (corporation, partnership, proprietorship) residing in the United States and having principal office and place of business at _____ (Street and number) _____ , (City) _____ , (State or territory, ZIP code) and being engaged in the marketing or handling of products, fabrics, or related materials subject to the Flammable Fabrics Act, as amended, and regulations thereunder.

Hereby guarantee(s) that with regard to all the products, fabrics, or related materials

[described as follows: _____

_____

_____]

    (If guaranty is limited to certain products, fabrics, or related materials, list the general categories here. If guaranty is not so limited, leave these lines blank.)

hereafter marketed or handled by the undersigned, and for which flammability standards have been issued, amended, or continued in effect under the Flammable Fabrics Act, as amended, reasonable and representative test as prescribed by the Consumer Product Safety Commission have been performed, which shows that the products, fabrics, or related materials conform to such of the above-mentioned flammability standards as are applicable thereto.

Dated, signed, and executed this _____ day of _____ ,
19 ____ , at _____ (City), _____ (State or Territory).

(Impression of   _____
  corporate seal,   (name under which business is
    if corporation)   conducted)

(If firm is a   _____
  partnership list   (Signature of proprietor, partner, or
  partners below)   authorized official of corporation)

State of _____ , ss:
County of _____

On this _____ day of _____ , 19 _____ , before me personally appeared the said _____ , (Signer of guaranty) proprietor, partner (strike nonapplicable words) _____ (If corporation, give title of signing official) of _____ , (Firm name) to me personally known, and acknowledged the execution of the foregoing instrument on behalf of the firm, for the uses and purposes therein stated.

(Impression of   _____
  notary seal   Notary Public in and for
  required here)   County of _____ State of
                         _____ . My commission
                         expires _____

Any seller residing in the United States can give a continuing guaranty to a buyer applicable to any product, fabric, or related material sold or to be sold by the seller to the buyer. Such continuing guarantees are good for three years and are renewable. The continuing guarantee must be executed in duplicate before a notary.

Form for Continuing Guaranty from Seller to Buyer

The undersigned, _____ , a _____ . (Corporation, partnership, proprietorship) residing in the United States and having its principal offices and place of business at _____ , _____ (Street and number) _____ , (City), _____ (State or territory, ZIP code), and being engaged in the marketing or handling of products, fabrics, or related materials subject to the Flammable Fabrics Act, as amended, and Regulations thereunder.

Hereby guarantee(s) to _____ (Name and address), buyer, that with regard to all the products, fabrics, or related materials [described as follows: _____

_____

_____]

    (If guaranty is limited to certain products, fabrics, or related materials, list the general categories here. If guaranty is not so limited, leave these lines blank.)

hereafter sold or to be sold to buyer by the undersigned, and for which flammability standards have been issued, amended, or continued in effect under the Flammable Fabrics Act, as amended, reasonable and representative tests as prescribed by the Consumer Product Safety Commission have been performed show that the products, fabrics, or related materials, at the time of their shipment or delivery by the undersigned, conform to such of the above-mentioned flammability standards as are applicable thereto.

Dated, signed, and executed this _____ day of _____ , 19 ____ , at _____ (City), _____ (State or Territory).

(Impression of   (name under which business is
  corporate seal,   conducted)
  if corporation)

(If firm is a   (Signature of proprietor, partner, or
  partnership list   authorized official of corporation)
  partners below)

State of _____ , ss:
County of _____

On this _____ day of _____ , 19 _____ , before me personally appeared the said _____ , (Signer of guaranty) proprietor,
partner (strike nonapplicable words) _____ (If corporation, give
title of signing official) of _____ , (Firm name) to me personally
known, and acknowledged the execution of the foregoing instrument on
behalf of the firm, for the uses and purposes therein stated.

(Impression of	Notary Public in and for
notary seal	County of _____ State of
required here)	_____ . My commission
	expires _____

Red Flag: A guarantee furnished by a person who is not a resident of the
United States is not a bar to prosecution and provides no immunity.

Key Point: No representation shall be made in advertising or other marketing
materials that the government guarantees that any product, fabric, or related
material conforms to a flammability standard in effect under the act.

Special Labeling Requirements

All items of children's sleepware shall be labeled with precautionary instructions
to protect the items from agents or treatments which are known to cause significant
deterioration of their flame resistance. Such labels must be permanently affixed
to the item.

LABELING CHECKLIST

_____ Are warranty rules complied with (see Chapter 14)?

_____ Are promotional program guides complied with (see Chapter 11)?

_____ Does the label identify the product?

_____ Does the label show the name and address of the manufacturer,
packer, or distributor?

_____ Does the label conform to Federal Trade Commission requirements
for stating the net quantity of the contents?

_____ Does the label use approved abbreviations?

_____ Does the label meet trademark and trade name requirements?

_____ Does the label meet Federal Trade Commission requirements for
"cents off," "introductory offer", and "economy size" promotions?

_____ Does the label conform to the requirements of any industry specific statutes or regulations?

_____ Do invoices conform to the requirements of any labeling act?

_____ Are proper record keeping practices in place?

TABLE 1

Products considered to be subject to the Fair Packaging and Labeling Act (not all inclusive).

Adhesives and sealants	Liquefied petroleum gas for
Aluminum foil cooking	other than heating
utensils	and cooking
Aluminum wrap	Lubricants for home use
Camera supplies	Photographic chemicals
Candles	Pressure sensitive tapes,
Christmas decorations	excluding gift tapes
Cordage	Solder
Disposable diapers	Solvents and cleaning for
Dry cell batteries	home use
Light bulbs	Sponges and chamois
	Waxes for home use

TABLE 2

Products which are not considered to be subject to the Fair Packaging and Labeling Act.

Antifreeze	Clothespins (wooden, plastic)
Artificial flowers and parts	Compacts and mirrors
Automotive accessories	Diaries and calendars
Automotive chemical products	Flower seeds
Automotive replacement parts	Footwear
Bicycle tires and tubes	Garden tools
Books	Gift ties and tapes
Brooms and mops	Glasses and glassware
Brushes (bristle, nylon, etc.)	Gloves (work type)
Cameras	Greeting cards
Chinaware	Hand tools
Christmas light sets	Handicraft and sewing thread
Cigarette lighters	Hardware

TABLE 2 *(Continued)*

Household cooking utensils	Rubber gloves (household)
Inks	Safety flares
Jewelry	Safety pins
Luggage	School supplies
Magnetic recording tape	Sewing accessories
Metal pails	Silverware, stainless
Motor oil (automobile)	steelware and pewterware
Mouse and rat traps	Small arms ammunition
Musical instruments	Smoking pipes
Paintings and wall plaques	Souvenirs
Photo albums	Sporting goods
Pictures	Toys
Plastic table cloths,	Typewriter ribbons
plastic placemats and	Woodenware
plastic shelf paper	

TABLE 3

Abbreviations which can be used in the required net quantity declaration. Plural and plural forms may be used.

Inch = in.	Pound = lb.
Feet or foot = ft.	Quart = qt.
Fluid = fl.	Square = sq.
Liquid = liq.	Weight = wt.
Ounce = oz.	Yard = yd.
Gallon = gal.	Avoirdupois = avdp.
Pint = pt.	Cubic = cu.

TABLE 4

Specific Labeling And Advertising Rules

The commodities listed in this table are subject to specific labeling requirements. Legal counsel should be consulted to ensure compliance with the applicable Federal Trade Commission rules.

TABLE 4 *(Continued)*
Specific Labeling And Advertising Rules

Binoculars	Household electric sewing
Care labeling of textiles	machines
Extension ladders	Leakproof dry cell batteries
Fiberglass curtains and	Leather belts
draperies	Ophthalmic goods
Gasoline octane numbers	Previously used motor oil
Home entertainment products	Sleeping bags
(amplifiers)	Size of television sets
Home insulation	Tablecloths
Home study and vocational	Transistor radios
schools	

TABLE 5
Approved Invoice Statement Forms

The undersigned hereby guarantees that the merchandise covered and delivered under this invoice is not misbranded, falsely invoiced, or falsely advertised under the Fur Products Labeling Act and applicable provisions of the Wool Products Labeling Act, and that reasonable and representative tests of such merchandise made under the procedures provided in Section 4 of the Flammable Fabrics Act show that it is not so highly flammable as to be dangerous when worn by individuals. The undersigned further warrants that the merchandise is properly labeled as to content as required by applicable Federal Trade Commission trade practice rules.

John Doe Company
Address _____

The undersigned hereby guarantees that the merchandise covered and delivered under this invoice is not misbranded, falsely invoiced, or falsely advertised under the Fur Products Labeling Act, and that reasonable and representative tests of such merchandise made under the procedures provided in Section 4 of the Flammable Fabrics Act show that it is not so highly flammable as to be dangerous when worn by individuals. The undersigned further warrants that the merchandise is properly labeled as to content as required by applicable Federal Trade Commission trade practice rules.

John Doe Company
Address _____

TABLE 5 *(Continued)*

Approved Invoice Statement Forms

The undersigned hereby guarantees that the merchandise covered and delivered under this invoice is not misbranded within the provisions of the Wool Products Labeling Act, and that reasonable and representative tests of such merchandise made according to the procedures provided in Section 4 of the Flammable Fabrics Act show that it is not so highly flammable as to be dangerous when worn by individuals. The undersigned further warrants that the merchandise is properly labeled as to content as required by applicable Federal Trade Commission trade practice rules.

John Doe Company
Address _____

The undersigned hereby guarantees that the merchandise covered and delivered under this invoice is not misbranded, falsely invoiced, or falsely advertised within the provisions of the Fur Products Labeling Act, and that reasonable and representative tests of such merchandise made according to the procedures provided in Section 4 of the Flammable Fabrics Act show that it is not so highly flammable as to be dangerous when worn by individuals.

John Doe Company
Address _____

The following conditions apply to the use of the approved invoice statements.

1. The guaranty or statement may be properly used only by guarantors who are residing in the United States.

2. Use of the invoice statement does not relieve the guarantor of the necessity of having the merchandise properly stamped, tagged, labeled, or identified with the fiber and other content information as required by the Wool and Fur Products Labeling Acts and the regulations issued thereunder, or as required by applicable trade practice rules.

3. The invoice statement is not to be construed as relieving anyone of the necessity of making invoice disclosures of true name and other information regarding the fur, as required by the Fur Products Labeling Act.

4. In respect to the Flammable Fabrics Act it is to be understood that

the invoice statement not only guarantees that the fabrics and fabrics contained in wearing apparel, have qualified under the reasonable and representative tests provided in the Act, but also that whatever further processing the goods have been subjected to after such tests has not affected the flammability thereof.

5. Where the invoice statement refers to FTC trade practice rules, it should be understood that the use of the statement does not prevent anyone from truthfully showing on the invoice itself the fiber and other content of the merchandise, if so desired, nor from making such disclosure on the invoice as may be required pursuant to purchase order or agreement with customers.

6. The invoice statements do not deprive anyone of the right to use separate invoice guarantees as provided by the relevant statutes mentioned, or from using a continuing guaranty filed with the commission as likewise provided by such statutes.

7. Although the invoice statements are made available for immediate use, they are to be regarded as subject to change by the commission at any time such change is deemed appropriate or necessary.

chapter sixteen

SALES BY MAIL

Mail-order sales, a rapidly growing means of marketing, are regulated by both the U. S. Postal Service and the Federal Trade Commission. Anyone contemplating marketing a product by mail should obtain a copy of the Domestic Mail Manual ($17) from the Superintendent of Documents, Washington, D. C. 20402. Purchasers will also receive updates to the manual when they are issued by the U. S. Postal Service.

The Domestic Mail Manual is a comprehensive compilation of regulations governing the use of the mails. Included in its coverage are such items as packaging, nonmailable matter, mail classifications, bulk mailing, and presorting.

In addition to the regulations promulgated by the U. S. Postal Service, the Federal Trade Commission has issued rules governing sales by mail. The most important of the Trade Commission rules are the "30-day" rule and the "negative option" rule. These are discussed in turn.

30-DAY RULE

In simple terms the Federal Trade Commission Mail Order or 30-day rule makes it an unfair method of competition and an unfair and deceptive practice for a seller to use the mails to solicit a sale unless they have a reasonable basis for believing that the goods will be shipped within a time stated in the solicitation or within 30 days if no time is stated in the solicitation. It is also unlawful to notify a buyer of an inability to make timely shipment without giving the buyer an opportunity to cancel. Finally, the rule also makes it unlawful to fail to make a prompt refund when the buyer elects to cancel the order. Now let's take a more detailed look at the provisions of the 30-day rule.

Failure to Ship

The failure to ship portion of the Federal Trade Commission rule specifically addresses three matters.

1. Solicitation without a reasonable basis to believe orders will be shipped within the time stated in the solicitation or within 30 days if no time is stated in the solicitation
2. Providing a purchaser with a revised shipping date unless the seller has a reasonable basis for representing the revised shipping date
3. Informing the buyer that the seller can make no representations regarding a revised shipping date unless the seller has a reasonable basis for informing the buyer and the seller informs the buyer of the reason or reasons for the delay

Key Point: If the Federal Trade Commission brings an action to enforce this part of the 30-day rule, the seller cannot establish a reasonable basis for its actions unless it has records or other documentary proof establishing the use of systems and procedures that assure the shipment of merchandise in the ordinary course of business within the applicable time frame.

Option to Cancel

When a seller is unable to ship merchandise within the applicable time, it is unlawful for the seller to fail to offer the buyer an option to either consent to a delay in shipment or to cancel the order and receive a prompt refund. The option must be clear and conspicuous and must be made to the buyer within a reasonable time after the seller first becomes aware of the inability to timely ship the merchandise. The option must also provide a revised shipping date or inform the buyer that the seller is unable to make any representation regarding the length of delay in shipping the merchandise.

When the revised date is no more than 30 days beyond the original date, the option notice shall inform the buyer that unless notice of cancellation is received prior to the revised shipping date, the buyer will be deemed to have agreed to the revised shipping date.

However, when the revised shipping date is more than 30 days after the original date or where the seller is unable to provide a definite revised shipping date, the offer of the option shall expressly inform the buyer that their order will automatically be deemed to have been cancelled unless:

1. The seller has actually shipped the merchandise within 30 days without receipt of a notice of cancellation

2. The seller has received from the buyer a response consenting to the shipping delay within the 30-day period

Key Point: If the seller is unable to provide a definite revised shipping date, the buyer must be informed that they have a continuing right to cancel their order.

A seller who provides a definite revised shipping date may at the same time or at a later time request the buyer's consent to any unanticipated delay beyond the definite revised shipping date. In requesting the buyer's consent to further delay, the seller must also inform the buyer that they retain the right to cancel their order at any time after the definite revised shipping date but prior to actual shipment.

Key Point: If the seller is unable to ship on or before the definite revised shipping date, the seller must offer the buyer a renewed option to consent to further delay or to cancel the order and receive a prompt refund. The renewed option must be offered within a reasonable time after the seller becomes aware that it will be unable to make timely shipment and prior to the definite revised shipping date. The terms of the renewed option must track the terms of the original option.

30-DAY RULE SEQUENCE CHART

Solicitation	Must ship by time stated in solicitation or within 30 days
First Notification (a reasonable time after learning of inability to make timely shipment and prior to 30 days or time stated in solicitation)	Inform buyer of revised shipping date or explain why a revised date cannot be given Provide option to cancel and receive prompt refund

30-DAY RULE SEQUENCE CHART *(Continued)*

Second Notification (a reasonable time after learning of inability to make timely shipment and in any event prior to any termination or revised shipping date)	Inform buyer of new revised shipping date or explain why a revised date cannot be given Provide a renewed option to cancel and receive prompt payment

Option to Cancel

Whenever the seller is required to offer the buyer an option to cancel, the seller must also furnish the buyer with adequate means to exercise the option at seller's expense.

Key Point: The seller should provide the buyer with a written means of exercising the option at the seller's expense such as through the use of business reply mail or a postage prepaid card.

Key Point: Whenever a seller is unable to make a timely shipment, the seller may elect to consider the order cancelled and to notify the buyer of this decision together with a prompt refund within a reasonable time after seller becomes aware of their inability to make timely shipment.

Red Flag: In any Federal Trade Commission enforcement action, evidence that the seller failed to provide the notice of the option in writing and by first class mail will create a rebuttable presumption that the seller failed to give notice of the option.

What a Seller Must Do When the Buyer Cancels

It is an unfair method of competition and an unfair and deceptive practice for a seller to fail to treat an order as cancelled and to make a prompt refund whenever:

1. The seller receives a cancellation notice pursuant to any option, renewed option, or continuing option prior to the time of actual shipment
2. The seller has notified the buyer of inability to make shipment and has indicated intention not to ship

3. The seller has neither shipped the goods within 30 days of the order or the time stated in the solicitation nor has the seller offered the buyer the required option

4. The seller has not shipped the goods and has not received the buyer's consent to a delayed shipment in the required time period

When the buyer cancels the seller must make prompt refund.

How to Make Refunds Under the 30-Day Rule

The Federal Trade Commission regulations defines which types of payments or credits are acceptable refunds. Accordingly when the buyer has tendered full or partial payment for goods by cash, check, or money order a refund must be made by cash, check, or money order within seven working days.

When the seller has extended credit to the buyer, a refund may be by a copy of a credit memorandum or the like or an account statement reflecting the removal or absence of any remaining charge from the goods from the buyer's account mailed by first class mail within the billing cycle.

When the buyer has utilized third-party credit, the refund should be in the form of a credit memo or the like to the third-party creditor which will remove the charge from the buyer's account. If no charge to the buyer's account has yet been made, the seller must send a statement mailed by first-class mail within one billing cycle to the buyer from the seller acknowledging the cancellation of the order and representing that the seller has not taken any action regarding the order which will result in a charge to the buyer.

30-DAY RULE CHECK LIST

_____ Was there a reasonable belief that goods could be shipped within 30 days or within the time stated at the time the sale was solicited?

_____ If timely shipment was not made was buyer given option to cancel?

_____ If a revised shipping date was given to buyer, was this a reasonable basis for representing the revised shipping date?

_____ Was a prompt refund or credit made upon receipt of notice of cancellation?

_____ If seller cancels because of an inability to make a timely shipment was a prompt refund made?

USING NEGATIVE OPTION PLANS

A negative option mail-order marketing plan is one in which the seller periodically sends subscribers a notice stating that certain merchandise will be shipped by a certain date unless the subscriber notifies the seller that the merchandise is not wanted. Book clubs and record and tape clubs frequently make use of negative option plans. It is obvious that negative option marketing is susceptible to great abuse. Accordingly, the Federal Trade Commission has issued a rule governing the use or negative option plans.

How to Use a Negative Option Plan

Lawful use of a negative option plan requires a seller to make certain disclosures and to give certain notifications. The disclosures which must be made clearly and conspicuously in the promotional material are:

1. The part of the sales plan that requires the buyer to notify the seller, in a particular fashion, that the buyer does not want to purchase a particular selection

2. Any obligation on the part of the buyer to make a minimum number of purchases

3. The right of a subscriber who has satisfied the minimal obligations to cancel their membership at any time

4. Whether billing charges will include an amount for postage and handling

5. The fact that the subscriber will have at least 10 days to mail any form contained in or accompanying an announcement identifying the next selection to the seller

6. The fact that the seller will credit the return of any selection sent to a subscriber, and guarantee to the Postal Service or the subscriber postage to return selections to the seller when the announcement did not arrive in time to afford the subscriber ten days in which to mail their form to the seller

7. The frequency with which announcements and forms will be sent to the subscriber and the maximum number that will be sent during a 12-month period.

The notification which must be sent to the subscriber before any selection is mailed must conform to the following requirements:

1. There must be an announcement identifying the selection.

2. There must be a form contained in or accompanying the announcement which clearly and conspicuously discloses that the subscriber will receive the selection identified in the announcement unless they notify the seller that they do not want the selection. The form must also disclose the procedures for using the form to instruct the seller that the selection is not wanted. Further the form must specify either a return date or a mailing date for exercising the negative option.

3. The announcement and form must be mailed at least 20 days prior to a return date or 15 days prior to a mailing date or provide a mailing date at least ten days after the announcement and form are received by the subscriber.

Red Flag: Whatever system is selected for mailing the announcement and form, the subscriber must be given at least ten days in which to exercise the negative option.

Unlawful Negative Option Plan Activities

In addition to the disclosure and notification requirements of the commission rule, certain practices sometimes engaged in by negative option plan marketers are declared to be unlawful. These additional unlawful activities are:

1. To refuse to credit the return of a selection, including postage when:

   a. A selection was shipped to a subscriber who has properly indicated that they did not want to receive the selection.

   b. The seller received a form after the return date but the form had been postmarked at least three days prior to the return date.

Key Point: This requires special training of mailroom personnel to ensure that the proper records are preserved to prove when late arriving forms were postmarked.

   c. The announcement and form are not received by the subscriber in time to afford them at least ten days in which to mail the form.

   d. Prior to the date of shipment of the selection, the seller has received a notice of cancellation of membership from a subscriber who has completed any minimum contract obligations.

Red Flag: Only the first selection sent after notice of cancellation is received is subject to return. Any future selections sent to a cancelled subscriber are unordered merchandise which the subscriber may keep at no cost.

Key Point: If the seller knows that the subscriber is entitled to return the selection for any of the above reasons, it is an unfair and deceptive act or practice for the seller to fail to notify the buyer of their right to return the selection for full credit if the subscriber desires to do so.

It is also unlawful to fail to terminate promptly the membership of a canceling contract-complete subscriber. Further, it is unlawful to ship substituted merchandise without the express consent of the subscriber. The form accompanying the announcement may be used to provide the subscriber a means of consenting to the shipment of substituted merchandise.

Shipment of Bonus Merchandise

Many negative option marketing plans use introductory and bonus merchandise offers or inducements to subscribers to enter or remain in the plan. It is an unfair and deceptive practice to refuse to ship such merchandise within four weeks unless the seller is prevented from making the shipment due to unforseen circumstances beyond their control. In which case, the seller must make a reasonably equivalent alternative offer to the seller.

The subscriber may refuse the reasonably equivalent alternative offer of introductory merchandise and cancel his subscription. If the subscriber returns any of the introductory merchandise already received, the seller must honor the cancellation.

NEGATIVE OPTION CHECKLIST

_____ Are required disclosures made?

_____ Was the proper notification given to the subscriber?

_____ Was timely notification given?

_____ Was promised bonus merchandise shipped within four weeks?

_____ Has proper credit been given to a subscriber who has rightfully returned a selection?

AVOIDING MAIL FRAUD

It is a violation of federal law to use the U. S. Mail to conduct a fraudulent scheme. Moreover, it is also a crime to use a false or fictitious name or address for the purpose of promoting or conducting mail fraud. It should not be necessary to dwell unduly on the contours of federal mail fraud. The basic elements of mail fraud are easily stated.

1. A scheme to defraud

2. Use of the mail for the purpose of carrying out the scheme

3. An intent to defraud

Key Point: Statements that are patently false or are made with a reckless indifference to their truth or falsity can be the equivalent of an intent to defraud.

Red Flag: Misleading advertising material can result in mail fraud.

Mere product "puffing" is not a scheme to defraud under the statute when the purchaser gets the article actually intended to be purchased. However, "puffing" does become fraudulent when the advertised product inherently fails to perform as claimed in the "puffing." Even gross exaggerations as to the merits and performance of a product may not constitute fraud if they are accompanied by a bona fide offer to refund the purchase price to dissatisfied purchasers.

chapter seventeen

UNFAIR PRACTICES

From time to time in other chapters of this book various marketing practices have been referred to as unfair trade practices in violation of the Federal Trade Commission Act. This chapter discusses a miscellany of other marketing practices which have been held to be unfair practices. Practices which are "unfair" because they are deceptive are discussed in Chapter 18, Misrepresentation. Practices discussed in Chapters 17 and 18 are often referred to as "dirty tricks" and in an appropriate case can be strong evidence of an intent to monopolize in a Sherman Act case.

BRIBERY AND PAYOLA

It should not require extended discussion to make the point that bribery is an unfair practice. In the context of the marketing function, bribery is most likely to occur in the form of payments made to employees of a customer. The Federal Trade Commission has used the term "commercial bribery" to refer to the practice of a seller of goods secretly paying money or making gifts to employees or agents of another to induce them to promote the purchase of the seller's goods by their own employers. The commercial harm from bribery is that the sale of the goods is not based on the merits of the product. Rather, the goods are sold because of the corruption of the purchaser's employees.

Payola is somewhat different from the commercial bribery discussed above.

Payola is the payment of money by record manufactures and distributors to disc jockeys to induce the disc jockeys to play and thereby promote certain records. Payola is not unlawful if the payor requires that a public disclosure of the payment is made at the time the record is played.

USING COERCION, INTIMIDATION, AND SCARE TACTICS

The use of coercion, intimidation, or various scare tactics to induce a customer to purchase a seller's goods is an unfair trade practice. This is true whether the practices are directed toward customers, prospective customers, competitors, suppliers, or recipients of unsolicited goods. Some unfair activities include:

1. Threatening lawsuits to collect payment for merchandise which had not been ordered
2. Threats to compete with a prospective purchaser unless the purchaser bought a particular good or service
3. A threat by a publisher to print derogatory material about a party unless the party contributed to the publication

In certain circumstances, the use of more than one sales talk to a prospective buyer in a single day may be unfair "relay salesmanship."

The use of horror stories and horror pictures to sell fire alarms and false representations of the danger of fire and explosion from the continued use of an existing furnace have been challenged.

Falsely threatening to turn matters over to a collection agency when in fact there was no intent to use a collection agency was held to be an unfair practice.

DOOR-TO-DOOR SALES

The Federal Trade Commission has issued a rule which makes it an unfair act or deceptive practice for a seller of consumer goods or services with a purchase price of more than $25 who sells its product away from its place of business to fail to furnish the buyer with certain information. The information which must be furnished to the buyer includes rules governing the buyer's right to cancel within three business days of the purchase. Moreover, if the buyer's right to cancel is exercised, the seller must promptly refund any down payment by the buyer. (See Chapter 14, Warranties, for a discussion of the requirement to disclosure warranties in door-to-door sales).

Key Point: Sales subject to the Truth-in-Lending Act and Regulation Z are exempt from the FTC rule covering door-to-door sales.

Key Point: The rule does not apply to telephone sales.

The FTC Rule was issued by the Commission to address five problems associated with sales made away from the seller's principal place of business:

1. deception by the seller in getting inside the consumer's home
2. high-pressure sales tactics
3. misrepresentation as to quality, price, or characteristics of the product
4. high price for low quality merchandise
5. nuisance created by the uninvited visit of the salesperson to the home

The rule requires that the buyer be given two copies of a completed form entitled either "Notice of Right to Cancel" or "Notice of Cancellation" which shall contain in ten-point bold face type statements informing the buyer about:

1. The right to cancel and how to cancel
2. The seller's obligation to return to the buyer any property traded in, payments made, and any negotiable instruments executed by the buyer
3. The obligations of the buyer and seller with regard to the product purchased

The cancellation notice may be shortened to eliminate references to inapplicable matters, e. g., return of trade-in property when seller does not take trade-ins.

The notice of cancellation must be furnished in such a manner that the buyer may use one copy to give notice to the seller while at the same time the buyer can retain one copy of both the notice and the contract for his or her own records.

Harassment of Competitors

Actions taken for the sole purpose of harassing a competitor are unfair. Examples of such activities include threatening to file lawsuits, filing groundless lawsuits, and sending large numbers of fictitious requests for estimates, specifications, and prices to a competitor.

Appropriation of a Competitor's Efforts

Taking for one's own use the results of the efforts of a competitor may be an unfair practice. Examples of such practices include the use of photographs of a competitor's product in advertising with the implication that it was the advertiser's product, the use of letters of recommendation actually given to a competitor and duplicating a competitor's product.

ENTICING A COMPETITOR'S EMPLOYEES

Ordinarily there is nothing unlawful in hiring one or even several employees from a competitor. However, it can become unlawful if it is done with the purpose of injuring the competitor through the use of false, misleading, or derogatory statements. For example, enticing away a competitor's employees by false statements regarding the competitors financial soundness is unfair.

Inducing a Breach of a Competitor's Contracts

It is an unfair practice to interfere with a competitor's relationships with its customers by inducing the customers to breach their contracts. Such inducements can include offering to sell goods at reduced or cut-rate prices for the purpose of injuring a competitor. Another method of inducing a contractual breach is by making false and misleading statements about the competitor to the customer. Harassing a competitor's customers to induce them to stop dealing with the competitor is also an unfair practice.

PHYSICAL INTERFERENCE WITH A COMPETITOR'S GOODS OR PROPERTY

It should come as no surprise that the unauthorized interference with the goods or property of a competitor is an unfair practice. Examples of such activities include

1. Collecting and destroying a competitor's catalogs or sales materials
2. Appropriating a competitor's containers
3. Removing a competitor's name from the competitor's products
4. Tampering with a competitor's products

5. Removing a competitor's product from the dealer's or consumer's premises

Acquisition of a Competitor's Trade Secrets

Certain methods of obtaining the trade secrets of a competitor are unfair practices. These unfair methods of acquiring a competitor's trade secrets may generally be thought of as methods of industrial espionage. Such espionage activities would include placing an employee in the competitor's business, bribing employees, secretly procuring customer lists, and the like. However, at least one court has held that it was not unlawful to employ agents to obtain information by posing as prospective customers where the information obtained was no more than that which the competitors regularly made available to customers.

Failure to Fill Orders Promptly or Shipment of Substitute Goods

A continued failure to fill orders within a reasonable time is an unfair trade practice. Special rules apply to failure to fill orders by mail-order sellers (see chapter 16).

Shipping or invoicing goods which are different from those ordered has also been held to be an unfair practice.

Payments of Push Money

Push money is money paid by a supplier to a retailer's sales staff to induce them to push or promote the supplier's product. Payments of push money are not unfair if the retailer consents to the payments. However, if the payments are made without the retailer's consent and knowledge it is an unfair practice.

Payments of push money are also unlawful in the following situations:

1. When any benefits to the salesperson is dependent on a lottery

2. When the payment requires or contemplates a practice which intentionally and unduly hampers the sale of competitor's products

3. When the effect of the payment is to substantially lessen competition or tends to create a monopoly

4. When similar payments are not accorded to sales persons or competing retailers on proportionately equal terms as required by the Robinson-Patman Act

Secret Rebates

The payment of secret rebates to a purchaser is an unfair practice because it is destructive of competition on the merits.

Avoiding Unfair Practices

Most unfair practices described thus far fall within the purview of dirty tricks. They are not practices that result from a lack of knowledge or occur by inadvertence. Rather, they are the result of overaggressive and shady sales efforts. The best company defense against such practices is to clearly communicate to all sales and marketing personnel that the firm intends to conduct its business in a lawful and upright manner.

Lotteries

The use of lotteries in marketing products is unlawful under the Federal Trade Commission Act and the use of the U. S. Mail to mail lottery tickets or related materials is a federal crime. However the U. S. Mail may be used to transmit materials relating to a lawful state-conducted lottery. Lotteries have often been used in the sale of candy. In upholding a Federal Trade Commission decision prohibiting a marketing lottery the Supreme Court said:

> . . . here the competitive method is shown to exploit consumers, children, who are unable to protect themselves. It employs a device whereby the amount of the return they receive from the expenditure of money is made to depend on chance. Such devices have met with condemnation through-out the community. Without inquiring whether, as respondent contends, the criminal statutes imposing penalties on gambling, lotteries and the like, fail to reach this particular practice in most or in any of the states, it is clear that the practice is the sort which the common law and criminal statutes have long deemed contrary to public policy. For these reasons a large share of the industry holds out against the device, despite the ensuing loss in trade, or bows reluctantly to what it brands unscrupulous. It would seem a gross perversion of the normal meaning of the word, which is the first criterion of statutory construction, to hold that the method is not "unfair."

A lottery may be found to exist even if the purchaser always receives something of value for money. While a manufacturer may not be responsible for how the distributor sells the product, the manufacturer must not package the product or present it in a manner that suggests the use of a lottery for its sale.

In the context of candy sales, lottery schemes have generally fallen into one of four categories: (1) the candy may have been packaged or assembled for lottery purposes, (2) candy wrappers may have different colors or different colored centers with persons finding special colors being entitled to a prize, (3) sales of candy with the price to be paid indicated on the inside of the wrapper, and (4) the use of punch boards in distributing candy. Punch board use has been condemned even when the consumer was assured of obtaining five cents worth of candy for five cents paid but through the use of a punch board might obtain a greater amount of candy.

Clearly these forms of lottery sales would be unlawful if adopted for use with products other than candy. For example, it has been held unlawful to use a punch board for the sale of hosiery. The key elements of a lottery method of sale are chance and price.

GENERAL GUIDES FOR UNFAIR PRACTICES

There is no concise definition of what constitutes an unfair trade practice. Many unfair practices have been described in this book. However, the restlessly inventive human mind is certain to devise new marketing plans which the Federal Trade Commission and the courts have not yet considered. The following rule of thumb may be applied to test novel marketing proposals. Unfair practices are those that are:

A. Opposed to good morals because of:
   1. Deception
   2. Bad faith
   3. Fraud
   4. Oppression
B. Against public policy because of a dangerous tendency to
   1. Create a monopoly
   2. Unduly hinder competition

State Laws

Many practices that are unfair practices under the Federal Trade Commission Act are also violative of state laws. For example, the state of Hawaii makes the payment of certain rebates an unfair trade practice. Legal counsel should be consulted regarding state law.

chapter eighteen

HOW TO AVOID MISREPRESENTATION PRACTICES

Misrepresentation in the marketing of goods and services is made unlawful by section 5 of the Federal Trade Commission Act which prohibits unfair or deceptive acts in commerce. The law prohibits practices that are injurious to the public whether or not there is any harm to competition. Accordingly, misrepresentation applies to many activities that would not be unlawful under the antitrust laws. Occasional acts of misrepresentation as well as established methods of conduct are covered by the act.

Key Point: Section 12 of the Federal Trade Commission Act makes it unlawful to disseminate any false advertising relating to food, drugs, devices, and cosmetics.

The act's broad language makes it applicable to almost any business activity. Many marketing activities in which misrepresentation can occur are discussed separately in Chapters 11 to 15. This chapter will discuss general rules relating to misrepresentation and specific practices not covered previously.

Deception

To be unlawful an act need not actually deceive anyone. It is sufficient if the challenged conduct has the capacity or tendency to deceive. In determining whether there is a capacity or tendency to deceive the commission and courts will consider the effect of the representation on the "average", "ordinary" public which includes ignorant, unthinking, credulous, and unsophisticated persons. However, the effect of the representation on very stupid persons will not be considered.

The representation considered as a whole is tested for deception rather than each separate part. If a word or term is ambiguous and one meaning would be false then the word or term is deceptive. A higher standard of care is required in labeling than is required in advertising a product.

Key Point: A representation may not be deceptive and therefore not a misrepresentation but still be an unfair practice.

Key Point: Misrepresentation may result from a failure to disclose a material fact.

Because the standards for deception are so broad, various guides and rules have been promulgated for use in determining what various words and phrases mean in an industry context and how they can be used lawfully. For example, Federal Trade Commission Trade Practice Conference Rules are drafted by the Federal Trade Commission on an industrywide basis with cooperation of the industry.

In addition to Federal Trade Commission Guides, Rules, and Regulations, the commission and courts have considered dictionary definitions, consumer surveys—whether conducted by the marketer or an independent agency—definitions promulgated by the U. S. Bureau of Standards, and testimony of individual members of the general public in determining whether a representation is deceptive.

Many unfair and deceptive practices are the result of conscious decision making by the marketer. These can best be avoided by creating a business environment of good citizenship. On the other hand, many acts of misrepresentation may occur through inadvertence. To avoid inadvertent misrepresentations, it is helpful to consult legal counsel and to refer to the various Federal Trade Commission Rules, Guides, and Policy statements. Some Federal Trade Commission Rules, Guides, and Policies have been discussed elsewhere in this book but others are too specific to be covered here. Let's now turn to some specific areas of deception.

TELEMARKETING FRAUD

It has been estimated that telemarketing frauds have bilked consumers out of at least $1 billion a year. The Federal Trade Commission has mounted a major attack against telemarketing fraud including initiating a number of cases in U. S. District Courts. From 1983 to mid-1988, the Federal Trade Commission has obtained court orders against 165 individuals and businesses, including six criminal convictions, and has obtained over $90 million in redress for defrauded consumers.

Numerous legislative proposals dealing with telemarketing are being considered by Congress. It is virtually certain that some legislative action will be taken within the next few years. Moreover, it is likely that the Federal Communications Commission will investigate such practices as computer-generated phone calls. Until specific legislation is passed, telemarketing fraud will be attacked under the existing law preventing unfair and deceptive practices. Legislation most likely will include a 30-day rule similar to that applicable to sales by mail.

An example of how the Federal Trade Commission is using existing law to combat telemarketing fraud is a complaint filed against a telemarketer of coins. The commission alleged that the telemarketer misrepresented the grade and investment value of the coins sold by telephone. According to the Federal Trade Commission, the telemarketer told prospective purchasers that coins could appreciate 500 to 1000 percent in ten years when in fact the consumer could expect to recover only a fraction of the purchase price. The court issued a temporary restraining order.

In another case brought by the Federal Trade Commission, a travel service using telemarketing was held to have misrepresented the cost of its travel packages, obtained credit card numbers under false pretenses, and then billed consumers' credit card accounts without authorization. The court stated that it would order the payment of refunds to the injured consumers.

USING CONTESTS LEGALLY

The use of contests in product marketing is not illegal. However, it is an unfair practice to misrepresent the various features of the contest. Some rather common-sense rules apply to the use of contests as a marketing method:

1. Cash prizes cannot be promised, unless cash in the amount promised is actually paid.

2. If a person must purchase or sell merchandise to win a prize, it is an unfair practice to represent that the prize can be obtained solely by solving a puzzle, composing a rhyme, or making a correct guess.

3. When merchandise certificates are awarded as prizes, their value cannot be misrepresented, nor can their value be nullified by price increases.

4. A promotional scheme should not be held out to be a contest when no contest is involved.

5. A contest should not be represented as a part of an advertising scheme unless it is.

6. The odds of winning a prize should not be misrepresented.

7. It is improper to represent that a particular person will judge the contest unless a definite commitment to act as judge has been obtained from that person.

8. It is improper to use puzzles so simple to solve as to remove them from the category of a contest when the winning of a prize depends on purchasing a product.

Key Point: Although the use of contests is legal, lotteries are illegal (see Chapter 17).

Key Point: Special rules apply to the use of games of chance in connection with the retail of food and gasoline.

MERCHANDISE CERTIFICATES

The use of merchandise certificates is lawful so long as their is no misrepresentation as to the brand, style, quantity, quality, or value of the merchandise that may be redeemed. Moreover the place of redemption may not be misrepresented. Any limitations on the time of redemption must be disclosed.

Key Point: Use of the term "gift certificate" is a misrepresentation if the certificate cannot be redeemed without making a purchase unless disclosure of the purchase requirement is made.

ORIGINALITY OR EXCLUSIVENESS

As one might expect, it is a misrepresentation to claim falsely that one originated a product, or some part of it or that the product itself is original. Similarly, it is a misrepresentation to make false claims that a product is the only one which possesses certain characteristics or performs certain functions. False claims that the seller has exclusive rights to sell a product or that the seller is the sole manufacturer or distributor are unlawful.

Examples of claims that have been prohibited are:

1. Only "genuine aspirin"

2. Claiming to offer information not available from any other source

3. Claiming to be the only book of its kind distributed solely through ministers, physicians, and marriage counselors

4. Substantially different from anything else on the market

5. Made by an exclusive process

FREE TRIAL EXAMINATION

A marketing program may offer a free trial examination period so long as all conditions restricting the free trial examination are disclosed. Any cost to the consumer, must be disclosed. When a free home trial examination is offered, the product must actually be made available for trial in the home.

Key Point: Advertisement of a "free trial" is considered by the Federal Trade Commission to be a guarantee that the full purchase price will be refunded at the option of the purchaser.

METHOD OF MANUFACTURING

The method or process used to manufacture or prepare an article for sale should not be misrepresented. For example, products made by machine should not be advertised as "handmade" nor should ready-made products be offered as "custom-made" or "tailor-made." Products produced in factories cannot be offered as "homemade." There should be no misrepresentations regarding the nature of work force used to produce the product such as "blind-made," "union-made," or "Indian-made."

REBUILT OR RECONDITIONED GOODS

For most products consumers want to buy new items rather than used ones. Some marketers have been tempted to take advantage of this predilection by passing off used goods as new. It is a violation of the Federal Trade Commission Act to misrepresent that used, second-hand, or rebuilt goods are new. Similarly it is unlawful to claim that a product made of used materials is new.

When a product is first introduced to the public as a "new" product, the Federal Trade Commission uses a six-month rule of thumb as the length of time it can be claimed as "new." Under exceptional circumstances the period may be longer than six months. The Federal Trade Commission has held that advertising a product as "new" implies that the product was recently developed, discovered, or invented. Therefore, after the product has been available for six months in some market areas, it cannot be advertised as "new" even when first introduced into a new market area.

Key Point: It is necessary to distinguish between claims that a product is "new" and claims that an individual item of merchandise is "new."

Rebuilt or Reconditioned

It is unlawful to represent goods as rebuilt when they have only been repaired. Similarly it is unlawful to claim items were factory rebuilds unless they were rebuilt in a factory.

Returned Merchandise

In some marketing programs a purchaser may use merchandise on a trial basis and if not satisfied return it to the seller. The question arises as to whether such returned items may then be sold as new. The Federal Trade Commission has issued a policy statement requiring clear and conspicuous disclosure of the prior use in all of the marketer's advertising, sales promotion literature, invoices, and packaging. The fact that there may be no qualitative difference between a "new" item and one that has been returned will not justify substituting returned goods for "new" goods. The commission recommends that sellers establish inventory controls to ensure that returned goods are not intermingled with new goods.

Key Point: Goods which have merely been inspected and not used may be sold as new goods.

PASSING OFF

It is unlawful misrepresentation to pass off a product of one manufacturer as that of another manufacturer. Such passing off may occur through the prominent display of the name of the other manufacturer in connection with the sale of the goods. Simulation of another manufacturers packaging, trade name, corporate name, and so on, can also be unlawful misrepresentation.

TESTS, SURVEYS, AND AWARDS

Claimed results of tests and surveys or awards received may be misrepresented also. The Federal Trade Commission has required disclosure of defects in testing or surveying methods. For example, a seller has been required to disclose that the tests relied on were not conducting in accordance with industry standards. Survey results cannot be used to represent a product unless the survey was conducted and the statistical result is fairly represented. Marketers should not engage in activities designed to bias the survey results.

A marketer should not claim that its product has won prizes, trophies, or other awards which imply comparative tests with competitive products unless such comparative testing actually occurred.

Similarly a product certification claim cannot be used unless the certifying organization was competent to make the certification.

When tests results are used to promote a product, the items tested must be representative of the items actually offered for sale.

chapter nineteen

USING TRADEMARKS AND COPYRIGHTS LEGALLY

The word, name, symbol, or devices a manufacturer selects to distinguish its product or service from its competitors stands at the very center of its marketing program. It is the focal point of advertising and promotional endeavors. The mark pictures in the mind of the consumer the quality of the product or service. In sum, it is the embodiment of the manufacturer's reputation.

It is surprising, in light of its significance, that little time may be given by many entrepreneurs to selection of and verifying the availability of a trademark, service mark, or trade name.

It is important to understand how trademark rights are acquired, the significance of federal registration of the mark; and as it relates to selection of a mark, the legal prerequisites to registration, as well as relevant commercial considerations in its selection.

ESTABLISHING OWNERSHIP OF A TRADEMARK

In most countries, rights in trademarks or trade names are acquired by registration with a designated governmental agency. However, in the United States actual and continuous use of the mark is the determining factor establishing mark ownership.

From a legal standpoint, rights in a mark are established on a first-come basis. The first proprietor to use a given mark in conjunction with the sale of products or services on labeling or promotional material is the owner of that mark. It is vitally important to document and maintain records of the date on which the first mark is used in commerce, both intrastate and interstate.

Under the Trademark Law Revision Act of 1988 it is no longer required that a trademark actually be used in interstate commerce before it can be registered. Now a person who has a bona fide intention, under circumstances showing good faith, to use a trademark in interstate commerce may apply to register a trademark on the principal registry; The application is made by:

1. Filing with the Patent and Trademark Office
2. On a written form prescribed by the Commissioner
3. Verified by the applicant
4. Specifying the applicant's citizenship and domicile
5. Stating applicant's bona fide intent to use the trademark in interstate commerce
6. The goods in connection with which the trademark will be used
7. The manner in which the trademark will be used
8. Stating that the applicant feels entitled to use the mark and that to the best of his or her knowledge or belief no one else has the right to use the mark in commerce
9. Filing a drawing of the mark
10. Paying the prescribed fees

During the trademark examination period an applicant who has made use of the mark in commerce may claim the benefits of such use in commerce by amending the application to show such use.

After notice of allowance of the application for registration, the applicant has six months to file with the Patent and Trademark Office a verified statement that the mark is in use in interstate commerce and specifying the first date of use in interstate commerce. The statement must also show the goods used with the mark and the manner in which it was used. On request, the period for filing the verified statement of actual use in commerce may be extended for a total period of 24 months.

Continuous use of the mark is important to maintain ownership interest in the mark because the law provides that discontinuing use constitutes an abandonment of the mark and of the owner's claim to ownership.

In addition to continuity of use, the manufacturer must constantly monitor the quality of the products or services sold under the mark if he is to protect his ownership of the mark. The manufacturer must always be alert to protect the quality of the product or service associated with his mark. The law recognizes the right of the public to rely on the mark for the purpose of judging the quality of product or service and assuring them of substantial consistency in their purchases.

Almost every franchise agreement and many other distributorship agreements include a license in favor of the franchisee or distributor to use the trademark. It is important to again emphasize that the mark represents the manufacturer's good will. Failure to maintain sufficient control over the franchisee or distributor to ensure the public consistent quality of the products or services sold under the mark, may result in a finding that the mark has been abandoned. This factor highlights the absolute necessity of an effective screening process for prospective franchisees and distributors. Personal character and background are of far more significance than is the ability to purchase the franchise. Will the licensee cooperate with your policing efforts to ensure high quality? Remember, you are entrusting every franchisee or distributor you accept with your reputation.

Key Point: Any written distribution agreement should set forth the extent of the distributor's right to use the supplier's trademark.

WHEN YOU SHOULD REGISTER YOUR TRADEMARK

As previously stated, registration does not create ownership rights in a mark. Ownership depends on continuous use. Regardless of whether a mark is registered, the first person or entity to use the mark has superior rights and may be entitled to an injunction and damages in an infringement suit.

However, substantial advantages arise by virtue of federal registration. These are:

1. If the right to use the mark is challenged in court, and it is registered, the law presumes ownership and exclusive right to use the mark lies in the registrant. The party challenging the registered mark must prove that his or her rights are superior. If proof of first date of use is inadequate it will not prevail, even if in fact it is true.

   Key Point: Document the time of first use.

2. Unless the mark was acquired by fraud, or has been abandoned, or has been abused by using it in a way that misrepresents the true source of the products or services, or unless it becomes the common descriptive name of an article or substance (usually a problem only where the products consists of something unique, i.e., not previously

available); the right to use the registered mark becomes uncontestable except in those areas where an actual user was utilizing the mark prior to the registrant's use of the mark.

3. If the mark is registered no one can claim that they did not know of its use because the law declares that everyone has notice of the registrant's claim to ownership of a registered mark.

4. If someone uses the registered mark without permission or uses a confusingly similar mark, a court has the authority to award three times the amount of actual damages. Also you can stop importation of products bearing an infringing mark.

HOW TO REGISTER A MARK

The proposed mark must be submitted in accordance with specifications set out in the application for registration which can be obtained from the U. S. Patent and Trademark Office in Washington DC. The filing fee is nominal. While application is pending and if you are satisfied regarding the mark's availability, you can continue to use your mark and the designation "TM" or "Brand" to distinguish it for advertising, labeling, or promotional activities. The designation "R" cannot be used until the mark is registered with the U. S. Patent and Trademark Office.

HOW TO SELECT A TRADEMARK

It is obvious that prudence requires a diligent search prior to the use of a mark in order to determine whether that mark or one similar to it is being or has been used by another. The extent of such a search is limited only by the business judgment of the intended user and the resources he is willing to expend. Considerations should include the anticipated extent of use of the mark and the geographic distribution of the products or services bearing the mark.

Before commencement of a nationwide search, using trademark search firms, the manufacturer should do a preliminary search using the resources available. Inquiry can be made of sales and other company representatives who might have considerable knowledge of the existent competition's marks, products, or services. Trade journals, trade directories, telephone directories, and technical dictionaries are good sources of information. If the preliminary search doesn't show any conflicting mark, a search firm should be retained to search the U. S. Patent and Trademark Office records for:

1. Principal register

2. Supplemental register

3. Pending applications

4. Cancelled registrations

5. Abandoned registrations

Relevant State Trademark Registers and corporate records should also be examined.

Key Point: If a conflicting mark is found but appears to be abandoned, it may still be in use. Further search is necessary. On the other hand, the existence of a registered mark does not necessarily mean it is not available. Use may have been terminated. Further search is again necessary.

It is extremely important to remember that, regardless of how thorough the search, there can be no guarantee that all trademarks were located, particularly unregistered marks. Nevertheless, searches by reputable search firms will provide sufficient data for a reasonable business decision. The search should take only a few weeks and, unless it becomes complicated, will involve only a moderate fee.

The search will assist in identifying potential conflicts with a prior user or the user of a mark similar enough to cause confusion to buyers.

An evaluation of the availability of the proposed mark includes analysis of physical likeness of marks, and similarities in products or services represented by similar marks. A detailed analysis of mark evaluation is beyond the scope of this text. The involvement of competent legal counsel is crucial at this stage of mark selection.

The legal standard for infringement is that the challenged mark is "likely" to cause confusion, mistake, or deception in the mind of the consumer. If such result is only a "possibility" the infringement action will fail. The potential consequences of failing to adequately search the availability of the mark could be disastrous. Apart from obvious legal expenses in defending an infringement action which, if lost, could result in financial liability, the marketing program would suffer a loss of good will established by use of the mark and the cost of changing to another trademark.

What constitutes a good mark? Certainly the mark should be designed or formulated in such a way to speak favorably to the targeted customer. This makes sense since a mark is supposed to enhance product or service recognition in the eye of the intended customer so that it can be requested or recommended. Technical trademarks or complicated trademarks, for example, are difficult to pronounce, are likely to be ineffective unless potential customers are highly educated. Easily readable and enunciated marks should be given preference. The age and income of the potential consumers should be considered. A visually recognized mark is more effective.

In picking a logo a manufacturer should consider how well the mark will reproduce on newspaper print, television, or other advertising media. Poor newsprint quality can ruin the effectiveness of finely detailed logos and they may not reproduce well on television without being greatly magnified.

HOW MUCH PROTECTION DOES A TRADEMARK PROVIDE?

The degree of protection afforded by a trademark depends in part on the nature of the word chosen as a trademark. For example a word made up especially to represent a product such as "Kodak" is entitled to greater protection than is a word or symbol closely related to or descriptive of the product to which it is applied.

A generic term cannot be protected as a trademark. For example, the word "beer" cannot be claimed as a trademark because according it trademark protection would prevent competitors from describing their own products.

Key Point: If a term is necessary to describe a product characteristic that a competitor has a right to copy, a manufacturer may not effectively preempt competition by claiming that term as its own.

The purpose of a trademark is to identify the source of the product, i.e., the manufacturer, and not to identify the type of product. Thus in order to show that a proposed trademark is not generic, it must be shown that the primary significance of the term in the minds of the consuming public is not the product but the producer.

The following names have been held to be generic:

Chocolate fudge

Christian Science Church

Bead bath

Bundt

Computer learning center

Murphy bed

Warehouse foods

Rack O'pork

National High School Cheerleading Championship

Wickerware

Surgincenter

Note: A word may be generic in one context but not in another. For example "seats" was held not to be generic when used as a name for a reservation service but would be generic if used in connection with chairs, couches, or bleachers.

Marks that are merely descriptive are not protected unless they have acquired a secondary meaning. Descriptiveness of a mark exists if the mark informs the consumer of the function of the product, the product's intended purpose, the characteristics or qualities of the product, or the effect of the product on the user. A secondary meaning of a descriptive mark that may make the mark protectable exists when, in the mind of the consumer, the mark identifies the origin of the product as well as describing the product.

A mark does not acquire a secondary meaning merely by being associated with a popular product. Rather, it must be shown that the primary significance of the mark to the consumer is to identify the origin of the product. A secondary meaning is usually created by extensive advertising over time. However, one cannot prove a claim of secondary meaning simply by showing large advertising budgets.

If a mark is not federally registered, then whoever first uses the mark in a new territory acquires the right to use the mark in that territory. A trademark knows no boundaries because it is trade and not territory that is protected. A senior user of a mark can exclude a junior user only if the senior user can establish that its use of a mark had acquired a secondary meaning by the time the junior user used the mark.

Key Point: A valid trademark can over time become a generic term and thereby lose its right to protection under the Lanham Trademark Act. A nongeneric trademark becomes generic and loses its protected status when the principal significance of the trademark to the public becomes the indication of the nature of the article rather than the indication of the article's origin. However, federal registration of a trademark endows it with a strong presumption of validity including a specific presumption that it is not generic.

TRADE NAMES

A trade name is different from a trademark. A trade name is a name used by a firm to identify itself. Trade names are not eligible for registration under the Lanham Act, but are protected by the act, 15 U. S. C. section 25(a). However, if a trade name is also used to identify a product as a house mark, the name may be registered, for example, Ford Mustang.

SUBSTITUTING PRODUCTS

A dealer who substitutes another product in filling an order placed for a trade-marked product without informing the customer, may be guilty of trademark infringement and unfair trade practices. For example, it was held unlawful for a lounge and casino to substitute another cola-type beverage in response to specific orders for "Coke" or "Coca Cola" without first giving the customer oral notice that another cola would be served. An important issue in product substitution situations is whether the consumer was given effective notice that the requested trademark item was not being provided.

Good faith or lack of wrongful intent is not a defense to a trademark infringement claim. The basic policy behind the Lanham Act is to protect consumers from the likelihood of confusion. Therefore a determination of liability for infringement turns on the objective fact of likely customer confusion and not on the good faith of the infringer.

State unfair competition laws traditionally have been applied to trademark infringement, passing off one's goods as those of another, and misappropriation of good will by using the trade name or symbol of another.

DECEPTIVE USE OF TRADEMARKS

To use a trademark to deceive the public is an unlawful act under section 5 of the Federal Trade Commission Act. The fact that the trademark has been registered with the U.S. Patent Office is no defense and will not prevent the Federal Trade Commission from prohibiting its use as deceptive and misleading. Moreover, the owner of a trademark or trade name has a duty not to use or permit it to be used in a manner designed to deceive the public.

> *Example:* A firm which had a history of using the trademark "Sani-Onyx" for 20 years to describe a product which was not onyx was prohibited from using the trademark.

However, the Federal Trade Commission recognizes that a company may have a large investment in a legitimate trademark or trade name and that a prohibition of all use of the mark or name is a drastic measure. Accordingly, the Federal Trade Commission may order that the mark only be used in conjunction with other words or phrases that eliminate any deception that might arise from an unrestricted use of the trademark or trade name.

The Lanham Act may create a basis for a false advertising claim when a trademark or trade name is used. Section 43(a) of the Lanham Act provides in part that:

> Any person who shall . . . use in connection with any goods or services . . . any false description or representation including words or other symbols tending falsely to describe or represent the same, and shall cause such goods or services to enter into commerce shall be liable to a civil action . . . by any person who believes that he is or is likely to be damaged by the use of any such false description or representation.

For example, advertising to sell brand name products at a specified price when the brand name products were not available may constitute false advertising. However, it has been held that an advertisement to sell brand name tires at a specified price which contained disclaimers that because of space limitations some stores might not stock all tire sizes and advising consumers to call the stores to check availability was not false advertising.

COPYRIGHTS

Copyright law provides limited protection for a term of years to a variety of artistic creations including writings, photographs, drawings, plays, musical compositions, sound recordings, motion pictures, and works of art. However, not all items that might be claimed copyrightable are eligible for copyright protection.

Items Which Cannot Be Copyrighted

Some items that cannot be copyrighted are:

1. Ideas
2. Procedures
3. Processes
4. Systems
5. Methods of operation
6. Concepts

Items Which Can Be Copyrighted

Copyright protection can be had for original works of authorship that are fixed in a tangible medium of expression from which they can be reproduced or communicated. Works that can be copyrighted include:

1. Literary works
2. Musical works including lyrics
3. Dramatic works including musical accompaniment
4. Pantomines and choreographic works
5. Pictorial, graphics, and sculptures
6. Audiovisuals
7. Sound recordings
8. Motion pictures

Exclusive Rights

The exclusive rights vested in the holder of a copyright include the rights to:

1. Print, publish, reproduce, and sell the work
2. Translate or dramatize the work
3. Arrange or adapt the work
4. Perform the work in public for profit and to make and sell transcript

Acquiring a Copyright

There is no requirement that a work be registered in order to achieve copyright protection. Rather the statute merely requires that certain formalities be observed on first publication of the work. For writings, copyright protection is obtained by giving notice of copyright on the work by the word "copyright," "copr.," or "C" along with the name of the owner and the year in which the copyright is claimed. For musical works the symbol "P" is used along with the first year of publication and the name of the copyright owner.

appendix a

DISTRIBUTION CONTRACTS

Contracts with distributors may range from very informal oral agreements that consist of no more than accepting orders on an order-by-order basis to complex formal written franchise agreements that have been registered with the state. In most instances a manufacturer will prefer to have written agreements clearly specifying each party's rights. However, there may be valid reasons for not insisting on a written agreement. When there has been a long-standing oral relationship with a valued distributor, a manufacturer should consider whether insisting on a written distribution agreement will create dissension where none exists.

An important consideration both in drafting a written distribution agreement and in deciding whether to transform an oral agreement into a written agreement is the effect of laws regulating termination of the relationship. If state statutes regulate termination, it may only be necessary to ensure that any written agreement conforms to the state statute. If there is no state statute, the state common law may permit an order-to-order relationship to be terminated at will. In other states such a relationship may require reasonable notice for termination.

Key Point: Section 2-309 of the Uniform Commerical Code provides that a relationship of indefinite duration can be terminated on good faith and on reasonable notice at any time.

Contract Expectations

In preparing a distribution contract it is important to bear in mind that the supplier and distributor have different objectives. The distributor, for example, will want to have the most stringent restrictions possible on termination by the supplier, will want the written agreement to detail the supplier's obligations to provide advertising and promotion assistance, and also will want the contract to provide for the lowest possible performance levels.

On the other hand, the supplier will want the greatest possible freedom to terminate the distributor and will require high performance standards to push the distributor to exploit the product's market.

Contract Provisions

The actual contract provisions with distributors will depend on the nature of the product, type of distribution system, and character of the industry. Moreover, applicable state and federal law must be considered in deciding what matters should be covered in a written contract. However, at least the following items should be considered.

1. *Product.* The contract should specify what products or product lines offered by the supplier are available to the distributor. Whether the supplier will be permitted to carry new prodcuts developed by the supplier should also be spelled out in the contract.

2. *Territory.* The distribution contract should delineate the territory in which the distributor is authorized to sell the product. Any territorial or customer restraints should be placed in the contract. The contract should also address items such as areas of primary responsibility and restraints on transshipping the product. Moreover, the contract should indicate whether the distributor is being given an exclusive dealership and if so the extent of the exclusive dealership.

3. *Noncompete Clauses.* If the supplier is providing customer lists or proprietary information or other trade secrets, the contract should include a provision restraining the distributor from competing with the supplier after termination of the agreement. Noncompete clauses are clear restraints on competition and will not be enforced unless reasonably limited as to time and territory. Because most states have laws regulating the use of noncompete clauses, legal counsel should be consulted before drafting such a clause. The noncompete clause should expressly provide that the supplier may obtain injunctive relief to restrain the distributor from violating the contract provisions. Additionally the contract should state that both parties agree that actual damages will be difficult to ascertain and that therefore liquidated damages in a fixed amount may be awarded for breach of the contract.

4. *Distributor's Duties.* The distributor contract should not only describe the duties to stock the product, but also describe requirements for inventory and parts, training of sales personnel, warranty repairs, any postsale service needs, and development of the sales territory through promotions and advertising.

Key Point: A requirement that a distributor use its "best efforts" to promote a product is a higher standard than a requirement of "reasonable efforts."

Another distributor's duty to include in the contract is a sales quota. The contract may provide for different sales quotas at different time periods during the life of the contract.

5. *Marketing Plans.* A supplier may require its distributors to develop and submit annual marketing plans for the supplier's product. Follow-up reports on marketing activities may also be required.

6. *Supplier Advertising and Promotion.* The contract may describe the supplier's obligation to advertise and promote the product. If cooperative advertising is offered, the distribution agreement may address the distributor's right to participate in a cooperative advertising and promotional program.

7. *Protection of Trade Secrets.* In many distribution agreements a very important item will be the protection of trade secrets. Generally, the contract should provide that the distributor acquires no rights in the supplier's trade secrets. The distributor should be required to use the supplier's trade secret information only to promote sale of the supplier's product during the term of the agreement and to return all such information to the supplier on termination of the agreement.

8. *Trademarks.* If any trademarked products are covered by the agreement, the contract should indicate the extent of the distributor's right to use the supplier's trademark. The distributor may be required to take reasonable steps to protect the supplier's trademark. The supplier must also make provisions for ensuring the quality of any trademarked product.

9. *Business Opportunity Laws.* It may be possible to avoid application of state business opportunity laws by carefully drafting the distribtuon contracts. Whether it is worthwhile to structure a distribution system to avoid the business opportunities law is a matter of business judgment. Business opportunity laws usually are applied to distribution programs that involve vending machines, racks, or product displays. In most instances state business opportunity statutes can

be avoided by making no representations as to income expectations, by making no product buy-back promises and by leaving the distrtibutor to find the distribution locations. To be certain that no income expectation claim will be implied, it is safest to avoid offering any market projections.

10. *Obligations of the Supplier.* A distributor will want to pay particular attention to the requirements placed on the supplier by the distribution contract. Large distributors dealing with small suppliers often have great bargaining power. A distributor who is purchasing component parts may have particular concern with the supplier's ability to fill orders on a timely basis and the supplier's ability to ensure uniform quality. Among the items to consider in any enumeration of the supplier's duties are the following:

a. Minimum level of supplies avaiable

b. Technical assistance available to the distributor and its customers

c. Training offered to the distributor's employees

d. Supplier's quality control

e. Advertising and promotion to be provided by the supplier including national advertising and cooperative advertising

11. *Warranty Liability.* The sale of products to ultimate consumers may result in both express and implied warranties (see Chapter 14). In negotiating a distribution agreement, the supplier and the distributor will have conflicting objectives regarding warranties. A nonmanufacturing supplier will want to assure itself that it will not have a liability greater than the manufacturer's. The manufacturer will want to limit its warranty liability to the extent the law permits it to do so. However, it is a matter of business judgment whether marketing concerns dictate offering a more encompassing warranty to improve sales. The distributor may also have conflicting warranty interest. Strong warranties may increase sales. On the other hand, if quality is not consistent with the warranty, susbtantial expenses may be incurred in fulfilling the warranty.

   The distributor will want contract provisions to provide indemnification against third-party claims that may arise under warranty, product liability, infringement of patents, trademarks, or copyrights. The distributor's contract provisions should address its obligation if any to make warranty repairs and the obligations of the supplier or manufacturer to reimburse the distributor for warranty repairs.

12. *Contract Duration.* The duration of the distribution contract should be set forth. Duration may be for an indefinite period to continue until terminated on reasonable notice or for a specific time period. If the term is specific, the parties may wish to include contract language describing the right of the distributor to renew the agreement for a successive term. Renewal provisions should state clearly the circumstances for denial and the terms on which notice of intent to renew must be given. Moreover, a contract renewal provision should also list the rights of the supplier to change any terms such as price at the time of renewal.

Red Flag: Many state statutes regulate contract renewal rights. This is especially true with respect to franchise agreements.

13. *Price and Quantity.* The distributor contract should address the price at which the supplier will sell to the distributor. If the duration of the contract is for any substantial period, the price term should refer to sales at the supplier's then current price list. In the alternative, the contract may provide for sales at a certain percentage discount from the suppliers suggested retail price. The price term may also cover eligibility for quantity discounts and promotional discounts.

The contract may provide that the supplier will sell and the buyer will purchase a specific quantity during the agreement term. In the alternative, the supplier may contract to provide all distributor's requirements. The supplier may limit the quantity it must supply over a particular time period and it may also reserve the right to allocate supplies among distributors during periods of supply shortages.

14. *Termination Provisions.* Both the supplier and distributor will want the distribtuion contract to provide for termination of the contract. The conditions of termination may be suject to provisions of state law. Franchise agreements are often subject to state law termination provisions. Typically state statutes provide for notice of intent to terminate by the supplier or franchisor followed by a period of about 90 days in which the distributor may cure any default and thereby avoid termination. State law may also limit the causes of termination of the contract prior to the end of the contract term.

In negotiating the term provisions of a distribution agreeement the parties should at least consider the following matters.

A. *Termination Without Cause.* A contract could provide that either party might terminate the agreement at any time without cause on a certain number of days notice. Such a provision is unlikely to be acceptable if either party is required to make a substantial investment to accomplish the purposes of the contract.

B. *Failure to Comply with Performance Standards.* In most cases it will be the supplier who will want the right to terminate for failure of the distributor to comply with performance standards. However, there are circumstances in which the distributor is concerned with the quality of the supplier's performance.

The performances standards may be specified in the contract itself or if they are voluminous they may be placed in a separate document that is incorporated into the contract by reference. The performance standards will of course be specifically tailored to meet the needs of the parties, given the character of the product, the method of distribution, and custom and usage of the industry. Performance standards may be stated in a variety of ways including:

1. Quantity of product sold
2. Dollars of sales
3. Training of employees
4. Performance of warranty work
5. Cleanliness of premises
6. Methods of display
7. Quality control
8. Postsale service
9. Inventory maintenance
10. Maintenance of credit
11. Timely payment for orders
12. Exploitation of market

Red Flag: To state a performance standard in terms of "best efforts" is not recommended because it is inherently ambiguous and invites litigation.

Enforcement of performance standards should be done on a fair and impartial basis. Selective enforcement of performance standards may result in litigation claiming that the supplier conspired with others to cause the termination.

Red Flag: A selective enforcement of an unrealistic sales quota may violate the Automobile Dealer's Day in Court Act.

A supplier should stand ready to renegotiate the performance standards if changes in economic conditions, technology, methods of distribution, competition, or consumer preferences render the existing standards unrealistic or unfair.

Parties should also consider providing for remedies short of termination for failure to meet performance standards. For example, a distributor's failure to meet standards may create a right of the supplier to reduce the size of the distributor's territory or to appoint new distributors in the area served by the defaulting distributor. Default of timely payment provisions may be remedied by giving the supplier the right to require C. O. D. terms on future orders. The alternative remedy should be tailored to the particular default. If alternative remedies are permitted, the contract should state whether the supplier has the sole right to choose between termination and some less drastic remedy.

C. *Contract Breaches.* Both parties will want the right to terminate the agreement if the other party breaches the contract in a material fashion. The contract should provide for any right to notice and opportunity to cure the default prior to termination. It should also provide that failure to terminate for a particular breach does not constitute a waiver of the right to terminate for a similar breach later.

Red Flag: Before drafting termination provisions state law must be considered to check notice and right to cure requirements.

The parties may stipulate in the contract that some defaults cannot be cured and that termination may be had without opportunity for cure.

Key Point: The length of time between notice of termination and the date of termination need not be the same for all defaults. Some defaults may justify termination with little or no notice.

D. *Termianation Based upon Change in Business Ownership.* Frequently much of the value of the distributorship agreement to the supplier will be the obtaining of the services of a particular person. If that person is no longer associated with distribution outlet, the supplier will want to be free to seek a new distributor. On the other hand, the distributor may feel that much of the market value of the distributorship consists of supplier contracts. Therefore, both supplier and distributor need the contract to state whether the contract can be terminated on change in ownership of the distributor. Such contract clauses may permit the distribuor to transfer ownership freely to a certain class of persons, i.e., spouse or adult children, but require the supplier's agreement for transfers to others.

E. *Termination for Financial Reasons.* A supplier will want the right to terminate the agreement if the distributor encounters financial difficulties. A distributor with financial difficulties is likely to be slow to pay for orders and unable to properly promote the supplier's product. Financially insecure distributors may also be unable or unwilling to provide adequate postsale service. Suppliers will want the right to terminate if the distributor fails to make timely order payments or to comply fully with credit terms. A termination clause may be triggered by the failure to discharge a lien (other than a routine financing lien) insolvency or the inability to pay debts.

Red Flag: If a distributor files bankruptcy prior to termination by the supplier, the distributor has the right under section 365 of the Bankruptcy Code to either affirm or reject the contract. If it is affirmed, the supplier cannot terminate based on bankruptcy but could terminate for some other reason.

F. *Termination and Noncompetition Clauses.* Care should be taken to ensure that the termination clause and any noncompete clauses dovetail.

15. *Arbitration Provisions.* Parties should consider whether all, some, or no claims made under the contract should be subject to binding arbitration. If claims are made subject to arbitration, the agreement may specify the place of arbitration, the method of selection of arbitrators, and other arbitration details.

Recent Supreme Court decisions have opened the door to arbitration of even antitrust claims and RICO claims. Arbitration is given wide scope and there is only limited appeal from an arbitration decision. Discovery need not be permitted and the normal rules of evidence do not apply. Therefore an arbitration clause should be drafted with great care and consideration.

CONSIGNMENT CONTRACTS

Consignment contracts are often used by start-up companies that have not established consumer acceptance of their product. Consignment contracts help these companies obtain distribution outlets because the consignment allows the distributor to shift inventory costs, and risks of credit, catastrophe, and obsolescence to the supplier.

The essence of a consignment agreement is that the suppleir makes the distributor his agent for the sale of goods but retains ownership and control of the goods even while they are in the hands of the agent. The sales agent has only limited rights to deal in the goods—primarily to transfer title and possession in accordance with the consignor's instructions.

To ensure that a contract will in fact create a consignment relationship and not some conditional sales or financing arrangement, the contract should provide that:

1. Any unsold merchandise can be returned to the consignor without obligation.

2. Legal title remains with the supplier until sale on which it passes directly to the purchaser.

3. The supplier controls the price, terms, and conditions of sale.

4. The consignee is required to keep the supplier's goods segregated from other goods which it may hold.

5. All receipts from the sale should be held in trust for the supplier in a special account or they should be remitted to the supplier immediately.

6. Records of the consignment goods should be kept separately from records of other goods.

7. The consignee should be required to render periodic accountings.

8. The supplier be permitted to inspect the goods and the relevant records at the consignee's place of business.

9. The consignee must return the goods on demand of the supplier at any time.

10. The supplier is liable for actions taken by the consignee within the scope of actual or implied agency authority.

11. All shipping documents must refer to the goods as consigned goods.

Red Flag: Under the Uniform Commercial Code consigned goods may be subject to the claims of the consignee's creditors while the goods are in the hands of the consignee, unless the consignor complies with the special requirements of UCC section 2-326(3). Under the UCC, the supplier may give notice to potential creditors of the consignee by posting signs. This method is not reliable. Rather, the supplier should file an Article 9 financing satement signed by the consignee. The supplier should also obtain a signed security agreement.

True consignment arragements will not be subject to the price discrimination provisions of the Robinson-Patman Act because no sale is involved.

SAMPLE DISTRIBUTION CONTRACT

The sample contract shown below should be considered as illustrative only. It should not simply be copied as is. Each supplier and distributor must carefully consider their needs and the needs of the industry in drafting specific contract provisions. Legal counsel should be sought in preparing the distribution agreement.

AGREEMENT

Agreement made this _____ day of _____ 19 ____ , by and between Supplier, a Colorado corporation with its principal place of business at 17 Base Street, Gold Hill, Colorado, and Distributor, a Texas corporation, with its principal place of business at 1000 Dynasty Street, Dallas, Texas.

Whereas, Supplier has developed a product for the removal of nostril hair which is unique; and

Whereas, Distributor, desires to sell the product developed by Supplier;

Now therefore, it is agreed that in consideration of the mutual promises contained herein, Supplier agrees to sell its product to Distributor for sale in the territory described in this agreement, and Distributor agrees to buy Supplier's product for resale within the sales territory described herein.

1. *Best Efforts.* Distributor agrees to use its best efforts to actively promote and sell the full line of products offered for sale by Supplier.

2. *Prices.* Distributor agrees to purchase from Supplier sufficient quantities of product to meet customer demand. Prices and credit terms shall be in accordance with Supplier's then current price list which may be changed from time to time by the Supplier. A copy of the Supplier's price list as of the date of this agreement is attached. All orders received by Supplier from Distributor are received subject to acceptance by Supplier in its sole and absolute discretion. Supplier shall incur no liability to Distributor if it is unable to supply the product for any reason. However, Supplier shall attempt to fill such orders as are received.

3. *Sales Force.* Distributor shall maintain a sales force of sufficient size to exploit the market potential of product throughout Distributor's territory. The sales force shall be well trained and competent to demonstrate product to prospective buyers. Distributor shall send at least one sales representative each year to Supplier's training seminar. Sales force shall be well versed in Supplier's promotional and ad-

vertising programs and shall pursue such programs diligently and in a manner which reflects positively on the high quality reputation of product. Distributor shall be responsible for developing a marketing plan for product each year. Supplier shall have the right to review Distributor's marketing plan.

4. *Compliance with Law.* In order to maintain the high reputation of product, Distributor shall conduct its business at all times in full compliance with all applicable federal, state, and local laws and regulations and with the highest commercial standards.

5. *Sales Reports.* Prior to the fifteenth day of each month of the term of this agreement, Distributor shall report to Supplier the quantity of each class or style of product sold by Distributor the preceding month. Failure to make such report may be deemed by Supplier a default of this agreement. If Supplier gives Distributor notice of default of this paragraph, Distributor shall have 10 days in which to cure the default. Failure to cure the default within 10 days of receipt of notice of default shall constitute a material breach of this agreement and shall constitute grounds for termination in accordance with paragraph 13 of this agreement.

6. *Inventory Reports.* Every three months, Distributor shall report its level of product inventory to Supplier. The inventory report shall be due by the fifteenth day of the months of April, July, October, and January.

7. *Sales Territory.* Distributor agrees to concentrate its sales efforts in its sales territory. Distributor further agrees that it will not sell Supplier's products either directly or indirectly to customers located outside of its sales territory without the express written consent of Supplier. Supplier may act in its sole discretion in giving or withholding consent to sales outside of Distributor's sales territory.

7. (Alternative) Distributor agrees to use its best efforts to promote, sell, and service products within its sales territory. Distributor further agrees that its primary responsibility is to service retail customers within its sales territory and that it shall concentrate its sales efforts in its territory. Distributor hereby acknowledges that concentrating its sales efforts within its sales territory is essential to the promotion, sale, and servicing of products.

8. *Credit Program Eligibility.* In order to maintain eligibility for Supplier's credit program, Distributor shall furnish to Supplier detailed profit-and-loss statements and year-end balance sheets. These financial statements shall be provided to Supplier as soon as they are available from Distributor's auditors.

9. *Performance Standard.* Distributor and Supplier through good faith negotiations and consultations based upon their knowledge of the market conditions in sales territory and the characteristics and prices of product have determined that the fair and reasonable performance standard for sale to be achieved by Distributor within sales territory during the term of this agreement is as follows:

Year	Product Type	Quantity
1st	A	
	B	
2nd	A	
	B	
3rd	A	
	B	

For each successive year of this agreement the performance standard shall be adjusted to reflect population trends within the sales territory. Such adjustment shall reflect the product saturation level reflected in the performance standard for the third year of this agreement.

Distributor agrees that these performance standards are fair and reasonable and are essential to fulfillment of Distributor's obligations in this agreement. Distributor agrees that its failure to meet these performance standards is a default under this agreement which is not susceptible to cure and is therefore a material breach of this agreement and shall constitute good cause for termination or nonrenewal of this agreement.

10. *Assignment.* Distributor may not assign any of its rights or obligations hereunder. Assignment shall include mergers, reorganizations, and consolidations. Supplier shall have the right to terminate this agreement if a person not a shareholder of Distributor at the time of execution of this agreement shall acquire 30 percent or more of the stock of Distributor.

Distributor represents that at the time of entering into this agreement its only substantial shareholders are:

Name   *Percentage of Stock Owned*

_____   _____

_____   _____

_____   _____

11. *No Fee Paid.* Distributor has not paid and will not pay any fee to supplier in connection with entering into this agreement or any prior agreement with Supplier or its predecessors. Distributor acknowledges that its rights under this agreement and the operations of its business are not substantially related to the use of any trademark, trade name, logo, service mark, or other commercial symbol of Supplier or its products. [This clause is intended to negate any argument that this contract constitutes a franchise.]

12. *Distributor Independence.* Distributor represents that its business is not dependent on product from Supplier for its continuation.

13. *Termination.* Termination of this agreement may occur as follows:
    a. On the expiration of the term of this agreement without renewal.
    b. Either party may terminate this agreement without cause on 30 days written notice or such longer period as may be required by

applicable law. Such notice period shall apply to the initial term and any renewal term of this agreement.

c. This agreement shall terminate automatically and without notice on the happening of the following: insolvency, bankruptcy, assignment for the benefit of creditors, application for the appointment of a receiver, or appointment of a receiver for the Distributor. Provided, however, that Supplier may waive such termination in writing within five business days of being informed of any such event.

d. Either party may terminate this agreement by giving 30 days written notice of election to terminate for default for the events stated below; provided, however, that the defaulting party shall have 20 days from receipt of such notice to cure the default:

   i. For failure of a party to comply with any term or provision of this agreement other than the performance standards

   ii. For failure of either party to pay any sums due under the terms of this agreement within five days following the date on which sum is due and payable

   iii. For becoming insolvent or unable to pay debts as they become due, or having a negative net worth.

e. This agreement shall terminate immediately on written notice of either party to the defaulting party given at any time after the occurrence of any of the following events:

   i. Conviction of any officer, director, or substantial or principal shareholder of the defaulting party for any offense substantially related to the business being conducted in connection with this agreement or related to the business of the terminating party

   ii. Failure of the defaulting party to comply with any federal, state, or local law or regulation relating to the purposes of this agreement, or which in the opinion of qualified legal counsel advising the terminating party is deemed to be an illegal or unfair trade practice under any federal, state or local law

   iii. The defaulting party voluntarily grants a lien, other than in the ordinary course of business, or inventory

   iv. Filing false data or reports required by this agreement

   v. The defaulting party fails to act in good faith or in a commercially acceptable manner in fulfilling its obligations under this agreement

   vi. The loss for a period of 15 days or more of any license or permit required by law for a party to carry out its obligations under this agreement or to maintain its status as a corporation whether such loss or suspension be the result of inadvertent or negligent failure to renew or because of action by state authorities to suspend, cancel or revoke the permit or license

f. Supplier may terminate this agreement immediately on notice to the Distributor for the following reasons:

   i. Abandonment of the distributorship

ii. Failure of Distributor to meet the performance standards established pursuant to agreement at any time within 90 days after the conclusion of any performance period

iii. Any change in control of the Distributor

iv. Any change in the active management of the Distributor which the Supplier believes will have a material effect on the ability of the Distributor to sell and promote products aggressively. The parties acknowledge that this agreement is in the nature of a personal service agreement and its value to Supplier lies in continuation of Distributor under the same management that it had at the signing of this agreement. Changes in management include the incapacity for a period of 30 days or the death of a principal officer, partner, or manager.

v. The breach of any warranty or representation made in this agreement by the Distributor

Parties acknowledge and agree that the terms of this agreement pertaining to termination are fair and reasonable and that these termination provisions are essential to protect the interests of both parties. The parties further agree that the occurrence of any events permitting termination under this agreement shall be deemed "good cause" and shall be "just and sufficient cause" within the meaning of any applicable law or regulation governing the parties right to terminate this agreement.

14. *Posttermination Inventory.* On termination of this agreement pursuant to paragraph 13, Supplier shall have the option, to be exercised at its sole discretion, to repurchase from Distributor any products, display cases, catalogs, or other promotional materials at the price originally paid by Distributor to Supplier for such items.

15. *Rights Following Termination.* Following termination pursuant to paragraph 13, neither party shall have any rights against the other under this agreement except as expressly provided in this agreement.

16. *Mutual Release.* Parties acknowledge and agree that at the date of signing this agreement neither of them has any claim for damages for breach of contract or otherwise against the other party. As a part of the consideration for entering into this agreement, any and all claims against the other party whether known or unknown are forever fully discharged and released.

Red Flag: Some states have statutes which specifically govern the release of unknown claims (see, for example, California Civil Code section 1542).

17. *Waiver.* The failure of either party to enforce any provision of this agreement shall not constitute a waiver of that party's right to require performance of that provision thereafter.

18. *Choice of Law.* This agreement shall be construed in accordance with the laws of the state of _____ .

19. *Entire Agreement.* The parties acknowledge that this agreement contains the entire agreement of the parties and supersedes and merges

all prior and contemporaneous agreements and understandings whether written or oral. Representations not contained in this agreement made by the representative or agent of either party shall be null, void, and of no effect. This agreement may be modified or amended only by written agreement signed by both parties.

In witness whereof, the parties have executed this agreement on the _____ day of _____ , 19 ____ .

Supplier
by: _____

Distributor
by: _____

Key Point: The foregoing sample distribution agreement is intended only to suggest some of the common agreement terms. Some distribution arrangements will require more detailed provisions, others less. Each contract should be tailored to fit the unique situation it will govern. Moreover, some industries have traditional modes of doing business and terms of art which must be considered in negotiating and drafting agreements.

SAMPLE ANTITRUST COMPLIANCE PROCEDURE PLAN

RELATIONS WITH COMPETITORS

General

Under section one of the Sherman Act, it is illegal for a busineess to conspire with its competitors in such a way as to restrain trade. As a result, contact with competitors provides the greatest opportunity for trade violations.

Therefore, it is essential to understind the laws that govern relationships with competitors in order to ensure compliance.

Violations

Any arrangements that unreasonably restrain trade have been made illegal by section one of the Sherman Act. Vioations that deal with relations between competitors include:

1. *Price Fixing.* Any agreements or understanding between competitors to raise, lower, peg, or stabilize prices.

2. *Limitation of Supply.* Any agreement or understanding between competitors to restrict the volume of goods they will produce or make available for sale.

3. *Allocation of Business.* Any agreement or understanding between competitors that each shall confine business to a different geographic area, to a different line of merchandise, or to different customers or classes of customers.

4. *Boycotts.* Any agreement or understanding between suppliers and/ or customers that they will not sell to or purchase from particular outsiders.

It should be noted that a violation of section one does not depend on achievement of the parties' objectives. Instead, a crime is committed the moment they agree, combine, or conspire—regardless of the results. It makes no difference whether this agreement be written or oral, express or implied, formal or informal; they are all illegal. In legal terms, any "meeting of the minds" constitutes an agreement.

General Rule

Because the previous agreements have been made illegal under the Sherman Act, the following company policy has been set. No employee shall enter into any discussion or enter into any understanding or agreement with competitors concerning:

1. Future prices
2. Costs
3. Profits
4. Product or service offerings
5. Terms or conditions of sale
6. Deliveries
7. Production facilities or capacity
8. Production or sales volume
9. Market share
10. Customer allocation of selection
11. Sales territories
12. Distribution methods or channels

The following guidelines have also been established in order to comply with antitrust laws dealing with restraint of trade.

Trade Associations

While trade associations and professional committees can perform useful and legitimate functions in facilitating the exchange of information on such industry matters as technological developments or government regulations, there is always the risk that member companies will be charged with having used the association to reach unlawful agreements. Therefore, as a company policy, if a competitor begins to discuss prices, terms of sale, and so on, any representative must refuse to participate and leave the meeting if such discussion is not stopped immediately.

Obtaining Competitive Information

A company is entitled to keep up with competitive developments by means of any public information available (e. g., published specifications or trade journals). However, any improper means to acquire confidential competitive information is forbidden.

Any information about competitive proposals or products marked "proprietary" or "confidential" or any other confidential material is not to be received or examined by any employee.

Commenting on Competitors

As a general rule, it is company policy to emphasize the quality of its products and to abstain from making degrading comments about competitors or their products.

There are a number of specific practices to which a representative must adhere to.

1. Do not make comments about a competitor's character. For example, do not tell a customer that a competitor's sales representative is immoral or untrustworthy.

2. Avoid references to a competitor's business troubles or weak points. For example, do not mention financial difficuties, lawsuits, or government investigations involving the competitor.

3. Make no statements about the specifications, quality, utility, or value of a competitors product unless the statement is based on current public information or factual data.

4. Sell on capabilitites, quality, know-how, and benefits to the customer and not on the competitor's deficiencies.

RELATIONS WITH CUSTOMERS

General

Customers, being one of our most imprtant assets, are to be treated with the utmost of care. A customer must be allowed to act independently, without company imposing any restrictive agreements. Company is free to choose its own customers, but the sales manager must be consulted before the company refuses to sell to any customer (whether or not the company has done business with the party in the past) other than for valid credit reasons. Because this whole area is so important, an understanding of the laws involved is necessary.

Violations

A number of practices in relation to customers have been determined to be illegal under the Sherman Act.

1. *Price Fixing.* In addition to being an agreemtnt between competitors to raise prices, price fixing is also any agreement or understanding between supplier and customer as to the price at which the customer may resell the good purchased from the supplier.
2. *Tying Agreements.* Any agreement imposed by a seller who enjoys a substantial market position with respect to a particular product, which compels the buyer of that product to also purchase a different (or tied) product.
3. *Refusals to Deal.* A supplier may not cut off a customer in furtherance of a wrongful objective (maintain resale prices).
4. *Reciprocity.* The practice of purchasing goods from another concern on the condition that it purchases different goods from you.
5. *Exclusive Dealing.* Any agreement or understanding where a purchaser agrees to buy exclusviely from a particular supplier for a significant period of time.

General Rules

1. Deal fairly, equally, and openly with all customers.
2. Respect the customers' freedom to conduct their business as they see fit. Do not attempt to exercise control over their resale prices, their handling of competitive products, or their selection of their own customers.

3. Avoid the use of coercive practices in all relationships with customers. Never threaten supply termination for any reason other than good faith enforcement of the company's contractual rights.

4. Avoid discussion of resale prices with customer groups.

5. Refrain from putting any pressure on suppliers to buy company's products because we purchase theirs.

PRICE DISCRIMINATION

U. S. law prohibits discrimination in price or services between competing purchasers. However, price differentials may be justified when: (a) there is a cost savings in manufacture, sale or delivery resulting from a larger order; (b) the seller is meeting the equally low price of the competition (however, it may not go below the competitor's price—only match it or go above it);* or (c) the buyers are not in competition.

U. S. law also prohibits indirect discrimination in price where the effect may be to injure or lessen competition. This would include differences in terms or conditions of sale such as rebates, credits, allowances, or services. It is also illegal to furnish one customer who resells company's products with services or facilities unless they are made available to all competing customers on proportionately equal terms. This would include such things as advertising, displays, demonstrators, special packaging, and so on.

As a general rule, whatever is provided to one customer must be provided to all.

RELATIONS WITH SUPPLIERS

General

Suppliers of materials and services to company are a very important resource and always should be treated courteously and fairly. Company employees dealing with suppliers must use common sense, good judgment, and the highest standards of integrity. In order to maintain compliance with the antitrust laws, company has a number of policies.

---

* In this event, the customer must fill out a form verifying seller's price and the competitor's price (which will be met).

Violations

The same violations that relate to customers (described in the previous section) also apply to relations with suppliers. These include tying agreements, refusals to deal, reciprocity, and exclusive dealing. It is also illegal for a buyer to induce or knowingly receive a discriminatory price, as described in the Price Discrimination section of Relations with Customers.

General Rules

1. Company will not restrict a supplier from selling its products or services to the company's competitors or other parties.
2. Company will neither suggest nor imply that a supplier must buy company products in return for company's purchases.
3. Company employees shall not relate the problems or weaknesses of a supplier to another supplier or person outside the company.
4. Company will not encourage a supplier to grant, and company will not accept, a discriminatory discount or a price which does not represent a fair market value for goods or services of similar quality and quantity.

Obtaining Suppliers

When either new materials or services or additional suppliers for current materials or services are needed, interested suppliers shall be given equal consideration. Materials critical to a company product or process shall be evalutated as to their ability to meet technical specifications and expectations for quality and reliability before any purchase commitments are made. Likewise, the supplier's ability to provide a continuous flow of qualified materials shall also be evaluated.

Bids and Quotations

It is company's policy to arrive at an agreement which is fair to both buyer and seller and considers the long-term financial well being of both. Company will not disclose one supplier's prices or other confidential information to another supplier or person outside the company. Finally, purchasing decisions will be based on total long-term cost to company—recognizing the indirect costs associated with imperfect goods and services, as well as the value of a long term business relationship with company's suppliers.

CONSEQUENCES OF ANTITRUST VIOLATIONS

The consequences of violating antitrust laws can be extremely grave. Corporations are subject to substantial fines, heavy liability for damages, and crippling injunctions. In addition, company officials and other employees who authorize or participate in such activities may also be severely punished.

Treble Damages

Private parties who sustain injury to their business or property as the result of antitrust violations are entitled to recover three times the amount of the actual damage sustained, plus litigation costs and attorneys' fees.

Injunctions

Court injunctions or Federal Trade Commission "cease and desist" orders, designed to prevent future violations, are generally granted in civil antitrust proceedings where a breach of law has been found. This action could seriously hamper a company's legitimate acitivies because the injunctions often go far beyond prohibition of the precise types of conduct held to be illegal.

Criminal Penalties

In Sherman Act criminal cases, the convicted corporation may be fined up to $1 million for each offense; and the guilty individuals may also be fined or sent to jail for up to three years or sentenced to both punishments.

Company Action

Any employees of company found violating any antitrust laws may be subject to severe disciplinary action and possible expulsion.

GOVERNMENT REQUESTS FOR INFORMATION

It is company policy to cooperate with every reasonable request of federal, state and municipal investigators seeking information concerning company operations for antitrust enforcement or other purposes. If a representative of the Department of Justice or the Federal Trade Commission, a member of the FBI, or any representative of any other government agency requests an interview with any company personnel or seeks data or copies of documents or seeks access to files, he or she should be told that the company will cooperate, but that the matter must first be referred to the company president.

LITIGATION

The company president and the vice president of marketing should be notified immediately in the event antitrust litigation has begun or is threatened by or against the company, a competitor, customer, or supplier.

APPENDIX 1

I have read and fully understand all the guidelines set forth for all company employees in the Antitrust Compliance Procedure.

Signor _____

Date _____

"Meeting the Price" Documentation

Dealer _____

Address _____

Phone _____

Representative _____ Position _____

Date of Sale _____

Competitor _____

Company Product	Company Std. Dealer Price	Competitor's Product	Competitor's Price	Company Discount Price
_____	_____	_____	_____	_____
_____	_____	_____	_____	_____
_____	_____	_____	_____	_____
_____	_____	_____	_____	_____
_____	_____	_____	_____	_____
_____	_____	_____	_____	_____

Salesperson _____

Date _____

Employees may be required to sign a form stating that they have read and will observe the company's antitrust compliance policy. Some companies also require employees to answer a short questionnaire at least annually to ferret out potential problems. Typical questions asked on such a questionnaire include:

1. Has any competitor approached you or an employee you supervise to discuss prices or other competitive information?

2. Have you had any contacts with competitors at business meetings, trade associations, or other occasions which might cause antitrust concern?

3. Has the Product Department asked you to obtain knowledge of prospective price actions of competitors?

4. Are you aware of any attempts by our competitors to get advance information of our prospective price actions?

5. Have you been involved in any situation where our pricing or other business practices have been the subject of complaint by our customers, competitors or the government?

6. Has any customer attempted to persuade you not to quote or sell to another customer?

The questions are of course designed to alert management to any potential compliance problems before violations develop. They also serve to remind and to sensitize employees to antitrust hot spots.

QUARTERLY ANTITRUST COMPLIANCE
REVIEW QUESTIONNAIRE

Directions: Please check the appropriate response and make any needed clarifications. Explain all "YES" answers in the space provided.

1. Have you been approached by any competitor's representative with the intent of obtaining or communicating price or other competitive information?

    _____ YES   _____ NO

_____

_____

2. Have you observed anything in your sales activities or otherwise which leads you to suspect that our competitors are operating collusively with other competitors, or are otherwise in violation of the antitrust laws?

_____ YES _____ NO

_____

_____

3. A. Have there been any instances involving contacts with competitors either at business meetings, trade association activities, vendor–vendee relationships, or other occasions which might have raised antitrust concern?

_____ YES, _____ NO

B. In this connection, please indicate whether you are keeping a record of such unusual competitor contacts?

_____ YES _____ NO

_____

_____

4. Have there been any instances where you have done so or have been asked by any company employee to get word of prospective price actions to competitors?

_____ YES _____ NO

_____

_____

5. Are you aware of any attempts by competitors to get word of prospective price announcements to any other company employee besides yourself?

_____ YES _____ NO

_____

_____

6. Has any customer, competitor, or supplier attempted to persuade you not to quote or sell to another potential customer or buy from another potential supplier?

_____ YES _____ NO

_____

_____

7. Have there been any instances where reciprocity was a part of a transaction?

_____ YES   _____ NO

_____

_____

8. A. Have there been any instances where the company price was lowered to meet a competitor's price?

_____ YES   _____ NO

B. If so, please indicate if you have filled out the proper forms for such a pricing act.

_____ YES   _____ NO

_____

_____

9. Have you been aware of any situations which might give rise to concern that a company employee has violated the Antitrust Compliance Procedure?

_____ YES   _____ NO

_____

_____

10. Are you aware of any situation where our pricing or other business practices have been a subject of complaint from customers, competitors, or the government?

_____ YES   _____ NO

_____

_____

11. Are the specific provisions of the Antitrust Compliance Procedure being carefully followed?

_____ YES   _____ NO

_____

_____

appendix c

ABRIDGED COPY OF REGULATION Z

SUBPART A—GENERAL

§ 226.1 Authority, purpose, coverage, organization, enforcement and liability.

(a) Authority. This regulation, known as Regulation Z, is issued by the Board of Governors of the Federal Reserve System to implement the federal Truth in Lending and Fair Credit Billing Acts, which are contained in title I of the Consumer Credit Protection Act, as amended (15 U.S.C. 1601 et seq.). This regulation also implements title XII, section 1204 of the Competitive Equality Banking Act of 1987 (Pub. L. 100-86, 101 Stat. 552). Information-collection requirements contained in this regulation have been approved by the Office of Management and Budget under the provisions of 44 U.S.C. 3501 et seq. and have been assigned OMB No. 7100-0199.

(b) Purpose. The purpose of this regulation is to promote the informed use of consumer credit by requiring disclosures about its terms and cost. The regulation also gives consumers the right to cancel certain credit transactions that involve a lien on a consumer's principal dwelling, regulates certain credit card practices, and provides a means for fair and timely resolution of credit billing disputes. The regulation does not govern charges for consumer credit.

(c) Coverage.

(1) In general, this regulation applies to each individual or business that offers or extends credit when four conditions are met:

(i) the credit is offered or extended to consumers:

(ii) the offering or extension of credit is done regularly,[1]

(iii) the credit is subject to a finance charge or is payable by a written agreement in more than 4 installments; and

(iv) the credit is primarily for personal, family, or household purposes.

(2) If a credit card is involved, however, certain provisions apply even if the credit is not subject to a finance charge, or is not payable by a written agreement in more than 4 installments, or if the credit card is to be used for business purposes.

(d) Organization. The regulation is divided into subparts and appendices as follows:

(1) Subpart A contains general information. It sets forth:

(i) the authority, purpose, coverage, and organization of the regulation;

(ii) the definition of basic terms;

(iii) the transactions that are exempt from coverage; and

(iv) the method of determining the finance charge.

(2) Subpart B contains the rules for open-end credit. It requires that initial disclosures and periodic statements be provided. It also describes special rules that apply to credit card transactions, treatment of payments and credit balances, procedures for resolving credit billing errors, annual percentage rate calculations, rescission requirements, and advertising rules.

(3) Subpart C relates to closed-end credit. It contains rules on disclosures, treatment of credit balances, annual percentage rate calculations, rescission requirements, and advertising.

(4) Subpart D contains rules on oral disclosures, Spanish language disclosure in Puerto Rico, record retention, effect on state laws, state exemptions, and rate limitations.

(5) There are several appendices containing information such as the procedures for determinations about state laws, state exemptions and issuance of staff interpretations, special rules for certain kinds of credit plans, a list of enforcement agencies, and the rules for computing annual percentage rates in closed-end credit transactions.

(e) Enforcement and liability. Section 108 of the act contains the administrative enforcement provisions. Sections 112, 113, 130, 131, and 134 contain provisions relating to liability for failure to comply with the requirements of the act and the regulation. Section 1204(c) of Title XII of the Competitive Equality Banking Act of 1987, Pub. L. No. 100-86, 101 Stat. 552, incorporates by reference administrative enforcement and civil liability provisions of sections 108 and 130 of the act.

[As amended 52 F.R. 43181, Nov. 9, 1987]

§ 226.2 Definitions and rules of construction.

(a) Definitions. For purposes of this regulation, the following definitions apply:

(1) "Act" means the Truth in Lending Act (15 U.S.C. 1601 et seq.).

(2) "Advertisement" means a commercial message in any medium that promotes, directly or indirectly, a credit transaction.

(3) [ ]²

(4) "Billing cycle" or "cycle" means the interval between the days or dates of regular periodic statements. These intervals shall be equal and no longer than a quarter of a year. An interval will be considered equal if the number of days in the cycle does not vary more than 4 days from the regular day or date of the periodic statement.

(5) "Board" means the Board of Governors of the Federal Reserve System.

(6) "Business day" means a day on which a creditor's offices are open to the public for carrying on substantially all of its business functions. However, for purposes of rescission under §§226.15 and 226.23, the term means all calendar days except Sundays and the legal public holidays specified in 5 U.S.C. 6103(a), such as New Year's Day, Washington's Birthday, Memorial Day, Independence Day, Labor Day, Columbus Day, Veterans Day, Thanksgiving Day, and Christmas Day.

(7) "Card issuer" means a person that issues a credit card or that person's agent with respect to the card.

(8) "Cardholder" means a natural person to whom a credit card is issued for consumer credit purposes, or a natural person who has agreed with the card issuer to pay consumer credit obligations arising from the issuance of a credit card to another natural person. For purposes of §226.12(a) and (b), the term includes any person to whom a credit card is issued for any purpose, including business, commercial, or agricultural use, or a person who has agreed with the card issuer to pay obligations arising from the issuance of such a credit card to another person.

(9) "Cash price" means the price at which a creditor, in the ordinary course of business, offers to sell for cash the property or service that is the subject of the transaction. At the creditor's option, the term may include the price of accessories, services related to the sale, service contracts and taxes and fees for license, title, and registration. The term does not include any finance charge.(10) "Closed-end credit" means consumer credit other than "open-end credit" as defined in this section.

(11) "Consumer" means a cardholder or a natural person to whom consumer credit is offered or extended. However, for purposes of rescission under §§ 226.15 and 226.23, the term also includes a natural person in whose principal dwelling a security interest is or will be retained or acquired, if that person's ownership interest in the dwelling is or will be subject to the security interest.

(12) "Consumer credit" means credit offered or extended to a consumer primarily for personal, family, or household purposes.

(13) "Consummation" means the time that a consumer becomes contractually obligated on a credit transaction.

(14) "Credit" means the right to defer payment of debt or to incur debt and defer its payment.

(15) "Credit card" means any card, plate, coupon book, or other single credit device that may be used from time to time to obtain credit.

(16) "Credit sale" means a sale in which the seller is a creditor. The term includes a bailment or lease (unless terminable without penalty at any time by the consumer) under which the consumer:

(i) Agrees to pay as compensation for use a sum substantially equivalent to, or in excess of, the total value of the property and services involved; and

(ii) Will become (or has the option to become), for no additional consideration or for nominal consideration, the owner of the property upon compliance with the agreement.

(17) "Creditor" means:

(i) A person (A) who regularly extends consumer credit[3] that is subject to a finance charge or is payable by written agreement in more than 4 installments (not including a downpayment), and (B) to whom the obligation is initially payable, either on the face of the note or contract, or by agreement when there is no note or contract.

(ii) For purposes of §§ 226.4(c) (8) (discounts), 226.9(d) (Finance charge imposed at time of transaction), and 226.12(e) (Prompt notification of returns and crediting of refunds), a person that honors a credit card.

(iii) For purposes of Subpart B, any card issued that extends either open-end credit or credit that is not subject to a finance charge and is not payable by written agreement in more than 4 installments.

(iv) For purposes of Subpart B (except for the finance charge disclosures contained in §§ 226.6(a) and 226.7(d) through (g) and the right of rescission set forth in § 226.14) and Subpart C, any card issuer that extends closed-end credit that is subject to a finance charge or is payable by written agreement in more than 4 installments.

(18) "Downpayment" means an amount, including the value of any property used as a trade-in, paid to a seller to reduce the cash price of goods or services purchased in a credit sale transaction. A deferred portion of a downpayment may be treated as part of the downpayment if it is payable not later than the due date of the second otherwise regularly scheduled payment and is not subject to a finance charge.

(19) "Dwelling" means a residential structure that contains 1 to 4 units, whether or not that structure is attached to real property. The term includes an individual condominium unit, cooperative unit, mobile home, and trailer, if it is used as a residence.

(20) "Open-end credit" means consumer credit extended by a creditor under a plan in which:

(i) The creditor reasonably contemplates repeated transaction;

(ii) The creditor may impose a finance charge from time to time on an outstanding unpaid balance; and

(iii) The amount of credit that may be extended to the consumer during the term of the plan (up to any limit set by the creditor) is generally made available to the extent that any outstanding balance is repaid.

(21) "Periodic rate" means a rate of finance charge that is or may be imposed by a creditor on a balance for a day, week, month, or other subdivision of a year.

(22) "Person" means a natural person or an organization, including a corporation, partnership, proprietorship, association, cooperative, estate, trust, or government unit.

(23) "Prepaid finance charge" means any finance charge paid separately in cash or by check before or at consummation of a transaction, or withheld from the proceeds of the credit at any time.

(24) "Residential mortgage transaction" means a transaction in which a mortgage, deed of trust, purchase money security interest arising under an installment sales contract, or equivalent consensual security interest is created or retained in the consumer's principal dwelling to finance the acquisition or initial construction of that dwelling.

(25) "Security interest" means an interest in property that secures performance of a consumer credit obligation and that is recognized by state or federal law. It does not include incidental interests such as interests in proceeds, accessions, additions, fixtures, insurance proceeds (whether or not the creditor is a loss payee or beneficiary), premium rebates, or interests in after acquired property. For purposes of disclosure under §§ 226.6 and 226.18, the term does not include an interest that arises solely by operation of law. However, for purposes of the right of rescission under §§ 226.15 and 226.23, the term does include interests that arise solely by operation of law.

(26) "State" means any state, the District of Columbia, the Commonwealth of Puerto Rico, and any territory or possession of the United States.

(b) Rules of construction. For purposes of this regulation, the following rules of construction apply:

(1) Where appropriate, the singular form of a word includes the plural form and plural includes singular.

(2) Where the words "obligation" and "transaction" are used in this regulation, they refer to a consumer credit obligation or transaction, depending upon the context. Where the word "credit" is used in this regulation, it means "consumer credit" unless the context clearly indicates otherwise.

(3) Unless defined in this regulation, the words used have the meanings given to them by state law or contract.

(4) Footnotes have the same legal effect as the text of the regulation.

[As amended 47 F.R. 7392, Feb. 19, 1982; 48 F.R. 14886, Apr. 6, 1983]

§ 226.3 Exempt transactions.

This regulation does not apply to the following:

(a) Business, commercial, agricultural, or organizational credit.[4]

(1) An extension of credit primarily for a business, commercial or agricultural purpose.

(2) An extension of credit to other than a natural person, including credit to government agencies or instrumentalities.

(b) Credit over $25,000 not secured by real property or a dwelling. An extension of credit not secured by real property, or by personal property used or expected to be used as the principal dwelling of the consumer, in which the amount financed exceeds $25,000 or in which there is an express written commitment to extend credit in excess of $25,000.

(c) Public utility credit. An extension of credit that involves public utility services provided through pipe, wire other connected facilities, or radio or similar transmission (including extensions of such facilities), if the charges for service, delayed payment, or any discounts for prompt payment are filed with or regulated by any government unit. The financing of durable goods or home improvements by a public utility is not exempt.

(d) Securities or commodities accounts. Transactions in securities or commodities accounts in which credit is extended by a broker-dealer registered with the Securities and Exchange Commission or the Commodity Futures Trading Commission.

(e) Home fuel budget plans. An installment agreement for the purchase of home fuels in which no finance charge is imposed.

(f) Student loan programs. Loans made, insured, or guaranteed pursuant to a program authorized by Title IV of the Higher Education Act of 1965 (20 U.S.C. 1070 et seq.).

[As amended 48 F.R. 14886, Apr. 6, 1983]

§ 226.4 Finance charge.

(a) Definition. The finance charge is the cost of consumer credit as a dollar amount. It includes any charge payable directly or indirectly by the consumer and imposed directly or indirectly by the creditor as an incident to or a condition of the extension of credit. It does not include any charge of a type payable in a comparable cash transaction.

(b) Example of finance charge. The finance charge includes the following types of charges, except for charges specifically excluded by paragraphs (c) through (e) of this section.

(1) Interest, time price differential, and any amount payable under an add-on or discount system of additional charges.

(2) Service, transaction, activity, and carrying charges, including any charge imposed on a checking or other transaction account to the extent that the charge exceeds the charge for a similar account without a credit feature.

(3) Point, loan fees, assumption fees, finder's fees, and similar charges.

(4) Appraisal, investigation, and credit report fees.

(5) Premiums or other charges for any guarantee or insurance protecting the creditor against the consumer's default or other credit loss.

(6) Charges imposed on a creditor by another person for purchasing or accepting a consumer's obligation, if the consumer is required to pay the charges in cash, as an addition to the obligation, or as a deduction from the proceeds of the obligation.

(7) Premiums or other charges for credit life, accident, health, or loss-of-income insurance, written in connection with a credit transaction.

(8) Premiums or other charges for insurance against loss of or damage to property, or against liability arising out of the ownership or use of property, written in connection with a credit transaction.

(9) Discounts for the purpose of inducing payment by a means other than the use of credit.

(c) Charges excluded from the finance charge. The following charges are not finance charges:

(1) Application fees charged to all applicants for credit, whether or not credit is actually extended.

(2) Charges for actual unanticipated late payment, for exceeding a credit limit, or for delinquency, default, or a similar occurrence.

(3) Charges imposed by a financial institution for paying items that overdraw an account, unless the payment of such items and the imposition of the charge were previously agreed upon in writing.

(4) Fees charged for participation in a credit plan, whether assessed on an annual or other periodic basis.

(5) Seller's points.

(6) Interest forfeited as a result of an interest reduction required by law on a time deposit used as security for an extension of credit.

(7) The following fees in a transaction secured by real property or in a residential mortgage transaction, if the fees are bona fide and reasonable in amount:

(i) Fees for title examination, abstract of title, title insurance, property survey, and similar purposes.

(ii) Fees for preparing deeds, mortgages, and reconveyance, settlement, and similar documents.

(iii) Notary, appraisal, and credit report fees.

(iv) Amounts required to be paid into escrow or trustee accounts if the amounts would not otherwise by included in the finance charge.

(8) Discounts offered to induce payment for a purchase by cash, check, or other means, as provided in § 167(b) of the act.

(d) Insurance.

(1) Premiums for credit life, accident, health, or loss-of-income insurance may be excluded from the finance charge if the following conditions are met:

(i) The insurance coverage is not required by the creditor, and this fact is disclosed.

(ii) The premium for the initial term of insurance coverage is disclosed. If the term of insurance is less than the term of the transaction, the term of insurance also shall be disclosed. The premium may be disclosed on a unit-cost basis only in open-end credit transactions, closed-end credit transactions by mail or telephone under § 226.17(g), and certain closed-end credit transactions involving an insurance plan that limits the total amount of indebtedness subject to coverage.

(iii) The consumer signs or initials an affirmative written request for the insurance after receiving the disclosures specified in this paragraph. Any consumer in the transaction may sign or initial the request.

(2) Premiums for insurance against loss of or damage to property, or against liability arising out of the ownership or use of property.[5] may be excluded from the finance charge if the following conditions are met:

(i) The insurance coverage may be obtained from a person of the consumer's choice,[6] and this fact is disclosed.

(ii) If the coverage is obtained from or through the creditor, the premium for the initial term of insurance coverage shall be disclosed. If the term of insurance is less than the term of the transaction, the term of insurance shall also be disclosed. The premium may be disclosed on a unit-cost basis only in open-end credit transactions, closed-end credit transaction by mail or telephone under § 226.17(g), and certain closed-end credit transactions involving an insurance plan that limits the total amount of indebtedness subject to coverage.

(e) Certain security interest charges. If itemized and disclosed, the following charges may be excluded from the finance charge:

(1) Taxes and fees prescribed by law that actually are or will be paid to public officials for determining the existence of or for perfecting, releasing, or satisfying a security interest.

(2) The premium for insurance in lieu of perfecting a security interest to the extent that the premium does not exceed the fees described in paragraph (e)(1) of this section that otherwise would be payable.

(f) Prohibited offsets. Interest, dividends, or other income received or to be received by the consumer on deposits or investments shall not be deducted in computing the finance charge.

SUBPART B—OPEN-END CREDIT

§ 226.5 General disclosure requirements.

(a) Form of disclosures.

(1) The creditor shall make the disclosures required by this subpart clearly and conspicuously in writing,[7] in a form that the consumer may keep.[8]

(2) The terms "finance charge" and "annual percentage rate," when required to be disclosed with a corresponding amount of percentage rate, shall be more conspicuous than any other required disclosure.[9]

(b) Time of disclosures.

(1) Initial disclosures. The creditor shall furnish the initial disclosure statement required by § 226.6 before the first transaction is made under the plan.

(2) Periodic statement.

(i) The creditor shall mail or deliver a periodic statement as required by § 226.7 for each billing cycle at the end of which an account has a debit or credit balance of more than $1 or on which a finance charge has been imposed. A periodic statement need not be sent for an account if the creditor deems it uncollectibe, or if delinquency collection proceedings have been instituted, or if furnishing the statement would violate federal law.

(ii) The creditor shall mail or deliver the periodic statement at least 14 days prior to any date or the end of any time period required to be disclosedunder § 226.7(j) in order for the consumer to avoid an additional finance or other charge. A creditor that fails to meet this requirement shall not collect any finance or other charge imposed as a result of such failure.

(c) Basis of disclosures and use of estimates. Disclosures shall reflect the terms of the legal obligation between the parties. If any information necessary for accurate disclosure is unknown to the creditor, it shall make the disclosure based on the best information reasonably available and shall state clearly that the disclosure is an estimate.

(d) Multiple creditors; multiple consumers. If the credit plan involves more than one creditor, only one set of disclosures shall be given, and the creditors shall agree among themselves which creditor must comply with the requirements that this regulation imposes on any or all of them. If there is more than one consumer, the disclosures may be made to any consumer who is primarily liable on the account. If the right of rescission under § 226.15 is applicable, however, the disclosures required by §§ 226.6 and 226.14 shall be made to each consumer having the right to rescind.

(e) Effect of subsequent events. If a disclosure becomes inaccurate because of an event that occurs after the creditor mails or delivers the disclosures, the resulting inaccuracy is not a violation of this regulation, although new disclosures may be required under § 226.9(c).

§ 226.6 Initial disclosure statement.

The creditor shall disclose to the consumer, in terminology consistent with that to be used on the periodic statement, each of the following items, to the extent applicable.

(a) Finance charge. The circumstances under which a finance charge will be imposed and an explanation of how it will be determined, as follows:

(1) A statement of when finance charges begin to accrue, including an explanation of whether or not any time period exists within which any credit extended may be repaid without incurring a finance charge. If such a time period is provided, a creditor may, at its option and without disclosure, impose no finance charge when payment is received after the time period's expiration.

(2) A disclosure of each periodic rate that may be used to compute the finance charge, the range of balances to which it is applicable,[11] and the corresponding annual percentage rate.[12] When different periodic rates apply to different types of transactions, the types of transactions to which the periodic rates apply shall also be disclosed.

(3) An explanation of the method used to determine the balance on which the finance charge may be computed.

(4) An explanation of how the amount of any finance charge will be determined,[13] including a description of how any finance charge other than the periodic rate will be determined.

(b) Other charges. The amount of any charge other than a finance charge that may be imposed as part of the plan, or an explanation of how the charge will be determined.

(c) Security interests. The fact that the creditor has or will acquire a security interest in the property purchased under the plan, or in other property identified by item or type.

(d) Statement of billing rights. A statement that outlines the consumer's rights and the creditor's responsibilities under §§ 226.12(c) and 226.13 and that its substantially similar to the statement found in Appendix G.

§ 226.7 Periodic statement.

The creditor shall furnish the consumer with a periodic statement that discloses the following items, to the extent applicable:

(a) Previous balance. The account balance outstanding at the beginning of the billing cycle.

(b) Identification of transactions. An identification of each credit transaction in accordance with § 226.8.

(c) Credits. Any credit to the account during the billing cycle, including the amount and the date of crediting. The date need not be provided if a delay in crediting does not result in any finance or other charge.

(d) Periodic rates. Each periodic rate that may be used to compute the finance charge, the range of balances to which it is applicable,[14] and the corresponding annual percentage rate.[15] If different periodic rates apply to different types of transactions, the types of transactions to which the periodic rates apply shall also be disclosed.

(e) Balance on which finance charge computed. The amount of the balance to which a periodic rate was applied and an explanation of how that balance was determined. When a balance is determined without first deducting all credits and payments made during the billing cycle, that fact and the amount of the credits and payments shall be disclosed.

(f) Amount of finance charge. The amount of any finance charge debited or added to the account during the billing cycle, using the term "finance charge." The components of the finance charge shall be individually itemized and identified to show the amount(s) due to the application of any periodic rates and the amount(s) of any other type of finance charge. If there is more than one periodic rate, the amount of the finance charge attributable to each rate need not be separately itemized and identified.

(g) Annual percentage rate. When a finance charge is imposed during the billing cycle, the annual percentage rate(s) determined under § 226.14, using the term "annual percentage rate."

(h) Other charges. The amounts, itemized and identified by type, of any charges other than finance charges debited to the account during the billing cycle.

(i) Closing date of billing cycle; new balance. The closing date of the billing cycle and the account balance outstanding on that date.

(j) Free-ride period. The date by which or the time period within which the new balance or any portion of the new balance must be paid to avoid additional finance charges. If such a time period is provided, a creditor may, at its option and without disclosure, impose no finance charge when payment is received after the time period's expiration.

(k) Address for notice of billing errors. The address to be used for notice of billing errors. Alternatively, the address may be provided on the billing rights statement permitted by § 226.9(a)(2).

[As amended 46 F.R. 29246, June 1, 1981]

§ 226.8 Identification of transactions.

The creditor shall identify credit transactions on or with the first periodic statement that reflects the transaction by furnishing the following information, as applicable.[16]

(a) Sale credit. For each credit transaction involving the sale of property or services, the following rules shall apply:

(1) Copy of credit document provided. When an actual copy of the receipt or other credit document is provided with the first periodic statement reflecting the transaction, the transaction is sufficiently identified if the amount of the transaction and either the date of the transaction or the date of debiting the transaction to the consumer's account are disclosed on the copy or on the periodic statement.

(2) Copy of credit document not provided—creditor and seller same or related person(s). When the creditor and the seller are the same person or related persons, and an actual copy of the receipt or other credit document is not rpovided with the periodic statement, the creditor shall disclose the amount and date of the transaction, and a brief identification[17] of the property or services purchased.[18]

(3) Copy of credit document not provided—creditor and seller not same or related person(s). When the creditor and seller are not the same person or related persons, and an actual copy of the receipt or other credit document is not provided with the periodic statement, the creditor shall disclose the amount and date of the transaction; the seller's name; and the city, and state or foreign country where the transaction took place.[19]

(b) Nonsale credit. A nonsale credit transaction is sufficiently identified if the first periodic statement reflecting the transaction discloses a brief identification of the transaction;[20] the Truth in Lending amount of the transaction; and at least one of the following dates: the date of the transaction, the date of debiting the transaction to the consumer's account, or, if the consumer signed the credit document, the date appearing on the document. If an actual copy of the receipt or other credit document is provided and that copy shows the amount and at least one of the specified dates, the brief identification may be omitted.

[As amended 46 F.R. 29246, June 1, 1981]

§ 226.9 Subsequent disclosure requirements.

(a) Furnishing statement of billing rights.

(1) Annual statement. The creditor shall mail or deliver the billing rights statement required by § 226.6(d) at least once per calendar year, at intervals of not less than 6 months nor more than 18 months, either to all consumers or to each consumer entitled to receive a periodic statement under § 226.5(b)(2) for any one billing cycle.

(2) Alternative summary statement. As an alternative to the paragraph (a)(1) of this section, the creditor may mail or deliver, on or with each periodic statement, a statement substantially similar to that in Appendix G.

(b) Disclosures for supplemental credit devices and additional features.

(1) If a creditor, within 30 days after mailing or delivering the initial disclosures under § 226.6(a), adds a credit feature to the consumer's account or mails or delivers to the consumer a credit device for which the finance charge terms are the same as those previously disclosed, no additional disclosures are necesary. After 30 days, if the creditor adds a credit feature or furnishes a credit device (other than as a renewal, resupply, or the original issuance of a credit card) on the same finance charge terms, the creditor shall disclose, before the consumer uses the feature or device for the first time, that it is for use in obtaining credit under the terms previously disclosed.

(2) Whenever a credit feature is added or a credit device is mailed or delivered, and the finance charge terms for the feature or device differ from disclosures previously given, the disclosures required by § 226.6(a) that are applicable to the added feature or device shall be given before the consumer uses the feature or device for the first time.

(c) Change in terms.

(1) Written notice required. Whenever any term required to be disclosed under § 226.6 is changed or the required minimum periodic payment is increased, the creditor shall mail or deliver written notice of the change to each consumer who may be affected. The notice shall be mailed or delivered at least 15 days prior to the effective date of the change. The 15-day timing requirement does not apply if the change has been agreed to by the consumer, or if a periodic rate or other finance charge is increased because of the consumer's delinquency or default; the notice shall be given, however, before the effective date of the change.

(2) Notice not required. No notice under this section is required when the change involves late payment charges, charges for documentary evidence, or over-the-limit charges; a reduction of any component of a finance or other charge; suspension of future credit privileges or termination of an account or plan; or when the change results from an agreement involving a court proceeding, or from the consumer's default or delinquency (other than an increase in the periodic rate or other finance charge).

(d) Finance charge imposed at time of transaction.

(1) Any person, other than the card issuer, who imposes a finance charge at the time of honoring a consumer's credit card, shall disclose the amount of that finance charge prior to its imposition.

(2) The card issuer, if other than the person honoring the consumer's credit card, shall have no responsibility for the disclosure required by paragraph (d)(1) of this section, and shall not consider any such charge for purposes of §§ 226.6 and 226.7.

[As amended 46 F.R. 29246, June 1, 1981]

§ 226.10 Prompt crediting of payments.

(a) General rule. A creditor shall credit a payment to the consumer's account as of the date of receipt, except when a delay in crediting does not result in a finance or other charge or except as provided in paragraph (b) of the section.

(b) Specific requirements for payments. If a creditor specifies, on or with the periodic statement, requiremetns for the consumer to follow in making payments, but accepts a payment that does not conform to the requirements, the creditor shall credit the payment within 5 days of receipt.

(c) Adjustment of account. If a creditor fails to credit a payment, as required by paragraphs (a) and (b) of this section, in time to avoid the imposition of finance or other charges, the creditor shall adjust the consumer's account so that the charges imposed are credited to the consumer's account during the next billing cycle.

§ 226.11 Treatment of credit balances.

When a credit balance in excess of $1 is created on a credit account (through transmittal of funds to a creditor in excess of the total balance due on an account, through rebates of unearned finance charges or insurance premiums, or through amounts otherwise owed to or held for the benefit of a consumer), the creditor shall:

(a) Credit the amount of the credit balance to the consumer's account;

(b) Refund any part of the remaining credit balance within 7 business days from receipt of a written request from the consumer; and

(c) Make a good faith effort to refund to the consumer by cash, check, or money order, or credit to a deposit account of the consumer, any part of the credit balance remaining in the account for more than 6 months. No further action is required if the consumer's current location is not known to the creditor and cannot be traced through the consumer's last known address or telephone number.

§ 226.12 Special credit card provisions.

(a) Issuance of credit cards. Regardless of the purpose for which a credit card is to be used, including business, commercial, or agricultural use, no credit card shall be issued to any person except:

(1) In response to an oral or written request or application for the card; or

(2) As a renewal of, or substitute for, an accepted credit card.[21]

(b) Liability of cardholder for unauthorized use.

(1) Limitation on amount. The liability of a cardholder for unauthorized use[22] of a credit card shall not exceed the lesser of $50 or the amount of money, property, labor, or services obtained by the unauthorized use before notification to the card issuer under paragraph (b)(3) of this section.

(2) Conditions of liability. A cardholder shall be liable for unauthorized use of a credit only if:

(i) The credit card is an accepted credit card;

(ii) The card issuer has provided adequate notice[23] of the cardholder's maximum potential liability and of means by which the card issuer may be notified of loss of theft of the card. The notice shall state that the cardholder's liability shall not exceed $50 (or any lesser amount) and that the cardholder may give oral or written notification, and shall describe a means of notification (for example, a telephone number, an address, or both); and

(iii) The card issuer has provided a means to identify the cardholder on the account or the authorized user of the card.

(3) Notification to card issuer. Notification to a card issuer is given when steps have been taken as may be reasonably required in the ordinary course of business to provide the card issuer with the pertinent information about the loss, theft, or possible unauthorized use of a credit card, regardless of whether any particular officer, employee, or agent of the card issuer does, in fact receive the information. Notification may be given, at the option of the person giving it, in person, by telephone, or in writing. Notification in writing is considered given at the time of receipt or, whether or not received, at the expiration of the time ordinarily required for transmission, whichever is earlier.

(4) Effect of other applicable law or agreement. If state law or an agreement between a cardholder and the card issuer imposes lesser liability than that provided in this paragraph, the lesser liability shall govern.

(5) Business use of credit cards. If 10 or more credit cards are issued by one card issuer for use by the employees of an organization, this section does not prohibit the card issuer and the organization from agreeing to liability for unauthorized use without regard to this section. However, liability for unauthorized use may be imposed on an employee of the organization, by either the card issuer or the organization, only in accordance with this section.

(c) Right of cardholder to assert claims or defenses against card issuer.[24]

(1) General rule. When a person who honors a credit card fails to resolve satisfactorily a dispute as to property or services purchased with the credit card in a consumer credit transaction, the cardholder may assert against the card issuer all claims (other than tort claims) and defenses arising ot of the transaction and relating to the failure to resolve the dispute. The cardholder may withhold payment up to the amount of credit outstanding for the property or services that gave rise to the dispute and any finance or other charges imposed on that amount.[25]

(2) Adverse credit reports prohibited. If, in accordance with paragraph (c)(1) of this section, the cardholder withholds payment of the amount of credit outstanding for the disputed transaction, the card issuer shall not report that amount as delinquent until the dispute is settled or judgment is rendered.

(3) Limitations. The rights stated in paragraphs (c)(1) and (2) of this section apply only if:

(i) The cardholder has made a good faith attempt to resolve the dispute with the person honoring the credit card; and

(ii) The amount of credit extended to obtain the property or services that result in the assertion of the claim or defense by the cardholder exceeds $50, and the disputed transaction occurred in the same state as the cardholder's current designated address or, if not within the same state, within 100 miles from that address.[26]

(d) Offsets by card issuer prohibited.

(1) A card issuer may not take any action, either before or after termination of credit card privileges, to offset a cardholder's indebtedness arising from a

consumer credit transaction under the relevant credit card plan against funds of the cardholder held on deposit with the card issuer.

(2) This paragraph does not alter or affect the right of a card issuer acting under state or federal law to do any of the following with regard to funds of a cardholder held on deposit with the card issuer if the same procedure is constitutionally available to creditors generally: obtain or enforce a consensual security interest in the funds; attach or otherwise levy upon the funds; or obtain or enforce a court order relating to the funds.

(3) This paragraph does not prohibit a plan, if authorized in writing by the cardholder, under which the card issuer may periodically deduct all or part of the cardholder's credit card debt from a deposit account held with the card issuer (subject to the limitations in 226.13(d)(1)).

(e) Prompt notification of returns and crediting of refunds.

(1) When a creditor other than the card issuer accepts the return of property or forgives a debt for services that is to be reflected as a credit to the consumer's credit card account that creditor shall, within 7 business days from accepting the return or forgiving the debt, transmit a credit statement to the card issuer through the card issuer's normal channels for credit statements.

(2) The card issuer shall, within 3 business days from receipt of a credit statement, credit the consumer's account with the amount of the refund.

(3) If a creditor other than a card issuer routinely gives cash refunds to consumers paying in cash, the creditor shall also give credit or cash refunds to consumers using credit cards, unless it discloses at the time the transaction is consummated that credit or cash refund for returns are not given. This section does not require refunds for returns nor does it prohibit refunds in kind.

(f) Discounts: tie-in arrangements. No card issuer may, by contract or otherwise:

(1) Prohibit any person who honors a credit card from offering a discount to a consumer to induce the consumer to pay by cash, check, or similar means rather than by use of a credit card or its underlying account for the purchase of property or services; or

(2) Require any person who honors the card issuer's credit card to open or maintain any account or obtain any other service not essential to the operation of the credit card plan from the card issuer or any other person, as a condition of participation in a credit card plan. If maintenance of an account for clearing purposes is determined to be essential to the operation of the credit card plan, it may be required only if no service charges or minimum balance requirements are imposed.

(f) Relation to Electronic Fund Transfer Act and Regulation E. For guidance on whether Regulation Z or Regulation E applies in instances involving both credit and electronic fund transfer aspects, refer to Regulation E, 12 CFR 205.5(c) regarding issuance and 205.6(d) regarding liability for unauthorized use. On matters other than issuance and liability, this section applies to the credit aspects of combined credit/electronic fund transfer transactions, as applicable.

§ 226.13 Billing error resolution.[27]

(a) Definition of billing error. For purposes of this section, the term "billing error" means:

(1) A reflection on or with a periodic statement of an extension of credit that is not made to the consumer or to a person who has actual implied, or apparent authority to use the consumer's credit card or open-end credit plan.

(2) A reflection on or with a periodic statement of an extension of credit that is not identified in accordance with the requirements of §§ 226.7(b) and 226.8.

(3) A reflection on or with a periodic statement of an extension of credit for property or services not accepted by the consumer or the consumer's designee, or not delivered to the consumer or the consumer's designee as agreed.

(4) A reflection on a periodic statement of the creditor's failure to credit properly a payment or other credit issued to the consumer's account.

(5) A reflection on a periodic statement of a computational or similar error of an accounting nature that is made by the creditor.

(6) A reflection on a periodic statement of an extension of credit for which the consumer requests additional clarification, including documentary evidence.

(7) The creditor's failure to mail or deliver a periodic statement to the consumer's last known address if that address was received by the creditor, in writing, at least 20 days before the end of the billing cycle for which the statement was required.

(b) Billing error notice.[28] A billing error notice is a written notice[29] from a consumer that:

(1) Is received by a creditor at the address disclosed under § 226.7(k) no later than 60 days after the creditor transmitted the first periodic statement that reflects the alleged billing error;

(2) Enables the creditor to identify the consumer's name and account number; and

(3) To the extent possible, indicates the consumer's belief and the reasons for the belief that a billing error exists, and the type, date, and amount of the error.

(c) Time for resolution; general procedures.

(1) The creditor shall mail or deliver written acknowledgment to the consumer within 30 days of receiving a billing error notice, unless the creditor has complied with the appropriate resolution procedures of paragraphs (e) and (f) of this section, as applicable, within the 30-day period; and

(2) The creditor shall comply with the appropriate resolution procedures of paragraphs (e) and (f) of this section, as applicable, within 2 complete billing cycles (but in no event later than 90 days) after receiving a billing error notice.

(d) Rules pending resolution. Until a billing error is resolved under paragraphs (e) or (f) of this section, the following rules apply:

(1) Consumer's right to withhold disputed amount; collection action prohibited. The consumer need not pay (and the creditor may not try to collect) any portion of any required payment that the consumer believes is related to the

disputed amount (including related finance or other charges).[30] If the cardholder maintains a deposit account with the card issuer and has agreed to pay the credit card indebtedness by periodic deductions from the cardholder's deposit account, the card issuer shall not deduct any part of the disputed amount or related finance or other charges if a billing error notice is received any time up to 3 business days before the scheduled payment date.

(2) Adverse credit reports prohibited. The creditor or its agent shall not (directly or indirectly) make or threaten to make an adverse report to any person about the consumer's credit standing, or report that an amount or account is delinquent, because the consumer failed to pay the disputed amount or related finance or other charges.

(e) Procedures if billing error occurred as asserted. If a creditor determines that a billing error occurred as asserted, it shall within the time limits in paragraph (c)(2) of this section:

(1) Correct the billing error and credit the consumer's account with any disputed amount and related finance or other charges, as applicable; and

(2) Mail or deliver a correction notice to the consumer.

(f) Procedures if different billing error or no billing error occurred. If, after conducting a reasonable investigation,[31] a creditor determines that no billing error occurred or that a different billing error occurred from that asserted, the creditor shall within the time limits in paragraph (c)(2) of this section:

(1) Mail or deliver to the consumer an explanation that sets forth the reasons for the creditor's belief that the billing error alleged by the consumer is incorrect in whole or in part;

(2) Furnish copies of documentary evidence of the consumer's indebtedness, if the consumer so requests; and

(3) If a different billing error occurred, correct the billing error and credit the consumer's account with any disputed amount and related finance or other charges, as applicable.

(g) Creditor's rights and duties after resolution. If a creditor, after complying with all of the requirements of this section, determines that a consumer owes all or part of the disputed amount and related finance or other charges, the creditor:

(1) Shall promptly notify the consumer in writing of the time when payment is due and the portion of the disputed amount and related finance or other charges that the consumer still owes;

(2) Shall allow any time period disclosed under §§ 226.6(a)(1) and 226.7(j), during which the consumer can pay the amount due under paragraph (g)(1) of this section without incurring additional finance or other charges;

(3) May report an account or amount as delinquent because the amount due under paragraph (g)(1) of this section remains unpaid after the creditor has allowed any time period disclosed under §§ 226.6(a)(1) and 266.7(j) or 10 days (whichever is longer) during which the consumer can pay the amount; but

(4) May not report that any amount or account is delinquent because the amount due under paragraph (g)(1) of the section remains unpaid, if the creditor receives (within the time allowed for payment in paragraph (g)(3) of this section)

further written notice from the consumer that any portion of the billing error is still in dispute, unless the creditor also:

(i) Promptly reports that the amount or account is in dispute;

(ii) Mails or delivers to the consumer (at the same time the report is made) a written notice of the name and address of each person to whom the creditor makes a report; and

(iii) Promptly reports any subsequent resolution of the reported delinquency to all persons to whom the creditor has made a report.

(h) Reassertion of billing error. A creditor that has fully complied with the requirements of this section has no further responsibilities under this section (other than as provided in paragraph (g)(4) of this section) if a consumer reasserts substantially the same billing error.

(i) Relation to Electronic Fund Transfer Act and Regulation E. If an extension of credit is incident to an electronic fund transfer, under an agreement between a consumer and a financial institution to extend credit when the consumer's account is overdrawn or to maintain a specified minimum balance in the consumer's account, the creditor shall comply with the requirements of Regulation E. 12 CFR 305.11 governing error resolution rather than those of paragraphs (a), (b), (c), (e), (f), and (h) of this section.

§ 226.14 Determination of annual percentage rate.

(a) General rule. The annual percentage rate is a measure of the cost of credit, expressed as a yearly rate. An annual percentage rate shall be considered accurate if it is not more than 1/8 of 1 percentage point above or below the annual percentage rate determined in accordance with the selection.[31a]

(b) Annual percentage rate for initial disclosures and for advertising purposes. Where one or more periodic rates may be used to compute the finance charge, the annual percentage rate(s) to be disclosed for purposes of §§ 226.6(a)(2) and 226.16(b)(2) shall be computed by multiplying each periodic rate by the number of periods in a year.

(c) Annual percentage rate for periodic statements. The annual percentage rate(s) to be disclosed for purposes of § 226.7(d) shall be computed by multiplying each periodic rate by the number of periods in a year and, for purposes of § 226.7(g), shall be determined as follows:

(1) If the finance charge is determined solely by applying one or more periodic rates, at the creditor's option, either:

(i) By multiplying each periodic rate by the number of periods in a year; or

(ii) By dividing the total finance charge for the billing cycle by the sum of the balances to which the periodic rates were applied and multiplying the quotient (expressed as a percentage) by the number of billing cycles in a year.

(2) If the finance charge imposed during the billing cycle is or includes a minimum, fixed, or other charge not due to the application of a periodic rate, other than a charge with respect to any specific transaction during the billing cycle, by dividing the total finance charge for the billing cycle by the amount of

the balance(s) to which it is applicable[32] and multiplying the quotient (expressed as a percentage) by the number of billing cycles in a year.[33]

(3) If the finance charge imposed during the billing cycle is or includes a charge relating to a specific transaction during the billing cycle (even if the total finance charge also includes any other minimum, fixed, or other charge not due to the application of a periodic rate), by dividing the total finance charge imposed during the billing cycle by the total of all balances and other amounts on which a finance charge was imposed during the billing cycle without duplication, and multiplying the quotient (expressed as a percentage) by the number of billing cycles in a year,[34] except that the annual percentage rate shall not be less than the largest rate determined by multiplying each periodic rate imposed during the billing cycle by the number of periods in a year.[35]

(4) If the finance charge imposed during the billing cycle is or includes a minimum, fixed, or other charge not due to the application of a periodic rate and the total finance charge imposed during the billing cycle does not exceed 50 cents for a monthly or longer billing cycle, or the pro rata part of 50 cents for a billing cycle shorter than monthly, at the creditor's option, by multiplying each applicable periodic rate by the number of periods in a year, notwithstanding the provisions of paragraphs (c)(2) and (3) of this section.

(d) Calculations where daily periodic rate applied. If the provisions of paragraphs (c)(1)(ii) or (2) of this section apply and all or a portion of the finance charge is determined by the application of one or more daily periodic rates, the annual percentage rate may be determined either:

(1) By dividing the total finance charge by the average of the daily balances and multiplying the quotient by the number of billing cycles in a year; or

(2) By dividing the total finance charge by the sum of the daily balances and multiplying the quotient by 365.

[As amended 47 F.R. 756, Jan. 7, 1982; 48 F.R. 14886, Apr. 6, 1983]

§ 226.15 Right of rescission.

(a) Consumer's right to rescind.

(1)

(i) Except as provided in paragraph (a)(1)(ii) of this section, in a credit plan in which a security interest is or will be retained or acquired in a consumer's principal dwelling, each consumer whose ownership interest is or will be subject to the security interest shall have the right to rescind: each credit extension made under the plan; the plan when the plan is opened; a security interest when added or increased to secure an existing plan; and the increase when a credit limit on the plan is increased.

(ii) As provided in § 125(e) of the act, the consumer does not have the right to rescind each credit extension made under the plan if such extension is made in accordance with a previously established credit limit for the plan.

(2) To exercise the right to rescind, the consumer shall notify the creditor of the rescission by mail, telegram, or other means of written communication. Notice is considered given when mailed, or when filed for telegraphic transmission,

or, if sent by other means, when delivered to the creditor's designated place of business.

(3) The consumer may exercise the right to rescind until midnight of the third business day following the occurrence described in paragraph (a)(1) of this section that gave rise to the right of rescission, delivery of the notice required by paragraph (b) of this section, or delivery of all material disclosures,[36] whichever occurs last. If the required notice and material disclosures are not delivered, the right to rescind shall expire 3 years after the occurrence giving rise to the right of rescission, or upon transfer of all of the consumer interest in the property, or upon sale of the property, whichever occurs first. In the case of certain administrative proceedings, the rescission period shall be extended in accordance with § 125(f) of the act.

(4) When more than one consumer has the right to rescind, the exercise of the right by one consumer shall be effective as to all consumers.

(b) Notice of right to rescind. In any transaction or occurrence subject to rescission, a creditor shall deliver 2 copies of the notice of the right to rescind to each consumer entitled to rescind. The notice shall identify the transaction or occurrence and clearly and conspicuously disclose the following:

(1) The retention or acquisition of a security interest in the consumer's principal dwelling.

(2) The consumer's right to rescind, as described in paragraph (a)(1) of this section.

(3) How to exercise the right to rescind, with a form for that purpose, designating the address of the creditor's place of business.

(4) The effects of rescission, as described in paragraph (d) of this section.

(5) The date the rescission period expires.

(c) Delay of creditor's performance. Unless a consumer waives the right to rescind under paragraph (e) of this section, no money shall be disbursed other than in escrow, no services shall be performed, and no materials delivered until after the rescission period has expired and the creditor is reasonably satisfied that the consumer has not rescinded. A creditor does not violate this section if a third party with no knowledge of the event activating the rescission right does not delay in providing materials or services, as long as the debt incurred for those materials or services is not secured by the property subject to rescission.

(d) Effect of rescission.

(1) When a consumer rescinds a transaction, the security interest giving rise to the right of rescission becomes void, and the consumer shall not be liable for any amount, including any finance charge.

(2) Within 20 calendar days after receipt of a notice of rescission, the creditor shall return any money or property that has been given to anyone in connection with the transaction and shall take any action necessary to reflect the termination of the security interest.

(3) If the creditor has delivered any money or property, the consumer may retain possession until the creditor has met its obligation under paragraph (d)(2) of this section. When the creditor has complied with that paragraph, the

consumer shall tender the money or property to the creditor or, where the latter would be impracticable or inequitable, tender its reasonable value. At the consumer's option, tender of property may be made at the location of the property or at the consumer's residence. Tender of money must be made at the creditor's designated place of business. If the creditor does not take possession of the money or property within 20 calendar days after the consumer's tender, the consumer may keep it without further obligation.

(4) The procedures outlined in paragraphs (d)(2) and (3) of this section may be modified by court order.

(e) Consumer's waiver of right to rescind. The consumer may modify or waive the right to rescind if the consumer determines that the extension of credit is needed to meet a bona fide personal financial emergency. To modify or waive the right, the consumer shall give the creditor a dated written statement that describes the emergency, that specifically modifies or waives the right to rescind and that bears the signatures of the consumers entitled to rescind. Printed forms for this purpose are prohibited.

(f) Exempt transactions. The right to rescind does not apply to the following:

(1) A residential mortgage transaction.

(2) A credit plan in which a state agency is a creditor.

§ 226.16 Advertising.

(a) Actually available terms. If an advertisement for credit states specific credit terms, it shall state only those terms that actually are or will be arranged or offered by the creditor.

(b) Advertisement of terms that require additional disclosures. If any of the terms required to be disclosed under § 226.6 is set forth in an advertisement, the advertisement shall also clearly and conspicuously set forth the following:

(1) Any minimum, fixed, transaction, activity or similar charge that could be imposed.

(2) Any periodic rate that may be applied expresed as an annual percentage rate as determined under § 226.14(b). If the plan provides for a variable periodic rate, that fact shall be disclosed.

(3) Any membership or participation fee that could be imposed.

(c) Catalogs and multiple-page advertisements.

(1) If a catalog or other multiple-page advertisement gives information in a table or schedule in sufficient detail to permit determination of the disclosures required by paragraph (b) of this section, it shall be considered a single advertisement if:

(i) The table or schedule is clearly and conspicuously set forth; and

(ii) Any statement of terms set forth in § 226.6 appearing anywhere else in the catalog or advertisement clearly refers to that page on which the table or schedule begins.

(2) A catalog or multiple-page advertisement complies with this paragraph if the table or schedule of terms includes all appropriate disclosures for a rep-

resentative scale of amounts up to the level of the more commonly sold higher-priced property or service offered.

SUBPART C—CLOSED-END CREDIT

§ 226.17 General disclosure requirements.

(a) Form of disclosure.

(1) The creditor shall make the disclosures required by this subpart clearly and conspicuously in writing, in a form that the consumer may keep. The disclosures shall be grouped together, shall be segregated from everything else, and shall not contain any information not directly related[37] to the disclosures required under § 226.18.[38] The itemization of the amount financed under § 226.18(c)(1) must be separate from the other disclosures under that section.

(2) The terms "finance charge" and "annual percentage rate," when required to be disclosed under § 226.18(d) and (e) together with a corresponding amount or percentage rate, shall be more conspicuous than any other disclosure, except the creditor's identity under § 226.18(a).

(b) Time of disclosures. The creditor shall make disclosures before consummation of the transaction. In certain residential mortgage transactions, special timing requirements are set forth in § 226.19(a). In certain variable-rate transactions, special timing requirements for variable-rate disclosures are set forth in § 226.19(b) and § 226.20(c). In certain transactions involving mail or telephone orders or a series of sales, the timing of disclosures may be delayed in accordance with paragraphs (g) and (h) of this section.

(c) Basis of disclosures and use of estimates.

(1) The disclosures shall reflect the terms of the legal obligation between the parties.

(2) If any information necessary for an accurate disclosure is unknown to the creditor, it shall make the disclosure based on the best information reasonably available and shall state that the disclosure is an estimate.

(3) The creditor may disregard the effects of the following making calculations and disclosures.

(i) That payments must be collected in whole cents.

(ii) That dates of scheduled payments and advances may be changed because the scheduled date is not a business day.

(iii) That months have different numbers of days.

(iv) The occurrence of leap year.

(4) In making calculations and disclosures, the creditor may disregard any irregularity in the first period that falls within the limits described below and any payment schedule irregularity that results from the irregular first period:

(i) For transactions in which the term is less than 1 year, a first period not more than 6 days shorter or 13 days longer than a regular period;

(ii) For transactions in which the term is at least 1 year and less than 10 years, a first period not more than 11 days shorter or 21 days longer than a regular period; and

(iii) For transactions in which the term is at least 10 years, a first period shorter than or not more than 32 days longer than a regular period.

(5) If an obligation is payable on demand, the creditor shall make the disclosures based on an assumed maturity of 1 year. If an alternate maturity date is stated in the legal obligation between the parties, the disclosures shall be based on that date.

(6)

(i) A series of advances under an agreement to extend credit up to a certain amount may be considered as one transaction.

(ii) When a multiple advance loan to finance the construction of a dwelling may be permanently financed by the same creditor, the construction phase and permanent phase may be treated as either one transaction or more than one transaction.

(d) Multiple creditors; multiple consumers. If a transaction involves more than one creditor, only one set of disclosures shall be given and the creditors shall agree among themselves which creditor must comply with the requirements that this regulation imposes on any or all of them. If there is more than one consumer, the disclosures may be made to any consumer who is primarily liable on the obligation. If the transaction is rescindable under § 226.23, however, the disclosures shall be made to each consumer who has the right to rescind.

(e) Effect of subsequent events. If a disclosure becomes inaccurate because of an event tht occurs after the creditor delivers the required disclosures, the inaccuracy is not a violation of this regulation, although new disclosures may be required under paragraph (f) of this section, § 226.19, or § 226.20

(f) Early disclosures. If disclosures are given before the date of consummation of a transaction and a subsequent event makes them inaccurate, the creditor shall disclose the changed terms before consummation, if the annual percentage rate in the consummated transaction varies from the annual percentage rate disclosed under § 226.18(e) by more than 1/8 of 1 percentage point in a regular transaction, or more than 1/4 of 1 percentage point in a irregular transaction, as defined in § 226.22(a).

(g) Mail or telephone order delay in disclosures. If a creditor receives a purchase order or a request for an extension of credit by mail, telephone, or any other written or electronic communication without face-to-face or direct telephone solicitation, the creditor may delay the disclosures until the due date of the first payment, if the following information for representative amounts or ranges of credit is made available in written form to the consumer or to the public before the actual purchase order or request:

(1) The cash price or the principal loan amount.

(2) The total sale price.

(3) The finance charge.

(4) The annual percentage rate and if the rate may increase after consummation, the following disclosures:

      (i) The circumstances under which the rate may increase.

      (ii) Any limitations on the increase.

      (iii) The effect of an increase.

    (5) The terms of repayment.

(h) Series of sales-delay of disclosures. If a credit sale is one of a series made under an agreement providing that subsequent sales may be added to an outstanding balance, the creditor may delay the required disclosures until the due date of the first payment for the current sale, if the following two conditions are met:

    (1) The consumer has approved in writing the annual percentage rate or rates, the range of balances to which they apply, and the method of treating any unearned finance charge on an existing balance.

    (2) The creditor retains no security interest in any property after the creditor has received payments equal to the cash price and any finance charge attributable to the sale of that property. For purposes of this provision, in the case of items purchased on different dates, the first purchased is deemed the first item paid for; in the case of items purchased in the same date, the lowest priced is deemed the first item paid for.

    (i) Interim student credit extensions. For each transaction involving an interim credit extension under a student credit program, the creditor need not make the following disclosures: the finance charge under § 226.18(d), the payment schedule under § 226.18(g), the total of payments under § 226.18(h), or the total sale price under § 226.18(j).

    [As amended 52 F.R. 48670, Dec. 24, 1987]

§ 226.18 Content of disclosures.

For each transaction, the creditor shall disclose the following information as applicable:

    (a) Creditor. The identity of the creditor making the disclosures.

    (b) Amount financed. The "amount financed," using that term, and a brief description such as "the amount of credit provided to you or on your behalf." The amount financed is calculated by:

    (1) Determining the principal loan amount or the cash price (subtracting any downpayment);

    (2) Adding any other amounts that are financed by the creditor and are not part of the finance charge; and

    (3) Subtracting any prepaid finance charge.

    (c) Itemization of amount financed.

    (1) A separate written itemization of the amount financed, including:[39]

      (i) The amount of any proceeds distributed directly to the consumer.

      (ii) The amount credited to the consumer's account with the creditor.

      (iii) Any amounts paid to other persons by the creditor on the consumer's behalf. The creditor shall identify those persons.[40]

(iv) The prepaid finance charge.

(2) The creditor need not comply with paragraph (c)(1) of this section if the creditor provides a statement that the consumer has the right to receive a written itemization of the amount financed, together with a space for the consumer to indicate whether it is desired, and the consumer does not request it.

(d) Finance charge. The "finance charge," using that term, and a brief description such as "the dollar amount the credit will cost you."[41]

(e) Annual percentage rate. The "annual percentage rate," using that term, and a brief description such as "the cost of your credit as a yearly rate."[42]

(f) Variable rate.

(1) If the annual percentage rate may increase after consummation in a transaction not secured by the consumer's principal dwelling or in a transaction secured by the consumer's principal dwelling with a term of one year or less, the following disclosures:[43]

(i) The circumstances under which the rate may increase.

(ii) Any limitations on the increase

(iii) The effect of an increase.

(iv) An example of the payment terms that would result from an increase.

(2) If the annual percentage rate may increase after consummation in a transaction secured by the consumer's principal dwelling with a term greater than one year, the following disclosures.

(i) The fact that the transaction contains a variable-rate feature.

(ii) A statement that variable-rate disclosures have been provided earlier.

(g) Payment schedule. The number, amounts, and timing of payments scheduled to repay the obligation.

(1) In a demand obligation with no alternate maturity date, the creditor may comply with this paragraph by disclosing the due dates or payment periods of any schedule interest payment for the first year.

(2) In a transaction in which a series of payments varies because a finance charge is applied to the unpaid principal balance, the creditor may comply with this paragraph by disclosing the following information:

(i) The dollar amounts of the largest and smallest payments in the series.

(ii) A reference to the variations in the other payments in the series.

(h) Total of payments. The "total of payments," using that term, and a descriptive explanation such as "the amount you will have paid when you have made all scheduled payments."[44]

(i) Demand feature. If the obligation has a demand feature, that fact shall be disclosed. When the disclosures are based on an assumed maturity of 1 year as provided in § 226.17(c)(5), that fact shall also be disclosed.

(j) Total sale price. In a credit sale, the "total sale price," using that term, and a descriptive explanation (including the amount of any downpayment) such as the total price of your purchase on credit, including your downpayment of $." The total sale price is the sum of the cash price, the items described in the paragraph (b)(2), and the finance charge disclosed under paragraph (d) of this section.

(k) Prepayment.

(1) When an obligation includes a finance charge computed from time to time by application of a rate to the unpaid principal balance, a statement indicating whether or not a penalty may be imposed if the obligation is prepaid in full.

(2) When an obligation includes a finance charge other than the finance charge described in paragaph (k)(1) of this section, a statement indicating whether or not the consumer is entitled to a rebate of any finance charge if the obligation is prepaid in full.

(l) Late payment. Any dollar or percentage charge that may be imposed before maturity due to a late payment, other than a deferral or extension charge.

(m) Security interest. The fact that the creditor has or will acquire a security interest in the property purchased as part of the transaction, or in other property identified by item or type.

(n) Insurance. The items required by § 226.4(d) in order to exclude certain insurance premiums from the finance charge.

(o) Certain security interest charges. The disclosures required by § 226.4(e) in order to exclude form the finance charge certain fees prescribed by law or certain premiums for insurance in lieu of perfecting a security interest.

(p) Contract reference. A statement that the consumer should refer to the appropriate contract document for information about nonpayment, default, the right to accelerate the maturity of the obligation, and prepayment rebates and penalties. At the creditor's option, the statement may also include a reference to the contract for further information about security interests and, in a residential mortgage transaction, about the creditor's policy regarding assumption of the obligation.

(q) Assumption policy. In a residential mortgage transaction, a statement whether or not a subsequent purchaser of the dwelling from the consumer may be permitted to assume the remaining obligation on its original terms.

(r) Required deposit. If the creditor requires the consumer to maintain a deposit as a condition of the specific transaction, a statement that the annual percentage rate does not reflect the effect of the required deposit.[45]

[As amended 52 F.R. 48670, Dec. 24, 1987]

§ 226.19 Certain residential mortgage and variable-rate transactions.

(a) Residential mortgage transactions subject to RESPA.

(1) Time of disclosures. In a residential mortgage transaction subject to the Real Estate Settlement Procedures Act (12 U.S.C. 2601 et seq.) the creditor shall make good faith estimates of the disclosures required by § 226.18 before consummation, or shall deliver or place them in the mail not later than three business days after the creditor receives the consumer's written application, whichever is earlier.

(2) Redisclosure required. If the annual percentage rate in the consummated transaction varies from the annual percentage rate disclosed under

§ 226.18(e) by more than ⅛ of 1 percentage point in a regular transaction of more than ¼ of 1 percentage point in an irregular transaction, as defined in § 226.22, the creditor shall disclose the changed terms no later than consummation or settlement.

(b) Certain variable-rate transactions .[45a] If the annual percentage rate may increase after consummation in a transaction secured by the consumer's principal dwelling with a term greater than one year, the following disclosures must be provided at the time an application form is provided or before the consumer pays a non-refundable fee, whichever is earlier.[45b]

(1) The booklet titled Consumer Handbook on Adjustable Rate Mortgages published by the Board and the Federal Home Loan Bank Board, or a suitable substitute.

(2) A loan program disclosure for each variable-rate program in which the consumer expresses an interest. The following disclosures, as applicable, shall be provided:

(i) The fact that the interest rate, payment, or term of the loan can change.

(ii) The index or formula used in making adjustment, and a source of information about the index or formula.

(iii) An explanation of how the interest rate and payment will be determined, including an explanation of how the index is adjusted, such as by the addition of a margin.

(iv) A statement that the consumer should ask about the current margin value and current interest rate.

(v) The fact that the interest rate will be discounted, and a statement that the consumer should ask about the amount of the interest rate discount.

(vi) The frequency of interest rate and payment changes.

(vii) Any rules relating to changes in the index, interest rate, payment amount, and outstanding loan balance including, for example, an explanation of interest rate or payment limitations, negative amortization, and interest rate carryover.

(viii) An historical example, based on a $10,000 loan amount, illustrating how payments and the loan balance would have been affected by interest rate changes implemented according to the term of the loan program. The example shall be based upon index values beginning in 1977 and be up-dated annually until a 15-year history is shown. Thereafter, the example shall reflect the most recent 15 years of index values. The example shall reflect all significant loan program terms, such as negative amortization, interest rate carryover, interest rate discounts, and interest rate payment limitations, that would have been affected by the index movement during the period.

(ix) An explanation of how the consumer may calculate the payments for the loan amount to be borrowed based on the most recent payment shown in the historical example.

(x) The maximum interest rate and payment for a $10,000 loan originated at the most recent interest rate shown in the historical example assuming the maximum periodic increases in rates and payments under the program; and the initial interest rate and payment for that loan.

(xi) The fact that the loan program contains a demand feature.

(xii) The type of information that will be provided in notices of adjustments and the timing of such notices.

(xiii) A statement that disclosure forms are available for the creditor's other variable-rate loan programs.

[As amended 52 F.R. 48670, Dec. 24, 1987]

§ 226.20 Subsequent disclosure requirements

(a) Refinancings. A refinancing occurs when an existing obligation that was subject to this subpart is satisfied and replaced by a new obligation undertaken by the same consumer. A refinancing is a new transaction requiring new disclosures to the consumer. The new finance charge shall include any unearned portion of the old finance charge that is not credited to the existing obligation. The following shall not be treated as a refinancing:

(1) A renewal of a single payment obligation with no change in the original terms.

(2) A reduction in the annual percentage rate with a corresponding change in the payment schedule.

(3) An agreement involving a court proceeding.

(4) A change in the payment schedule or a change in collateral requirements as a result of the consumer's default or delinquency, unless the rate is increased, or the new amount financed exceeds the unpaid balance plus earned finance charge and premiums for continuation of insurance of the types described in § 226.4(d).

(5) The renewal of optional insurance purchased by the consumer and added to an existing transaction, if disclosures relating to the initial purchase were provided as required by this subpart.

(b) Assumptions. An assumption occurs when a creditor expressly agrees in writing with a subsequent consumer to accept that consumer as a primary obligor on an existing residential mortgage transaction. Before the assumption occurs, the creditor shall make new disclosures to the subsequent consumer, based on the remaining obligation. If the finance charge originally imposed on the existing obligation was an add-on or discount finance charge, the creditor need only disclose:

(1) The unpaid balance of the obligation assumed.

(2) The total charges imposed by the creditor in connection with the assumption.

(3) The information required to be disclosed under § 226.18(k), (l), (m), and (n).

($) The annual percentage rate originally imposed on the obligation.

(5) The payment schedule under § 226.18(g) and the total of payments under § 226.18(h) based on the remaining obligation.

(c) Variable-rate adjustments.[45c] An adjustment to the interest rate with or without a corresponding adjustment to the payment in a variable-rate transaction subject to § 226.19(b) is an event requiring new disclosures to the consumer. At least once each year during which an interest rate adjustment is implemented without an accompanying payment change, and at least 25, but no more than 120, calendar days before a payment at a new level is due, the following disclosures, as applicable, must be delivered or placed in the mail:

(1) The current and prior interest rates.

(2) The index values upon which the current and prior interest rates are based.

(3) The extent to which the creditor has foregone any increase in the interest rate.

(4) The contractual effects of the adjustment, including the payment due after the adjustment is made, and a statement of the loan balance.

(5) The payment, if different from that referred to in paragraph (c)(4) of this section, that would be required to fully amortize the loan at the new interest rate over the remainder of the loan term.

[As amended 52 F.R. 48671, Dec. 24, 1987]

§ 226.21 Treatment of credit balances.

When a credit balance in excess of $1 is created in connection with a transaction (through transmittal of funds to a creditor in excess of the total balance due on an account, through rebates of unearned finance charges or insurance premiums, or through amounts otherwise owed to or held for the benefit of a consumer), the creditor shall:

(a) Credit the amount of the credit balance to the consumer's account;

(b) Refund any part of the remaining credit balance, upon the written request of the consumer; and

(c) Make a good faith effort to refund to the consumer by cash, check, or money order, or credit to a deposit account of the consumer, any part of the credit balance remaining in the account for more than 6 months, except that no further action is required if the consumer's current location is not known to the creditor and cannot be traced through the consumer's last known address or telephone number.

§ 226.22 Determination of annual percentage rate.

(a) Accuracy of annual percentage rate.

(1) The annual percentage rate is a measure of the cost of credit, expressed as a yearly rate, that relates the amount and timing of value received by the consumer to the amount and timing of payments made. The annual percentage rate shall be determined in accordance with either the actuarial method or the United States Rule method. Explanations, equations and instructions for determining the annual percentage rate in accordance with the actuarial method are set forth in Appendix J to this regulation.[45d]

(2) As a general rule, the annual percentage rate shall be considered accurate if it is not more than ⅛ of 1 percentage point above or below the annual percentage rate determined in accordance with paragraph (a)(1) of this section.

(3) In an irregular transaction, the annual percentage rate shall be considered accurate if it is not more than ¼ of 1 percentage point above or below the annual percentage rate determined in accordance with paragraph (a)(1) of this section.[46]

(b) Computation tools.

(1) The Regulation Z Annual Percentage Rate Tables produced by the board may be used to determine the annual percentage rate, and any rate determined from those tables in accordance with the accompanying instructions complies with the requirements of this section. Volume I of the tables applies to single advance transactions involving up to 480 mothly payments or 104 weekly payments. It may be used for regular transactions and for transactions with any of the following irregularities: an irregular first period, an irregular first payment, and an irregular final payment. Volume II of the table applies to transactions involving multiple advances and any type of payment or period irregularity.

(2) Creditors may use any other computation tool in determining the annual percentage rate if the rate so determined equals the rate determined in accordance with Appendix J, within the degree of accuracy set forth in paragraph (a) of this section.

(c) Single add-on rate transactions. If a single add-on rate is applied to all transactions with maturities up to 60 months and if all payments are equal in amount and period, a single annual percentage rate may be disclosed for all those transactions, so long as it is the highest annual percentage rate for any such transaction.

(d) Certain transactions involving ranges of balances. For purposes of disclosing the annual percentage rate referred to in § 226.17(g)(4) (Mail or telephone orders-delay in disclosures) and (h) (Series of sales-delay in disclosures), if the same finance charge is imposed on all balances within a specified range of balances, the annual percentage rate computed for the median balance may be disclosed for all the balances. However, if the annual percentage rate computed for the medium balance understates the annual percentage rate computed for the lowest balance by more than 8 percent of the latter rate, the annual percentage rate shall be computed on whatever lower balance will produce an annual percentage rate that does not result in an understatement of more than 8 percent of the rate determined on the lowest balance.

[As amended 48 F.R. 14886, Apr. 6, 1983]

§ 226.23 Right of recission.

(a) Consumer's right to rescind.

(1) In a credit transaction in which a security interest is or will be retained or acquired in a consumer's principal dwelling, each consumer whose ownership interest is or will be subject to the security interest shall have the right to rescind the transaction except for transactions described in paragraph (f) of this section.[47]

(2) To exercise the right to rescind, the consumer shall notify the creditor of the recission by mail, telegram or other means of written communication. Notice is considered given when mailed, when filed for telegraphic transmission, or, if sent by other means, when delivered to the creditor's designated place of business.

(3) The consumer may exercise the right to rescind until midnight of the third business day following consummation, delivery of the notice required by paragraph (b) of this section, or delivery of all material disclosures,[48] whichever occurs last. If the required notice or material disclosures are not delivered, the right to rescind shall expire 3 years after consummation, upon transfer of all the consumer's interest in the property, or upon sale of the property, whichever occurs first. In the case of certain administrative proceedings, the recission period shall be extended in accordance with § 125(f) of the act.

(4) When more than one consumer in a transaction has the right to rescind, the exercise of the right by one consumer shall be effective as to all consumers.

(b) Notice of right to rescind. In a transaction subject to recission, a creditor shall deliver 2 copies of the notice of the right to rescind to each consumer entitled to rescind. The notice shall be on a separate document that identifies the transaction and shall clearly and conspicuously disclose the following:

(1) The retention or acquisition of a security interest in the consumer's principal dwelling.

(2) The consumer's right to rescind the transaction.

(3) How to exercise the right to rescind, with a form for that purpose, designating the address of the creditor's place of business.

(4) The effects of recission, as described in paragraph (d) of this section.

(5) The date the recission period expires.

(c) Delay of creditor's performance. Unless a consumer waives the right of recission under paragraph (e) of this section, no money shall be disbursed other than in escrow, no services shall be performed and no materials delivered until the recission period has expired and the creditor is reasonably satisfied that the consumer has not rescinded.

(d) Effects of recission.

(1) When a consumer rescinds a transaction, the security interest giving rise to the right of recission becomes void and the consumer shall not be liable for any amount, including any finance charge.

(2) Within 20 calendar days after receipt of a notice of recission, the creditor shall return any money or property that has been given to anyone in connection with the transaction of the security interest.

(3) If the creditor has delivered any money or property, the consumer may retain possession until the creditor has met its obligation under paragraph (d)(2) of this section. When the creditor has complied with that paragraph, the consumer shall tender the money or property to the creditor or, where the latter would be impracticable or inequitable, tender its reasonable value. At the consumer's option, tender of property may be made at the location of the property

or at the consumer's residence. Tender of money must be made at the creditor's designated place of business. If the creditor does not take possession of the money or property within 20 calendar days agter the consumer's tender, the consumer may keep it without further obligation.

(4) The procedures outlined in paragraphs (d)(2) and (3) of this section may be modified by court order.

(e) Consumer's waiver of right to rescind. The consumer may modify or waive the right to rescind if the consumer determines that the extension of credit is needed to meet a bona fide personal financial emergency. To modify or waive the right, the consumer shall give the creditor a dated written statement that describes the emergency, specifically modifies or waives the right to rescind, and bears the signature of all the consumers entitled to rescind. Printed forms for this purpose are prohibited.

(f) Exempt transactions. The right to rescind does not apply to the following:

(1) A residential mortgage transaction.

(2) A refinancing or consolidation by the same creditor of an extension of credit already secured by the consumer's principal dwelling. The right of recission shall apply, however, to the extent the new amount financed exceeds the unpaid principal balance, any earned unpaid finance charge on the existing debt, and amounts attributed solely to the costs of refinancing or consolidation.

(3) A transaction in which a state agency is a creditor.

(4) An advance, other than an initial advance, in a series of advances or in a series of single-payment obligations that is treated as a single transaction under § 226.17(c)(6), if material disclosures have been given to the consumer.

(5) A renewal of optional insurance premiums that is not considered a refinancing under § 226.20(a)(5).

[As amended 47 F.R. 51732, Nov. 17, 1982; 51 F.R. 45299, Dec. 18, 1986]

§ 226.24 Advertising.

(a) Actually available terms. If an advertisement for credit states specific credit terms, it shall state only those terms that actually are or will be arranged and offered by the creditor.

(b) Advertisement of rate of finance charge. If an advertisement states a rate of finance charge, it shall state the rate as an "annual percentage rate" using that term. If the annual percentage rate may be increased after consummation, the advertisement shall state that fact. The advertisement shall not state any other rate, except that a simple annual rate or periodic rate that is applied to an unpaid balance may be stated in conjunction with, but not more conspicuously than, the annual percentage rate.

(c) Advertisement of terms that require additional disclosures.

(1) If any of the following terms is set forth in an advertisement, the advertisement shall meet the requirements of paragraph (c)(2) of this section.

(i) The amount or percentage of any downpayment.

(ii) The number of payments or period of repayment.

(iii) The amount of any payment.

(iv) The amount of any finance charge.

(2) An advertisement stating any of the terms in paragraph (c)(1) of this section shall state the following terms,[49] as applicable:

(i) The amount or percentage of the downpayment.

(ii) The terms of repayment.

(iii) The "annual percentage rate," using that term, and, if the rate may be increased after consummation, that fact.

(d) Catalogs and multiple page advertisements.

(1) If a catalog or other multiple-page advertisement gives information in a table or schedule in sufficient detail to permit determination of the disclosures required by paragraph (c)(2) of this section, it shall be considered a single advertisement if:

(i) The table or schedule is clearly set forth;

(ii) Any statement of the credit terms in paragraph (c)(1) of this section appearing anywhere else in the catalog or advertisement clearly refers to the page on which the table or schedule begins.

(2) A catalog or multiple-page advertisement complies with paragraph (c)(2) of this section if the table or schedule of terms includes all appropriate disclosures for a representative scale of amounts up to the level of the more commonly sold higher-priced property or services offered.

§ 226.25 Record retention.

(a) General rule. A creditor shall retain evidence of compliance with this regulation (other than advertising requirements under §§ 226.16 and 226.24) for 2 years after the date disclosures are required to be made or action is required to be taken. The administrative agencies responsible for enforcing the regulation may require creditors under their jurisdictions to retain records for a longer period if necessary to carry out their enforcement responsibilities under § 108 of the act.

(b) Inspection of records. A creditor shall permit the agency responsible for enforcing this regulation with respect to that creditor to inspect its relevant records for compliance.

§ 226.26 Use of annual precentage rate in oral disclosures.

(a) Open-end credit. In an oral response to a consumer's inquiry about the cost of open-end credit, only the annual percentage rate or rates shall be stated, except that the periodic rate or rates also may be stated. If the annual percentage rate cannot be determined in advance because there are finance charges other than a periodic rate, the corresponding annual percentage rate shall be stated, and other cost information may be given.

(b) Closed-end credit. In an oral response to a consumer's inquiry about the cost of closed-end credit, only the annual percentage rate shall be stated, except that a simple annual rate or periodic rate also may be stated if it is applied to an unpaid balance. If the annual percentage rate cannot be determined in advance, the annual percentage rate for a sample transaction shall be stated, and other cost information for the consumer's specific transaction may be given.

§ 226.27 Spanish language disclosures.

All disclosures required by this regulation shall be made in the English language, except in the Commonwealth of Puerto Rico, where creditors may, at their option, make disclosures in the Spanish language. If Spanish disclosures are made, English disclosures shall be provided on the consumer's request, either in substitution for or in addition to the Spanish disclosures. This requirement for providing English disclosures on request shall not apply to advertisement subject to §§ 226.16 and 226.24 of this regulation.

§ 226.28 Effect on state laws.

(a) Inconsistent disclosure requirements.

(1) State law requirements that are inconsistent with the requirements contained in chapter 1 (General provisions), chapter 2 (Credit transactions), or chapter 3 (Credit advertising) of the act and the implementing provisions of this regulation are preempted to the extent of the inconsistency. A state law is inconsistent if it requires a creditor to make disclosures or take actions that contradict the requirements of the federal law. A state law is contradictory if it requires the use of the same term to represent a different amount or a different meaning than the federal law, or if it requires the use of a term different from that required in the federal law to describe the same item. A creditor, state, or other interested party may request the Board ot determine whether a state law requirement is inconsistent. After the Board determines that a state law is inconsistent, a creditor may not make disclosures using the inconsistent term or form.

(2)

(i) State law requirements are inconsistent with the requirements contained in §§ 161 (Correction of billing errors) or 162 (Regulation of credit reports) of the act and the implementing provisions of this regulation and are preempted if they provide rights, responsibilities, or procedures for consumers or creditors that are different from those required by the federal law. However, a state law that allows a consumer to inquire about an open-end credit account and imposes on the creditor an obligation to respond to such inquiry after the time allowed in the federal law for the consumer to submit written notice of a billing error shall not be preempted in any situation where the time period for making written notice under this regulation has expired. If a creditor gives written notice of a consumer's rights under such state law, the notice shall state that reliance on the longer time period available under state law may result in the loss of important rights that could be preserved by acting more promptly under federal law; it shall also explain that the state law provisions apply only after expiration of the time period for submitting a proper written notice of a billing error under the federal law. If the state disclosures are made on the same side of a page as the required federal disclosures, the state disclosures shall appear under a demarcation line below the federal disclosures, and the federal disclosures shall be identified by a heading indicating that they are made in compliance with federal law.

(ii) State law requirements are inconsistent with the requirements contained in chapter 4 (Credit billing) of the act (other than §§ 161 or 162) and the implementing provisions of this regulation and are preempted if the creditor cannot comply with state law without violating federal law.

(iii) A state may request the Board to determine whether its law is inconsistent with chapter 4 of the act and its implementing provisions.

(b) Equivalent disclosure requirements. If the board determines that a disclosure required by state law (other than a requirement relating to the finance charge or annual percentage rate) is substantially the same in meaning as a disclosure required under the act or this regulation, creditors in that state may make the state disclosure in lieu of the federal disclosure. A creditor, state, or other intrested party may request the Board to determine whether a state disclosure is substantially the same in meaning as a federal disclosure.

(c) Request for determination. The procedures under which a request for a determination may be made under this section are set forth in Appendix A.

§ 226.29 State exemptions.

(a) General rule. Any state may apply to the Board to exempt a class of transactions within the state from the requirements of chapter 2 (Credit transactions) or chapter 4 (Credit billing) of the act and the corresponding provisions of this regulation. The Board shall grant an exemption if it determines that:

(1) The state law is substantially similar to the federal law or, in the case of chapter 4, affords the consumer greater protection than the federal law; and

(2) There is adequate provision for enforcement.

(b) Civil liability.

(1) No exemptions granted under this section shall extend to the civil liability provisions of §§ 130 and 131 of the act.

(2) If an exemption has been granted, the disclosures required by the applicable state law (except any additional requirements not imposed by federal law) shall constitute the disclosures required by this act.

(c) Applications. The procedures under which a state may apply for an exemption under this section are set forth in Appendix B.

[As amended 46 F.R. 29246, June 1, 1981]

SUBPART D—MISCELLANEOUS

§ 226.30 Limitation on rates.

A creditor shall include in any consumer credit contract secured by a dwelling and subject to the act and this regulation the maximum interest rate that may be imposed during the term of the obligation[50] when:

(a) In the case of closed-end credit, the annual percentage rate may increase after consummation, or

(b) In the case of open-end credit, the annual percentage rate may increase during the plan.

[As added 52 F.R. 43181, Nov. 9, 1987]

Note: The appendices to Regulation Z—not included here—cover the following topics:

Appendix A	Effect on State Laws
Appendix B	State Exemptions
Appendix C	Issuance of Staff Interpretations
Appendix D	Multiple Advance Construction Loans
Appendix E	Rules for Card Issuers That Bill on a Transaction-by-Transaction Basis
Appendix F	Annual Percentage Rate Computations for Certain Open-End Credit Plans
Appendix G	Open-End Model Forms and Clauses
Appendix H	Closed-End Model Forms and Clauses

Footnotes

1. The meaning of "regularly" is explained in defintion of "creditor" in § 226.2(A)
2. [Removed and reserved]
3. A person regularly extends consumer credit only if it extended credit more than 25 times (or more than 5 times for transactions secured by a dwelling) in the preceding calendar year. If a person did not meet these numerical standards in the preceding calendar year, the numerical standards shall be applied to the current calendar year.
4. Extensions of credit which are exempt under paragraph (A)(1) and (2) remain subject to § 226.12(A) and (B) governing the issuance of credit cards and the liability for their unauthorized use.
5. This includes single interest insurance if the insurer waives all right of subrogation against the consumer.
6. A creditor may reserve the right to refuse to accept, for reasonable cause, an insurer offered by the consumer.
7. The disclosure required by § 226.9(D) when a finance charge is imposed at the time of a transaction need not be written.
8. The alternative summary billing rights statement provided for in § 226.9(A)(2), and the disclosures made under § 226.10(B) about payment requirements need not be in a form that the consumer can keep.
9. The terms need not be more conspicuous when used under § 226.7(D) on periodic statements and under § 226.16 in advertisements.
10. Rescinded.
11. A creditor is not required to adjust the range of balances disclosure to reflect the balance below which only a minimum charge applies.
12. If a creditor is offering a varable rate plan, the creditor shall also disclose: (1) the circumstances under which the rate(s) may increase (2) any limitations on the increase and (3) the effect(s) of an increase.

13. If no finance charge is imposed when the outstanding balance is less than a certain amount, no disclosure is required of that fact or of the balance below which no finance charge will be imposed.

14. See footnotes 11 and 13.

15. If a variable rate plan is involved, the creditor shall disclose the fact that the periodic rate(s) may vary.

16. Failure to disclose the information required by this section shall not be deemed a failure to comply with the regulation if: (1) the creditor maintains procedures reasonably adapted to obtain and provide the information; and (2) the creditor treats an inquiry for clarification or documentation as a notice of a billing error, including correcting the account in accordance with § 226.13(E). This applies to transactions that take place outside a state, as defined in § 226.2(A), whether or not the creditor maintains procedures reasonably adapted to obtain the required information.

17. As an alternative to the brief identification, the creditor may disclose a number or symbol that also appears on the receipt or other credit document given to the consumer, if the number or symbol reasonably identifies that transaction with that creditor, and if the creditor treats an inquiry for clarification or documentation as a notice of a billing error, including correcting the accout in accordance with § 226.13(E).

18. An identification of property or services may be replaced by the seller's name and location of the transaction when: (1) the creditor and the seller are the same person; (2) the creditor's open-end plan has fewer than 15,000 accounts; (3) the creditor provides the consumer with point-of-sale documentation for that transaction; and (4) the creditor treats an inquiry for clarification or documentation as a notice of a billing error, including correcting the account in accordance with § 226.13(E).

19. The creditor may omit the address or provide any suitable designation that helps the consumer to identify the transaction when the transaction (1) took place at a location that is not fixed; (2) took place in the consumer's home; or (3) was a mail or telephone order.

20. See footnote 17.

21. For purposes of this section, "accepted credit card" means any credit card that a cardholder has requested or applied for and received, or has signed, used, or authorized another person to use to obtain credit. Any credit card issued as a renewal or substitute in accordance with this paragraph becomes an accepted credit card when received by the cardholder.

22. "Unauthorized use" means the use of a credit card by a person, other than the cardholder, who does not have actual, implied, or apparent authority for such use, and from which the cardholder receives no benefit.

23. "Adequate notice" means a printed notice to a cardholder that sets forth clearly the pertinent facts so that the cardholder may reasonably be expected to have noticed it and understood its meaning. The notice may be given by any means reasonably assuring receipt by the cardholder.

24. This paragraph does not apply to the use of a check guarantee card or a debit card in connection with an overdraft credit plan, or to a check guarantee card used in connection with cash advance checks.

25. The amount of the claim or defense that the cardholder may assert shall not exceed the amount of credit outstanding for the disputed transaction at the time the cardholder first notifies the card issuer or the person honoring the credit card of the existence

of the claim or defense. To determine the amount of credit outstanding for purposes of this section, payments and other credits shall be applied to: (1) late charges in the order of entry to the account, then to (2) finance charges in the order of entry to the account, and then to (3) any other debits in the order of entry to the account. If more than one item is included in a single extension of credit, credits are to be distributed pro rata according to prices and applicable taxes.

26.   The limitations stated in paragraph (C)(3)(ii) of this section shall not apply when the person honoring the credit card: (1) is the same person as the card issuer; (2) is controlled by the card issuer directly or indirectly; (3) is under the direct or indirect control of a third person that also directly or indirectly controls the card issuer; (4) controls the card issuer directly or indirectly; (5) is a franchised dealer in the card issuer's products or services; or (6) has obtained the order for the disputed transaction through a mail solicitation made or participated in by the card issuer.

27.   A creditor shall not accelerate any part of the consumer's indebtedness or restrict or close a consumer's account solely because the consumer has exercised in good faith rights provided by this section. A creditor may be subject to the forfeiture penalty under § 161(E) of the act for failure to comply with any of the requirements of this section.

28.   The creditor need not comply with the requirements of paragraphs (C) through (G) of this section if the consumer concludes that no billing error occurred and voluntarily withdraws the billing error notice.

29.   The creditor may require that the written notice not be made on the payment medium or other material accompanying the periodic statement if the creditor so stipulates in the billing rights statement required by §§ 226.6(D) and 226.9(A).

30.   A creditor is not prohibited from taking action to collect any undisputed portion of the item or bill; from deducting any disputed amount and related finance or other charges from the consumer's credit limit on the account; or from reflecting a disputed amount and related finance or other charges on a periodic statement, provided that the creditor indicates on or with the periodic statement that payment of any disputed amount and related finance or other charges is not required pending the creditor's compliance with this section.

31.   If a consumer submits a billing error notice alleging either the nondelivery of property or services under paragraph (A)(3) of this section or that information appearing on a periodic statement is incorrect because a person honoring the consumer's credit card has made an incorrect report to the card issuer, the creditor shall not deny the assertion unless it conducts a reasonable investigation and determines that the property or services were actually delivered, mailed, or sent as agreed or that the infomration was correct.

31a.   An error in disclosure of the annual percentage rate or finance charge shall not, in itself, be considered a vioation of this regulation if: (1) the error resulted from a corresponding error in a calculation tool used in good faith by the creditor; and (2) on discovery of the error, the creditor promptly discontinues use of that calculation tool for disclosure purposes, and notifies the Board in writing of the error in the calculation tool.

32.   If there is no balance to which the finance charge is applicable, an annual percentage rate cannot be determined under this section.

33. Where the finance charge imposed during the billing cycle is or includes a loan fee, points, or similar charge that relates to the opening of the account, the amount of such charge shall not be included in the calculation of the annual percentage rate.

34. See Appendix F regarding determination of the denominator of the fraction under this paragraph.

35. See footnote 33.

36. The term "material disclosure" means the information that must be provided to satisfy the requirements in § 226.6 with regard to the method of determining the finance charge and the balance on which a finance charge will be imposed, the annual percentage rate, and the amount or method of determining the amount of any membership or participation fee that may be imposed as part of the plan.

37. The disclosures may include an acknowledgment of receipt, the date of the transaction, and the consumer's name, address, and account number.

38. The following disclosures may be made together or separately from other required disclosures: the creditor's identity under § 226.18(F)(4), insurance under § 226.18(N), and certain security interest charges under § 226.18(O).

39. Good faith estimates of settlement cost provided for transaction subject on the Real Estate Settlement Procedures Act (12 U. S. C. 2601 et seq.) may be substituted for the disclosures required by paragraph (C) of this section.

40. The following payees may be described using generic or other general terms and need not be further identified: public officials or government agencies, credit reporting agencies, appraisers, and insurance companies.

41. The finance charge shall be considered accurate if it is not more than $5 above or below the exact finance charge in a transaction involving an amount financed of $1000 or less, or not more than $10 above or below the exact finance charge in a transaction involving an amount financed for more than $1000.

42. For any transaction involving a finance charge of $5 or less on an amount financed of $75 or less, or a finance charge of $7.50 or less on an amount financed of more than $75, the creditor need not disclose the annual percentage rate.

43. Information provided in accordance with §§ 226.18(F)(2) and 226.19(B) may be substituted for the disclosures required by paragraph (F)(1) of this section.

44. In any transaction involving a single payment, the creditor need not disclose the total of payments.

45. A required deposit need not include, for example: (1) an escrow account for items such as taxes, insurance, or repairs; (2) a deposit that earns not less than 5 percent per year; or (3) payments under a Morris Plan.

45a. Information provided in accordance with variable-rate regulations of other federal agencies may be substituted for the disclosures required by paragraph (b) of this section.

45b. Disclosures may be delivered or placed in the mail not later than three business days following receipt of a consumer's application when the application reaches the creditor by telephone, or through an intermediary agent or broker.

45c. Information provided in accordance with variable-rate subsequent disclosure regulations of other fedral agencies may be substituted for the disclosure required by paragraph (C) of this section.

45d. An error in disclosure of the annual percentage rate or finance charge shall not, in itself, be considered a violation of this regulation if: (1) the error resulted from a corresponding error in a calcuation tool used in good faith by the creditor and (2) on discovery of the error, the creditor promptly discontinues use of that calculation tool for disclosure purposes and notifies the Board in writing of the error in the calculation tool.

46. For purposes of paragraph (A)(3) of this section, an irregular transaction is one that includes one or more of the following features: multiple advances, irregular payment periods, or irregular payment amounts (other than an irregular first period or an irreglar first or final payment).

47. For purposes of this section, the addition to an existing obligation of a security interest in a consumer's principal dwelling is a transaction. The right of rescission applies only to the addition of the security interest and not the existing obligation. The creditor shall deliver the notice required by paragraph (B) of this section but need not deliver new material disclosures. Delivery of the required notice shall begin the rescission period.

48. The term "material disclosures" means the required disclosures of the annual percentage rate, the finance charge, the amount financed, the total of payments, and the payment schedule.

49. An example of one or more typical extensions of credit with a statement of all the terms applicable to each may be used.

50. Compliance with this section will constitute compliance with the disclosure requirements on limitation on increases in footnote 12 to §§ 226.6(A)(2) and 226.18(F)(2) until October 1, 1988.

INDEX